Archibald Clavering Gunter

The King's Stockbroker

Archibald Clavering Gunter

The King's Stockbroker

ISBN/EAN: 9783337000431

Printed in Europe, USA, Canada, Australia, Japan

Cover: Foto ©ninafisch / pixelio.de

More available books at **www.hansebooks.com**

The King's Stockbroker

The Sequel to "A Princess of Paris"

A Novel

BY

ARCHIBALD CLAVERING GUNTER

AUTHOR OF

"MR. BARNES OF NEW YORK," "THAT FRENCHMAN!"
"MISS NOBODY OF NOWHERE."

———

NEW YORK
THE HOME PUBLISHING CO.
3 EAST FOURTEENTH STREET
1894

CONTENTS.

BOOK I.

THE MECCA OF FINANCIERS.

BOOK II.

THE RAID OF THE POLICE.

4 CONTENTS.

BOOK III.

THE STRUGGLE ON THE QUINCAMPOIX.

4

BOOK IV.

JUGGLING WITH FATE.

BOOK V.

THE FLIGHT FROM FRANCE.

THE
KING'S STOCKBROKER.

BOOK I.

THE MECCA OF FINANCIERS.

CHAPTER I.

STEALING A GALLEY SLAVE.

It is the night of the 1st of June, 1719.

Upon the moonlit waters of the Mediterranean, just out of the port of Marseilles, a King's galley, *La Sylphide*, is rowing slowly into the harbor.

Behind her, the distant lights and fireworks from the Isle Pomègue give the last trace of the great water *fête* of Marseilles, that this day has been given to celebrate the making of the city a free port, and the arrival of the first great fleet from Louisiana, bearing the products of the new colony to France; upon which the Regent, the Duc d'Orleans, and his financier, Monseigneur Law, expect to build up the grandest commercial enterprise yet given to the world—that of the India Company.

The galley slaves are rowing slowly, for their day's work of transporting passengers to the island and towing the ships of the Mississippi squadron has been an awful one, under the burning sun.

The free sailors and soldiers are asleep upon the forecastle, tired with firing salutes and cheering for the Regent and Monseigneur Law.

Upon the center gangplank running through the low waist of the vessel the somnolent boatswain and his mates are not doing their usual flogging, and the cadence of the oars is languid.

Upon the high decorated poop at the stern, one or two under officers are asleep.

A little apart, upon this poop deck, is a creature just released from his chains, wearing the cap and camisole of a galley slave. Bending over him, with tears in his eyes, is a young man bedecked with the gorgeous uniform of a general of the army of France.

An officer of the galley approaches them.

"Hush! he is sleeping," whispers the general.

"Oh, ho! your *forçat*," laughs Lieutenant Polignac of the galley.

"Quiet! don't wake him!" mutters General le Comte d'Arnac, commandant of the port of Marseilles.

"*Tonnerre de Brest!* you take a good deal of interest in the poor devil," replies the officer of marine. "You give me a thousand crowns to-morrow morning to transfer a slave from the oar to your shore hospital for infectious diseases, in which, according to you, *mon general*, the last attendant galley slave died to-day. *Parbleu!* the man would live longer at the oar! One would think you wished him to die *soon*."

"Perhaps I do," remarks D'Arnac shortly, not anxious to give any one his secret.

"Oh, ho! just put him at the oar again, and for one hundred crowns our *comité* will guarantee he will not live the week through."

"No, I prefer for him to die my way."

"Which means not at all—you are so careful of his comfort," remarks Polignac slyly.

Raymond can see the man wink in the moonlight. After a minute's pause, he thinks perhaps a half confidence will be best.

"You have guessed it, my sea dog," he replies, clapping the lieutenant on the shoulder. "I want to make his lot as easy as is consistent with my duty. Would you not do the same if you suddenly discovered one who had fought by your side, a hero in the old Army of the Rhine, toiling with criminals on the oars of the galley?"

He gazes down at the shackled creatures plying the oars to which they are chained, in the low waist of the vessel almost at his feet, and mutters: "Would you not do a little to lighten his hard lot on earth—for I presume he is condemned for life?"

"Undoubtedly," remarks Polignac, "under the circumstances I would do the same, as far as consistent with duty."

Then the lieutenant walks forward to give the *comité* some further orders, wondering in his sailor mind what the deuce the whole affair means, but being very confident of the thousand crowns that have been promised him by the general commanding the port of Marseilles.

Looking at the wretches that row the King's galley, under the lashes of the boatswain and his mates, two hundred and ninety-seven of the three hundred that began the day's toil of this water *fête* at Marseilles, for two have died as they rowed, and one has just been released from his irons and lies upon the poop deck, the moonlight shining on his face and the young general bending over him, Polignac mutters: "*Tonn.. de Dieu!* a general of the army taking interest in a galley slave! It's as curious as the mermaid and the sea serpent."

But if Polignac, lieutenant of *La Sylphide*, is astonished, Raymond le Comte d'Arnac, general of the army of France, is not only astounded, but dazed and horrified, as he stands on the deck of the galley that is being swept into the harbor of Marseilles, and looking over the moonlit waters towards the Isle Pomègue sees the great *feu de joie* twinkling in the distance, and commences to appreciate what he is doing.

These lights of the celebration set him to thinking very deeply; he begins to realize the awful responsibility of the task he has set himself to do.

For Raymond le Comte d'Arnac, general of the army of France, has determined to steal from the galleys the wretched *forçat* upon whom he looks—well knowing that all the power of the Regent and all his clique of financiers, courtiers and officers of police will be against him.

But as he glances down on the face of his old comrade and sees it drawn with toil and pinched with want and suffering, he hears the pale, trembling lips of the sleep-

ing man murmur "TOGETHER !"   This word of
their friendship takes him back to the Army of the
Rhine, and he sees again the laughing, light-hearted
soldier of fortune, O'Brien Dillon, who saved his life
the night they stormed the lone bastion of Friburg;
and he remembers how they had been happy comrades
during the days at Rastadt.

Then he gazes back over the five years between that
time and this, and recollects how this man had married the
beautiful woman he had fought for by the camp fire, and
that his love for her had brought him to what he now is.

Raymond sees as in a dream his own attempt to
rescue this enchanting creature, who had been made the
bait to lure from the Regent of France the concessions
for Monseigneur Law, and how he himself had fallen
under her wondrous charms.

With this comes to him the remembrance of O'Brien
Dillon's return to Paris a general in the Austrian service
and count of the Empire, to again seek the wife of his
heart, not guessing that under the name of the beautiful
Hilda de Sabran she was mistress of the Regent of
France.   How, made rich by the spoils of the Turk, and
covered by the diamonds of the Ottoman Vizier, Dillon
I ad enjoyed a second honeymoon in the arms of
the siren who, though she loved him again for one short
evening, was ready to give him over to his enemies the
next morning, knowing that his was no nature to submit
to dishonor even from the Potentate of France; that she
must throw away her ambition and conceal her shame
from her husband, or permit those to do their will upon
him who, to keep the friendship of the Duc d'Orleans,
were willing to consign O'Brien Dillon to the oblivion
of death, or to a life-long prison.

This brings Raymond to the details of that curious
night at the Café St. Michel, where his Irish friend
was seized by a mob of apparently affrighted spectators,
after making his wonderful stroke at billiards—the first
massé shot ever made in public in the world.

That it was this shot that had been used to secretly
convict O'Brien Dillon of sorcery, Raymond has learned
from the muttered words of the creature lying before
him, faltered from pale lips before the sleep of intense
toil came upon the released slave of the oar.

Meditating upon this, D'Arnac concludes this conviction had probably been obtained under some old edict of the past century, not yet wiped out from the jurisprudence of the country.

For in France, in 1520, fires had burned for the execution of witches, wizards and sorcerers in every town, in every province, and for nearly two centuries thereafter necromancers, sorcerers and diaboles 'had suffered death at the stake as often as the superstitious wished. A few short years before this very night such transactions were not absolutely unusual.

Even as Raymond looks at the man, he knows enough about the still mysterious powers supposed to be transmitted from the evil one to be aware that half the galley slaves—marauders, thieves and bandits as they are—toiling under the lash of the boatswain, would shudder with fear at the thought that rowing beside them, suffering the same stripes, uttering the same shrieks, had been one accused of having intercourse with the devil.

"*Pardieu !*" mutters D'Arnac, looking at the motionless 'form, "if poor O'Brien had been a wizard, he could have used the black art to have escaped, and not needed me to assist him. If there is sorcery in the matter, it belongs to la Sabran, whose beauty bewitches all who come near her enchanting charms—to love her; most of them to their undoing."

Then thinking of the assignation he has even now with this beautiful creature who is waiting for him in vain on the Island Pomègue, he cogitates : "*Mon Dieu !* For this she will never forgive me ! "

With this he sets to thinking very hard and very desperately, for he imagines that the beautiful Hilda, who has twice been balked of his wooing, will hate him—not love him the more—for this night's desertion—and will use every means in her power to effect his downfall.

"If I make a false step, I am lost! I have so few friends to turn to," he reflects. "Even Cousin Charlie, who has betrayed this man, would destroy me. In stealing a galley slave unpardoned from the *bagne*, I am committing a crime from which even my rank will not save me, with every power of the clique about the Regent arrayed against me to urge my condemnation.

But steal him I will," he mutters, "and steal him by cunning, as I cannot use my power, Commandant, though I am, of the Port of Marseilles."

Meditating upon this, a sudden idea comes to Raymond, but with it comes the signal from the galley to the forts at the entrance of the basin, to lower the immense iron chain that is always raised at midnight to keep vessels from entering unsignalled.

The clanking of this barrier to the harbor warns him he must act quickly. Stepping to the sleeping galley slave D'Arnac attempts to awaken him, and is answered with a moan.

"Arise!" he whispers, shaking the sleeping *forçat*. "Wake up! You must act!"

To his assaults the pale lips give a subdued shriek: "I awake, *comité*—for the love of God, not the bastinado!—I awake!" And the shivering wretch, with every faculty nerved by fear, springs up, trembling, ready to take the oar.

Then, looking round in a half-dazed manner, O'Brien Dillon sees his comrade, and murmurs, "Raymond— *Mon Dieu!* I dreamt I was a galley slave." Here the cadence of the oars comes to him, mingled with a shriek brought by the *comité's* lash, and he trembles and, looking at himself, mutters: "No—not a dream—your face is a dream. They will drag me back!" then shuddering, clutches D'Arnac, moaning: "Friend of the sword, save a comrade from the cruel boatswain!"

And Raymond whispers in his ear: "You are safe—I am by your side. You remember?"

"Yes."

"You recall——"

"Yes! let me sleep—let me sleep! I am released from the irons—watch over me—let me sleep!" and the man, exhausted with the fearful toil of the day, sinks upon the deck.

But Raymond is at him again whispering: "Wake up!"

"Let me sleep!"

"Wake up for *revenge!*"

"For REVENGE!" And suddenly a giant rises up; no more the shrinking galley slave—but the man who will avenge his manhood's wrongs. And O'Brien Dillon says: "Where are they—my wife and my uncle Johnny Law, the financier of France?" His voice has an eager but horrible tone.

"They are not here. In order to escape, you must do as I direct. For ten minutes you must control yourself!" whispers Raymond. "Are you strong enough to swim one hundred yards?"

"One hundred yards? For revenge I could swim five miles!"

"Then, when I walk forward to speak to the lieutenant of the galley, utter the yell of the maniac and spring overboard. Dive deep and long, and make those stone stairs on the opposite side of the basin. You see them?"

"Yes."

"There I will meet you—you understand?"

"As well as I did at Friburg!" And the galley slave gives his hand to the general of the army, and whispers, "Together!"

"Yes, always together now!" mutters Raymond, tears dimming his sight, as he thinks of what this man had once been, and what he is.

Then as the galley sweeps into the basin of Marseilles, D'Arnac steps up to Lieutenant Polignac, who has gone forward along the center plank of the waist, and is talking to the *comité*, and says to him: "I will sign, as you suggested, a requisition for galley slave number one of the second oar."

"Yes, number 1392 of Toulon, unbranded," replies Polignac, looking over a book that he has just received from the boatswain, being a record of the *forçats* employed on the vessel.

"Unbranded?" chuckles the *comité*. "He's a rare bird; no *fleur-de-lys* on him! He came to us unbranded, and I had no orders as to what letter designating his crime should be put upon him. He's a strong devil and we'll miss him! But that matter you must settle with our captain, Monsieur le General."

Then he suddenly cries: "*Tonnerre de Brest!* but he's gone crazy!"

And Polignac echoes: "Your galley slave is a maniac!"

For at this moment, just as the vessel is dropping

anchor, O'Brien Dillon, rising from the poop deck, utters three or four demoniac yells, and springing over the side of the ship into the deep water of the basin, disappears from sight; and though they all run to the railings, and Polignac orders the sailors to look · out and see when the man rises, no living thing comes under their eyes in the basin of the harbor of Marseilles.

Then Polignac remarks: "*Tonn.. de Dieu!* General d'Arnac, it will not be necessary for you to write a receipt for the *forçat*; would you kindly attest this affair in the log-book?"

This Raymond does in the poop cabin, and it is the following record:

June 1, 1719.

Galley slave number 1392, of Toulon, being relieved from his irons to be placed upon shore duty at hospital for infectious diseases, suddenly went crazy, and springing overboard, was drowned, about midnight, in the harbor of Marseilles.

This over, D'Arnac steps to the gangway to leave the vessel, but Polignac is at his side, and whispers: "How about the thousand crowns *now?*"

"At my office at twelve to-morrow morning!" returns Raymond.

"Oh! I understand," chuckles the sea dog. "*Bon soir!* Monsieur le General. I hope the result of your excursion upon *La Sylphide* will be as pleasant to you as it has been profitable to me."

"God knows!" mutters D'Arnac, as he steps off the vessel, and with slashing tread, goes straight to his quarters, for into his mind has suddenly sprung a serious problem—how to clothe the *forçat* so he can pass unchallenged through the streets of the town?

"*Parbleu!* my quarters as commandant of the garrison are cursed with sentries!" Raymond mutters as he walks.

This he finds to be the case, for the sergeant of the guard seems unusually alert this night, and very wide awake; an activity which his superior would praise at any other time, but at this particular moment anathematizes under his breath.

Going to his own apartments D'Arnac discovers his lackeys are by no means so wakeful; every one of them are out on various junketings about town, as, with the instinct of servants, they have divined that when their master departed, he went for an all-night cruise.

Finding his flunkies absent, Raymond, after a little consideration, selects some clothes of his own that he has worn so long ago that their loss will hardly attract his valet's notice, and blessing God that the fashion for gentlemen still dictates their wearing wigs, hunts up an old peruke of his to cover the shaven head of his stolen galley slave. Carrying these under his long military overcoat, he departs again from his quarters.

Passing the saluting sergeant of the guard and the sentries he soon reaches the basin of the harbor of Marseilles, and coming to a little stone stairway leading up from the splashing water, sees reclining, sleeping again, the man registered that night as "*Forçat* number 1392, drowned in the harbor of Marseilles.*"

After one or two efforts, he succeeds in waking him, for these galley slaves were accustomed to sleep like dogs, and wake like dogs—to be aroused at any hour of the day or night that the vessel might be put in motion.

Shaking himself like a great water spaniel, O'Brien Dillon stands once more before his old comrade and friend.

"Clothe yourself in these! They are the dress of gentlemen, dear friend," whispers the latter.

"Bedad," answers O'Brien, "anything is better than the nothing I have worn." After a moment he adds: "Faith, it's about me usual method of toilet to dress myself after a bath!"

These words bring sudden joy to D'Arnac—the first he has had since he made his awful discovery—for in them he sees a flicker of the old Irish spirit. The words that come to him a moment after give him even greater hope.

"By Saint Patrick!" says the *forçat* who is rapidly putting himself in the habiliments of civil life, "ye've given me the fine clothes of a gentleman—that came from your heart, *ma bouchal!*" Then he says suddenly, with a shudder: "By me soul! you've put me in black! Is it a bad omen?"

"Oh," answers Raymond, "I forgot—. I've been in mourning for nearly a year for the Comte de Crevecœur, my uncle, who died in Paris."

With this O'Brien turns curious eyes upon his friend and whispers: "How long is it since the night I made that accursed shot at billiards?"

"Eighteen months," replies D'Arnac, after a pause of consideration.

"Eighteen *months*?" gasps Dillon. "By the powers of hell! it has seemed to me eighteen YEARS! Ah! the infernal click of the billiard balls that has been in my ears! The slash of the oars in the rowlocks, the snap of the boatswain's lash have been the click of the billiard balls. The screams of the tortured wretches have been the billiard balls to me. Oh, my God! But if I think of that time—it will make me the cur, when I have to be the lion—the lion hungry for revenge!" And his face in the moonlight is an awful one to look at.

Then trying to regain his spirits he attempts a chuckle: "And it's fine looking ye are, in your general's uniform and decorations. I was a general once and a count!" and his eyes gleam bright and lustrous as he mutters: "Give me a sword, and I'll be a general and a count again."

"Then be one!" and D'Arnac buckles his own weapon around his old comrade's waist, who cries and laughs over it, and pets it, and fondles its hilt, saying it is his friend, and now that he has a weapon in his hands, he feels a general once more.

At this Raymond grows more easy. He sees the indomitable spirit has not all been tortured out of this man; that in time O'Brien Dillon will become again the dashing soldier of the Rhine campaign.

"Come," he says, "I can't give you a general's quarters this evening."

"But ye'll give me the welcome of a friend!' mutters O'Brien as he strides beside Raymond.

"I want to ask you two questions, quick. It is for your safety as well as mine," remarks D'Arnac, anxiously. "Were you convicted by regular tribunal?"

"Faith, I'm afraid so. They took me in naked into the Conciergerie. I was charged within ten minutes after I arrived there with being a sorcerer and a wizard. The judges seemed to be ready for me. Your Cousin Charlie came in as Procureur du Roy, and proffered himself to me as my counsel, and told me not to say a word and he would fix everything. Then I heard a rigmarole about somebody that wasn't me—Paul Casanova—and of course I answered nothing and Cousin Charlie he answered nothing. Two minutes after I was chained and ironed, and in a van being driven out of Paris to a living hell!" Then he suddenly whispers, trembling: "God help me! Raymond! Save me! Don't let him see me! It is the *comité* coming—the cruel *comité!*"

And D'Arnac sees the gentleman walking at his side become a trembling *forçat* again and shrink behind him, as at a little distance they see pass before them the boatswain of the galley *La Sylphide*, whistling a merry strain, *en route* for some neighboring wine shop; but fortunately he doesn't see them.

"You are sure my cousin betrayed you?" asks Raymond the moment the man has disappeared.

"As I am a living wretch, despoiled of property and name, and degraded from my manhood, I know it—and now I know the reason of it. Uncle Johnny Law, the financier of France, and my wife, were sure from what I said to them on my return from Vienna that the minute I discovered that Madame la Comtesse Dillon (I'd made her that, hadn't I, my boy, by the sword?) was De Sabran, the mistress of the Regent of France, I would punish her unfaithfulness to me—that is the reason they made me what I am. Your cousin, Charlie de Moncrief, heard me tell of my wonderful shot at billiards I was to make that night. It was arranged for. The mob flew at me and cried 'sorcerer!' and 'demon!' and tore every bit of clothes from me, and robbed me of the diamonds that I had on me—so that I could not be identified. The judges were ready. The Procureur was on hand! So under an assumed name O'Brien Dillon, General of the Imperial Army and Count of the Empire, was condemned and smuggled away to the galleys of France—the doom of felons."

"My Heaven! the ineffable villain!" mutters Raymond. "Why, Charles de Moncrief came to me after he had assisted at your condemnation, and went with me to the office of the Lieutenant of Police to make inquiries about you."

"And you heard nothing?"

"Nothing from the police."

"Then the Lieutenant of Police is against me! Doesn't that prove what I have told you—that it is the power of France that is upon me? Raymond, my comrade, give me a little money—let me fly from here on my own account—else I will bring ruin upon you, my friend!"

And O'Brien Dillon holds out eager hands and would take money and disappear, perhaps forever, from the light of the world; but Raymond's grip is upon him, and his hand clutches his, and he mutters: "*Together*—the old word, O'Brien—TOGETHER—as at Friburg, when you saved my life!"

With that, the escaped *forçat* embraces the general of France with such a terrible grip that D'Arnac almost feels his bones crush together. And he knows that his comrade of the Rhine, from being a strong man, has become under the fearful exercise and training of the galleys, a very giant in strength.

"If I can get his mind as potent as his body," Raymond thinks, "together we will win our battle even against the power of France."

So, with more confidence than has come to him before in this adventure, D'Arnac conducts O'Brien Dillon past saluting sentries, into his quarters, and showing him a vacant room, and placing before him wine and provisions, hurriedly obtained from his sideboard, tells him to refresh himself, and then to lie down and sleep.

"Indade and I will! God of mercy! to think that I shall lie in a bed again this night—I, who have slept, it seems for ages, on the hard bench of the galley slave. I, who have—my God! Raymond—" and he bursts into tears that make his comrade weep also.

But eventually the Irish general is comforted, and goes to sleep like a child, sighing the long sighs of exhausted manhood; once more under the roof of man —once more with the comforts of man about him— once more with a man's hope in the world.

CHAPTER II.

THE TAVERN OF THE TURK'S HEAD.

UPON his own couch Raymond lies tossing a good deal of the night; sometimes thinking what a difference it would have been to him had not the galley slave whispered "Together!"; perchance with an awful long-ing for the beauty he now knows shall never be his, because he has determined that this woman, he once thought in his boyish way he loved, is a siren who leads men to destruction, and will destroy his life eventually, should he ever take her to his heart, as fully and perhaps as awfully as she has done that of the man who is sleeping in the adjoining room.

On awakening next morning, D'Arnac finds sudden movement is necessary.

A package comes to him which astounds and delights him, yet embarrasses him.

It is an order to relinquish his post as Commandant of Marseilles, and to return forthwith to Paris.

An official notification that he has been promoted to the rank of lieutenant general in the army of France, and has been made honorary lieutenant colonel of the *Musquetaires Noirs*, and commandant of a portion of the garrison of the capital, accompanies the epistle.

This promotion is so unexpected D'Arnac cannot guess to whose good offices it is due. A little consid-eration makes him think he owes it to his old chief of the Army of the Rhine, the Maréchal de Villars.

Upon it he must act at once.

He does so, leaving his office hurriedly to make arrangements for departure, but taking the precaution to lock the door of O'Brien Dillon's room, to prevent intrusion by any of his servants, most of whom are sleep-ing off the effects of their last night's festivity, and do not imagine their master has yet returned to his quarters.

Occupied about this, Raymond, passing the *Hôtel de Vilie*, sees the carriages of Monseigneur Law and his party drawn up ready to take departure from Mar-seilles.

The financier calls to him and says affably: "General d'Arnac, permit me to congratulate you upon your promotion!"

Law has had word of it by post also, and rather hints that it is owing to his good offices that the young man has received his important command, for this shrewd diplomatist imagines that it will be well to be *en rapport*, during the coming year, with any officer controlling a portion of the garrison of Paris.

He continues, rather eagerly: "Won't you join our party on this journey to the capital?"

"That will be impossible! I cannot turn over my command here in a minute," replies D'Arnac, anxious to get the affair over, for he sees the goddess that he had worshipped until to-day, the alluring Hilda de Sabran, is seated in the carriage immediately behind that of Monseigneur Law.

"You must join us," cries that beauty, overhearing the last portion of this conversation, during which she has been throwing veiled, yet pathetic glances at the dashing young general. "You missed our *fête* last night, but we claim you for the journey."

Then she waves a beckoning hand to him.

Thus compelled, D'Arnac approaches her carriage, and finding her alone in it, is forced to a *tête-a-tête* that he would like to avoid.

She whispers eagerly: "You will come with us?"

"Impossible!" he falters. "Official duties!" His look, which for the life of him he cannot control, gives this young lady pleasure. She is so enchanting a picture no man could withhold admiration.

"Official duties," she says bitterly, "kept you from me yesterday?" then whispers plaintively, lovingly: "Raymond, my darling—God help me! why did you forget me last night?" An awful longing in her soft voice, wistful tears in her blue eyes that have grown languid, looking for him who came not to her arms.

"Why?" stammers the young man. Then a sudden Machiavelian instinct coming to him, he mutters: "You see, your 'Uncle Johnny' was wiser than either of us; when he sent me away last evening, *he knew I could not get back to the Isle Pomègue.*"

"Ah, it was he!" and the beauty snaps the pearls she calls teeth very savagely together, and favors Uncle

Johnny's back with a look, that if he saw it, would make the financier jump.

On this Raymond gazes astonished; he had expected indignant anger from this slighted beauty, but she only gives pathetic entreaty in both voice and eyes to this man who is the first one in all her life to slight her marvelous loveliness and make her suffer the pang of jealous fear. Her rage is for others, Monseigneur Law, Raymond's *protégé*, la Quinault, the *comedienne* of the Français, but never D'Arnac.

Just at this instant the laughing Marquise de Prie, attended by the Prince de Conti, joins them from a neighboring shop, in which she has been making some purchases for the journey, and giving the promoted gentleman an elaborate courtesy, says: "Permit me to salute the colonel of the *Musquetaires Noirs*. That means all the Court balls *ex officio*. I claim the first minuet."

"With the greatest of pleasure," and Raymond bows, delighted at the opportune interruption.

"You had better join us, D'Arnac," remarks De Conti very affably, for even this prince of the blood thinks he may have use, in the near future, for a general commanding troops near Paris. "Egad! If you don't accept our offer, you will scarcely reach the capital for a year, unless you walk there. Every diligence seat is engaged for months ahead."

"I shall use my own chargers," answers Raymond, "though I am very much obliged to you for your kind invitation, Monsieur le Prince."

A moment after the carriages drive away; Hilda waving an adieu, with an entreaty in her eyes that would mean a great deal to D'Arnac, if he would accept their meaning.

Then he goes about his business again, and towards evening, his arrangements having been completed, deftly getting his galley slave out of Marseilles, the two take horse for Paris. ·

But were it not for D'Arnac's private means of conveyance they would be months reaching the capital. The rush to that city is so immense that every vehicle, every diligence, has been engaged far in advance to take the speculating crowd of financiers, from the world over, to the capital of France, which is growing even day by day under the great schemes of Monseigneur Law, in its crowds, in its riches, in its potency in the commercial world, in a luxury and extravagance that had been unheard of since the days when Ancient Rome conquered the world, and it in turn destroyed her by the effeminate voluptuousness it threw upon her.

In this gay capital, just at the corner of the Rue St. Denis and the Rue de Petit Lion, stands the hotel of Mr. Lanty Lanigan, a veteran in the French Army of the Rhine during the war of the Spanish succession and of the Imperial army on the banks of the Danube, opposed to the Turks, in which, following the fortunes of O'Brien Dillon, he had battled most valiantly both for love of fighting and for love of plunder.

Some two years before this, coming with his master in triumph to Paris, after the great battle of Belgrade, in which they had captured the Turkish Vizier and obtained a great ransom from him, as well as all the diamonds of himself and harem, amounting to some five hundred thousand crowns' worth of loot and plunder, Mr. Lanigan had disported himself with military ardor until the disastrous massé shot at billiards that his master had made at the Café St. Michel and the disappearance of O'Brien Dillon, Comte of the Empire and General in the Austrian service, from the sight of man.

Thereafter Mr. Lanigan, by assiduous attentions to Monseigneur Law at his bank on the Rue Vivienne, as well as various deft hints as to certain disclosures he might make the Regent in regard to the beautiful Hilda de Sabran being the wife of his lost master, had contrived to gain from the financier enough money to purchase the hostelry of the Turk's Head.

The house, three stories in height, topped by a sloping roof with dormer windows after the manner of that time, is quite extensive in its accommodations for wayfarers; part of the lower floor having been fitted up by its enterprising proprietor into a bright looking café, the floor of which is covered with the cleanest sawdust. Adjoining it is a pleasant wineshop, embellished by a billiard table.

If O'Brien Dillon has any unpleasant recollections of·

the famous massé shot evolved by the inventive mechanical genius of his Irish servant, Mr. Lanty has no such feelings with regard to it, and has made it, by means of his deft performance with a cue bearing a leather end, quite a resort of those who are devotees of the game, winning from them considerable money by his extraordinary execution of the marvelous shot which has now become recognized as a matter of mechanics—not magic.

The business of the tavern, café, and adjoining wine shop, has increased marvelously, as the town has filled up with strangers thronging to Paris to gain fortunes on the Rue Quincampoix, by speculating in the stocks of the India Company, now the great feature of financial Europe.

Within three months, Mr. Lanty Lanigan (generally known under the name of Lanty) has twice raised his charges, without losing a customer.

His hostelry he has decorated with an enormous Turk's head of most savage appearance and ferocious eyes, in honor of his triumph over the Ottoman, and has placarded under this sign the following ominous notice to travelers:

☞This is no poor man's Tavern!

None but the rich need apply

For entertainment for man or beast.

It is a bright, beautiful morning towards the end of June, 1719, when Lanty, walking out of his hostelry and taking a look up and down the Rue de Petit Lion and the Rue St. Denis, mutters to himself, gazing upon the great mass of people that throng the streets even at this early hour of the day: "Bedad, they're still crowding in like women to a wake! Divil take me, if I don't raise the charges on 'em agin!"

Then a sudden grin comes over his genial devil-may-care countenance, as he says: "Be me soul! here's luck! If it isn't that pretty little darlint Marie coming

down the street in the handsomest pair of red stockings
that ever made a man's heart beat faster !   I'm afeard
her father, that old Savoyard, Chambery, don't like
me as well as before he made ten millions on the Rue
Quincampoix.   But faix, if he made a hundred millions
I'd love his duck of a daughter all the same—perhaps a
little more.   Bedad ! I think me sword has done good
work for me with the young lady.   She's not used to
soldiers and gintlemin, and a man of the world impresses
her innocent soul."

Whereupon, assuming a martial manner, and bringing into prominence the hilt of a long Spanish rapier
that he always wears at his side, Mr. Lanigan strides up
to a very showy looking young woman who chances to
be passing the Turk's Head Inn just at this time.

"Ah, Marie, *acushla!*" he whispers in the easy manner that most Irishmen have towards the fair sex.   "Did
ye come out walking to see me this morning ?"

"Not *this* morning," says the girl saucily, "and I
did not see you at all; the sun was in my eyes."

"Faix, I know that I'm always dazzling," replies
Lanty, stealing the compliment from the sun.

"Pooh ! you're not dazzling to me," giggles the girl,
who has rustic, unformed but coquettish manners.
"What do you mean by ' *acushla ?*'   Is it a Dutch
compliment ?"

"Faix, don't ye know that's the Irish for darlint,—
ye little witch ?   Hav'nt I been calling you *acushla*
with me eyes ever since they first got sight of ye ?"
whispers Lanty with an enraptured ogle.

Whereupon the young lady elevates a coquettish nose
in the air and says: "You must not address me that
way.   My father wouldn't like it!"   Then she adds,
poutingly: "But I forgive you—it—it's the last chance
that you'll have !"

" 'The last chance I'll have ?'   What—what makes
ye think that ?" stammers Lanty, his spirit drooping a
little at this, for the young lady's charms of face and
manner and fortune have enraptured the ardent Irishman's soul.

"Because from now on I am going to be brought up
after the manner of the *noblesse*.   Father says he's rich
enough to give me the surroundings of a lady of fashion."

And mademoiselle flounts her petticoats out and takes her steps in the mincing manner of great ladies, displaying to Lanty's devouring eyes her very attractive red stockings and well shod feet.

"Bedad! then I'm just the man to put you into dacint society," says Lanty. "Who could do it better than the soldier and the gintlemin?"

"I'm afraid the soldier and the gentleman will see very little of me," returns Marie, laughingly, though there is a shade of concern in her voice. "I'm to have a governess and a maid servant with me on my next promenade. Will the soldier have the courage to face a governess and a maid servant?"

"Bedad! for you I'd have the courage to face a squadron of governesses and a regiment of maid servants! Do ye think I'm going to let yer old divil of a father put ye out of my way when I am just beginning to love ye?"

"*Love* me?" gasps the girl, growing red but pleased. "Love *me*, Mr. Lanty?"

"Aye, and MARRY ye," replies the Irishman. "Marie, *acushla!* ye're to be the future Mrs. Lanty Lanigan. Put that down in your prayer book and think of it when ye say yer *Ave Marias* ivery mornin', as I hope ye do, loike a good girl. Ye can tell yer father that with me compliments."

"Indeed, I shall do nothing of the kind—I dare not," says the girl. "My father talks of betrothing me to the rich Monsieur Potteau. He's worth five millions."

"Mother of Moses! the ex-footman of the Comte de Broglie!" gasps Lanty. "That's puttin' ye into society the same as an introduction to the divil is sending you to heaven. Be my soul, hasn't yer father enough money? What ye want in yer family now is a little good blood, which I am prepared to furnish to order; aye, and to shed it for ye," cries Lanty. "I'll run that footman through his flunky gizzard before he even kisses yer. Speaking of kisses, Marie, darlint, come into the back alley."

Then taking the girl by the arm in a very uncere-monious way, Mr. Lanty says: "Marie, answer me, as ye would yer patron saint: Which would ye sooner have, the dashing soldier, Mr. Lanigan, or the flunkey-bred footman of the Comte de Broglie?"

"Don't—don't ask me," gasps the girl.

"Bedad! that's the way I loike to have ye talk—agitated. Agitation shows emotion; emotion shows love. Marie, which would ye sooner have? Don't dally with me! WHICH? Look me in the eye and say it!"

"You," cries the girl, with a merry laugh.

"Then come into the back alley and give me a kiss!"

But breaking away from his restraining arms she hurries into the crowd, and in spite of Lanty's pursuit, her agile feet, in the great throng, outdistance and elude him.

At last the red stockings pass out of sight and he muses: "Bedad, I think I've got her. Now, for her father! Money is what will appeal to the provincial soul of the Savoyard Chambery, more than all the good blood of the Lanigans. Musha! up goes the prices in The Turk's Head! By Saint Patrick! won't I beggar my boarders!"

With this Shylock idea in his mind, going back to his duties as *maitre d'hôtel*, Lanty cries excitedly to a waiter who has brought complaint to him: "What's this about Monsieur le Baron de Boussier—complains of me raisin' the price of his apartments, does he? Tell the Baron, with me compliments, not to be so lazy and aristocratic, and go on the Rue Quincampoix and make some money. Faix, I've got a much better offer for his apartment from Le Pellouse, who was a butcher three weeks ago, and is now a millionaire Mississippian. By-the-bye, while we're thinkin' of it, make proclamation in the café that everything eatable and drinkable will be double from to-day on! Bedad, I'll also tell Monsieur Beauleau, that beggarly Swiss, I've popped up the cost of his garret room ten *livres* a day!"

For the price of living had risen with the increased population of Paris, which in two years had become greater by three hundred thousand people, and was augmenting at the rate of over a thousand a day. This concourse, under the primitive means of transportation at that time, was becoming even difficult to provision.

These various financial arrangements of Mr. Lanigan are by no means looked upon by his customers with pleasant eyes. Monsieur le Baron de Boussier twists his aristocratic moustache and exclaims : "*Parbleu!* At this rate, these stockbrokers are the only ones who will be able to afford bread and wine."

Various other exclamations of disgust come from people seated in the café at the announcement which is being made in strident voice by the waiter.

Hearing this, the Irish landlord steps in and remarks in his blandest tone : "The waiter made a mistake!"

"Of course it was a mistake!" cry some of the guests, delighted. And others laugh: "*Sacre bleu!* Your *garçon* is a *cochon!*"

"Faix, yes! He said I had doubled the price of provisions—it's an error—I told the imbecile to put 'em *three* times as high. I want ye all to know this is the capital of France, and yer livin' in an expensive city; and if ye think ye can foind cheaper rates, ye'd better apply next door, where they'll starve ye and charge ye more!"

At this there is a kind of "God help us!" groan from his customers.

But in the midst of the very pleasing scene Mr. Lanigan receives a shock that makes him oblivious of the price of provisions in Paris.

A young gentleman, in the handsome dress of an aristocrat of that day, who has been seated apparently waiting for something to turn up, for he has simply called for a bottle of *vin ordinaire*, and has dawdled over this, suddenly rises from his table, and walks up to his host, crying very savagely: "*Diable!* You dare raise the price of provisions, reptile?"

Turning upon him with a snarl of rage, for the Irishman's disposition is not a Christian one under provocation, Mr. Lanigan's eyes suddenly roll in his head, and he gasps: "Giniral d'Arnac!"

"Hush!" whispers the other, quickly. "Quarrel with me till I get you into another room!"

With this he suddenly bursts out into a jabber of French invective, and drags the astounded Lanty into a neighboring apartment.

Here Raymond suddenly whispers: "Keep cool!—I have got some good news for you."

"You—you have found him—alive?"

"Yes !"

"Holy St. Pathrick !" and such a wild howl of unutterable joy comes into the café that his customers spring up from their seats, but are sure that Mr. Lanigan has won his battle with his irate customer.

"Quiet !" mutters Raymond, "don't let your joy overcome you !" for there are tears in the Irish veteran's eyes, and he gasps, "Where did you find him ? What did they do to him that night ?"

"Restrain yourself," whispers the young officer, "for your old master's safety. No matter what your rage and indignation at his wrongs may be, keep your tongue quiet !"

"What happened to him ? By me soul, if they've hurt a hair of his wig I'll avenge him !" mutters the Irishman.

"To do that, keep quiet !"

"Faix, I'm still as a sarpint."

"Then listen," and Raymond gives him hurriedly but succinctly an account of how he had discovered his old master in the galleys, with the various details connected with it, which is broken in upon by little exclamations of horror, and sometimes a grinding of the teeth, and muttered curses from the sturdy Irishman, as he appreciates the horror of what has come to his old master.

As Raymond finishes he suddenly says: "Where is he ? Why didn't ye bring him in—sure wouldn't O'Brien Dillon get hospitality of me and protection by my life—if the ghost of old Richelieu were after him in person."

"He is not here. Monsieur d'Argenson, Lieutenant-General of police, has too many spies about to transport easily into Paris a man without a passport. I have left him outside the gates at Passy. You go there every morning ?"

"Yes, in a covered cart."

"You buy vegetables at the garden of a man named Shoteau ?"

"How did ye know that ?"

"My sister, la Marquise de Chateaubrien."

"Ah, yes. Faith, she's been a very good friend to me since I've been in business here—God bless her swate face !" mutters Lanty, for he has not been backward in asking for trade, and Mimi Chateaubrien has sent a good many customers to the Turk's Head Inn.

"Very well, at the garden of Shotcau, O'Brien Dillon will meet you. Then in your covered cart you can bring him to your inn and keep him quietly here."

"Faix, I would, but there's divil a vacant room in the house. Iverything is let, and I slape on the table meself," returns Lanty, rubbing his red head.

"You must make room."

"Very well, I'll raise that Papillon, the stockbroker, out of his apartments. Bedad, O'Brien Dillon shall have the best in the house. I'll put them at one hundred *livres* a day. Even that rich beast won't stand that price!"

"Then, don't let O'Brien leave his rooms until I have seen him. Come to me, at the Hôtel de Chateaubrien as soon as you have brought him here. I can depend upon you, Lanty ?"

"As in God !" is the modest assurance of the Irishman. "I'll have the cart ready in two minutes."

And he goes away, muttering : "Wirra ! wirra ! good God of Heaven! curse 'em! In the galleys—oh, me dear master!" Then he gnashes his teeth together and chuckles hideously : "By all the souls of the Saints, I pity Uncle Johnny Law, Madame Hilda and Cousin Charlie de Moncrief, if O'Brien Dillon is half the man he once was !"

But while doing this he is harnessing his donkey into his cart, and some five hours after comes to the great mansion of Raymond's widowed sister, the Hôtel de Chateaubrien on the Rue St. Honoré, and being ushered in by numerous flunkeys is there received by D'Arnac and Madame la Marquise, who appears very bright and charming this summer day, as she has thrown off mourning.

There is a look of intense interest in her face, for her brother has felt himself compelled to tell her of the treachery of De Moncrief to his friend, and his belief of Cousin Charlie's cowardly attempts at his own life by means of military duty, during the war upon the Rhine.

This revelation of the cold villainy of a man bound

to them by ties of blood, and whom she has until now at
least thought her brother's friend, has made her nervous and excited.

"Well?" cries Mimi anxiously, for she has become
enthused herself in Raymond's battle for his old
comrade.

"Well, bless your swate face, Mrs. Marquise," says
Lanty, "I've got him at the Turk's Head Inn. I
brought him in disguised with me cabbages."

"You came past the gates all right?" asks Raymond.

"Faix, and I did, but I'm afraid we'll have to be
moving him from my tavern very shortly."

"Why?"

"Because he's so very nervous, he trembles and
shivers at ivery click of the billiard balls in my café.
God help us! that a soldier should fear balls of any
kind."

"He must stand the click of the ivories for a day or
two, until I can find him other quarters!" mutters
D'Arnac, chewing his moustache.

"Bedad, I think we'll have to move him before."

"Pooh! billiard balls won't make him sick. He'll
get used to them in time."

"Nevertheless I think we'd better move him at
once!" persists Lanty.

"Impossible!"

"Quicker than lightning!"

"*Diable!* Why?"

"Because, by me soul, COUSIN CHARLIE'S SEEN HIM
ALREADY!" answers Lanty. "I thought I'd break the
news to you very gently," he mutters as he gazes on
Raymond who has grown deathly pale, and his sister
who has given a suppressed shriek and fallen shuddering into a chair.

CHAPTER III.

COUSIN CHARLIE SEES A GHOST.

"Charles de Moncrief has seen him!" whispers
Raymond, with white lips.

"Cousin Charlie!" gasps Mimi,

Then she falters up, and putting her arms about her brother says: "If they discover that you have abducted a galley slave what may they not do to you?"

"Ye're both almost as frightened," replies Lanty, "as Cousin Charlie was when he saw him?"

"You are sure he recognized him?"

"Faix, an' I'm afraid he did! Charlie nearly died in the café, and it took four strong brandies to revive him in the wine room. I didn't know what was the matter with him, as I was strengthening the old villain up."

"Quick! How did it occur?" mutters D'Arnac anxiously.

"Well, you see I raised the rent of his apartments, upon that stockbroker Papillon, to one hundred *livres* a day, and by me soul, hang me, if he didn't stand the raise! Oh, the money these creatures are making nowadays. So I jumped his rent to two hundred *livres* a day, and told him I wouldn't discuss it—he had no lease of the apartments, and Papillon went away cursing.

"Meantime I had got O'Brien Dillon in from Passy, and put him quietly into the rooms, and tucked him to bed with some pipes and tobacco at his elbow, and a whiskey bottle convanient, for he's not quite up to his old tune, though I've great hopes he'll soon become himself again. He took as natural to his pipe and whiskey as he ever did.

"With that I left him quietly asleep and came down to my business about the hotel, when, as bad luck would have it, your Cousin Charlie de Moncrief, who has some business with this stockbroker Papillon—some sly business I think it is, that he does not care about anyone's knowing about but himself—came to see him at his rooms, and inquiring in his sneaking way from one of the servant maids (who knew nothing about what I had been doing) she directed him to what she supposed were Papillon's apartments, and in he went.

"Faix, O'Brien Dillon must have been ashlape, otherwise that sneaking divil would never have got out alive. But I'm afraid he recognized him. The first I saw of him he came in staggering pale as if he'd seen a ghost, and as soon as he clapped eyes on me he gave a little shriek of horror and fainted dead away in the café, and

I like a fool looking at him didn't know the cause of it, and went to pouring brandy down the beast's throat, and every time he revived a little and saw me he nearly died again.

"Until finally I got him in a voiture and sent him off. But thinking over the matter, a frightful idea flashed through me, and I made inquiries, and found that Cousin Charlie had been in the room along with the master, and that the reason Monsieur Charlie de Moncrief needed so much brandy to keep him alive was his fearful interview with the sleeping goblin of O'Brien Dillon."

"We must get O'Brien out of town at once!" cries Raymond.

"Faix, I'll take him out as a cabbage agin," remarks Lanty, and turns to go.

But D'Arnac calls him back suddenly, and says: "No, on second thought Charles de Moncrief dare not sleep to-night if he guesses O'Brien Dillon is in town and free for vengeance. Dillon will be seized surely at the gates. I know enough of D'Argenson and his secret police to be aware of that. Have you no other place you can conceal him?"

"'Deed, an' I have. I've just bought L'Epée du Bois, Cabaret, and a very pretty turn I've made by it. I'll take him there for the present."

"Where is the place?"

"On the Rue de Venise, just out of the Quincampoix."

"Very well, I'll meet you there in two hours," replies Raymond.

Then the Irishman going away, his sister looks at D'Arnac, and her bright mind coming into the situation she says: "You may be safer than you imagine. Do you think the great policeman D'Argenson whose spies are everywhere would have let you bring Dillon into Paris *if he had not wished it?*" To this she adds anxiously: "What are you going to do?"

"I'm going to fight this affair open and in the light of day. I am a soldier, not a policeman!" says the young officer impetuously.

"Bravo! How?"

"By the Duc de Villars. He took great personal interest in his old officer. I shall ask him to see that justice is done to one of the bravest soldiers of his army.

If he cannot aid me I shall go to the German Embassador, for O'Brien Dillon is a Comte of the Empire, and general in the Austrian service."

"That's right, brother!" cries Mimi, her eyes sparkling. Then she adds eagerly: "If any little feminine artifice will help you, call upon Mimi de Chateaubrien. She is a widow and of course artful!"

Going away with her words in his ear, her kiss on his cheek, D'Arnac drives hurriedly to the residence of Hector de Villars, and, fortunately finding that grandee in, is immediately ushered into the presence of the Maréchal of France.

"I had been expecting you, my boy," says his old chief, kindly. "I am delighted to greet you as Lieutenant-General and Lieutenant-Colonel of the *Musquetaires Noirs*. Egad! you'll be a maréchal younger than I was. I was not a lieutenant-general till I was thirty, and you are only——"

"Twenty-six," remarks D'Arnac, and commences to thank De Villars for what he has done for him.

But that officer astonishes his *protégé* by saying: "Pooh! don't thank me—thank the Marquis d'Argenson, Keeper of the Seals and Lieutenant-General de Police."

"Thank *him?* He is my enemy—he is the friend of Law!" gasps Raymond, opening his eyes with astonishment.

"Nevertheless D'Argenson applied to the Regent for your appointment, and D'Orleans, remembering your saving Law's life at the Theatre Français, thought your promotion would please the King's stockbroker," remarks De Villars (applying a name to the financier that was becoming a popular one in France at that day). "Then," he continues, "they asked me, and I——"

"And you?"

"Oh, I told them you were a good soldier and a fine fighter."

"I am much obliged to you," interjects D'Arnac.

"But," chuckles De Villars, "I told them that, with the gallantry of youth, you had its impetuosity. Dost remember the elopement with Madame O Brien Dillon, eh, my youthful Bayard?"

"And it is this very impetuosity," breaks in Raymond,

"that brings me to you. I have come to you to right a wrong that has been done to a man who was once one of your favorite officers."

"*Diable!* Whose wrong?" growls the veteran, bristling up.

"O'Brien Dillon's! They made him a galley slave!"

"Good God! For what?"

"For making an uncommonly good shot at billiards."

"*Tonnerre de Dieu!* You don't mean it," mutters the maréchal, grinding his teeth.

"Yes, I do!" and Raymond gives a full account of the whole affair. Then he says: "What will you do for me?"

And De Villars puts him to despair. He remarks sententiously, "It is an affair of the police! The police should rectify it."

"The police—Impossible! They are friends of Law, and against my friend!"

"They *were* the friends of Law. Monsieur d'Argenson, I imagine, is now his enemy. Go to Monsieur d'Argenson and ask his advice, and I think it will be the advice of a friend. I imagine he wants your assistance in the army—and will.give you, in return, his aid as a policeman."

"But if he does not—if he should seize me in his office for conspiring to assist the escape of a galley slave!" mutters D'Arnac. "D'Argenson has arrested many a greater noble and higher officer than I am, in his day."

"If you are not back in one hour," returns the maréchal, "I will go to the Regent myself, and to the Austrian Embassador and, by my soul! it will be odd if Hector de Villars cannot get a little justice out of easy-going D'Orleans, even though his financier opposes it. But you should catch D'Argenson at his office at once."

"I will go!" mutters D'Arnac, desperately. "It's like putting my head in the lion's mouth, but I will go!"

"Very well," replies his chief, giving the young man a cordial grip of the hand, "if you are not back in one hour De Villars will then move on the enemy!"

Inspired by hope at the words of a man upon whose standard victory had so often perched, Raymond springs into his carriage again, and goes rushing through the streets of Paris, in which he cannot help noting the marvelous increase in the crowds of people in his year's absence —the wondrous multiplication of the equipages and their greater richness of liveries and trappings and adornment. But, shortly crossing into the Ile de la Cité, he comes to the Palais of Justice and the office of Monsieur, le Marquis d'Argenson, who, though Keeper of the Seals of France, still holds the spies, the *mouchards* and the sergeants de ville of Paris within his grasp.

There he is almost immediately ushered into the private office, and stands confronting Marc René d'Argenson, the greatest policeman and the poorest financier of his day; so poor a manipulator of funds that six years before, though he had held the power over all Paris as Lieutenant-General of Police for over a quarter of a century, on the death of Louis XIV. this man had suffered almost personal want, where others would have found themselves certainly prosperous—probably rich.

He has a clear, cold face, but peculiar sinister features, and dark eyes that have a marvelous flash *du diable*, giving him the common appellation of " The face of the *damné!* "

One of these devil's smiles comes over D'Argenson's mobile features as he sees Raymond enter his apartment, and, rising eagerly, extending a welcoming hand, he remarks: " I am glad to see you once more, General d'Arnac ! Permit me to congratulate you upon the high office to which you have recently been called. I think I may, without vanity, say that I have had something to do with your promotion."

" For which I have called to tender my thanks. Monsieur le Duc de Villars has just informed me of your kindness," returns D'Arnac.

" And you have called for *nothing else ?* " smiles the Minister of Police; though the contortion of his features makes the expression a sneer.

" Yes," answers Raymond, frankly.

" Oh, ho! I have been expecting you here for two hours," laughs D'Argenson. Then he says, significantly : " Ever since your old comrade of the Rhine campaign, O'Brien Dillon, Comte of the Empire, came in by the Port de Passy, concealed in cabbages."

At this there is a gasp of astonishment from D'Arnac.

" Do not fear," replies D'Argenson, " for your friend.

I imagine it is on his behalf that you come to me!"
The eyes of the great policeman gleam with triumphant
acuteness.   Then he adds tersely but affably: "If you
want me to be of real assistance to you, you must tell
me the whole matter."

"I will!" answers D'Arnac with military frankness,
for he commences to perceive De Villars' prognostications are coming true.

With this he attempts to relate the whole story of
O'Brien Dillon, commencing at his billiard shot in the
Café St. Michel.

"You may skip all that," interjects D'Argenson.   "I
am perfectly aware of the facts in his case until he
reached the galleys.   Tell me the rest."

This Raymond does, giving the complete account
of the affair, even to De Moncrief's recognition of
the escaped *forçat* in the tavern of the Turk's Head,
and Lanty's remarks upon the terrible fear and trembling it had brought upon the Procureur du Roy.   At
which the Lieutenant of Police bursts into shrieks of
diabolic laughter, crying: "I see him now! Poor little
De Moncrief!   He is doubtless too ill with terror to
venture out as yet.   But he will soon come to me with
his story, and a request for the arrest of the hiding
galley slave.   For, mark my words, Charles de Moncrief
would die a hundred deaths of apprehension under his
bedclothes if he thought O'Brien Dillon were alive and
free this night in Paris!"

"As he will be!   I trust in your good offices, Monsieur le Marquis," returns Raymond, anxiously.

"But not in Paris!"

"Why not?"

"O'Brien Dillon must be out of Paris within two
hours, to save a complication—that is, if you will take
my advice; though," remarks Monsieur d'Argenson,
smiling, "O'Brien Dillon is as safe here as you are!"

"How? When he was arrested and condemned by a
tribunal of justice?"

"O'BRIEN DILLON WAS NOT CONDEMNED! A naked
man was brought into the Conciergerie charged under
the name of Paul Casanova with being a sorcerer,
convicted under that name, and sentenced to the
galleys under that name—but that does not condemn

O'Brien Dillon, Comte of the Empire and general in the Austrian service. Still he had better leave Paris to prevent any complication between myself and Monseigneur Law, just at present. If you will take my advice, you will get your friend out of the capital, if possible within the hour—certainly within two! I will furnish you the necessary papers for his safe transport into Germany. When there, if he wishes to return," smiles the Marquis, "for revenge upon Monseigneur Law, who has twice ruined him, or to have it out with Charles de Moncrief, your cousin, who has brought him to the galleys, or to discipline Madame Hilda de Sabran, mistress of the Regent of France—but the wife of his bosom, who has been untrue to him with many gentlemen, and who even now I imagine adores a certain young general who blushes when he hears her name—let Dillon come here as some accredited officer of the Austrian government. I think he has interest enough with Prince Eugene of Savoy and the Imperial Court to obtain such an appointment. Then I feel he may be of use to both you and to *me!*"

And the face of the *damné* borrows a twist of the eyes from his master in Hades.

"Within two hours O'Brien Dillon is out of Paris *en route* for the Austrian border!" replies D'Arnac.

"You think he will become the old slashing soldier of fortune again?" queries D'Argenson so anxiously that Raymond knows that the officer of French police will have work for the officer of the Austrian army on his return to Paris.

"He has the spirit of an Irishman!" returns Raymond.

"And, *ma foi!* they throw off trouble like spaniels throw off water. Then *au revoir!*" remarks D'Argenson, who, while he has been talking, has been making out the necessary papers for Dillon. "I presume I shall have the pleasure of seeing you at the next court ball. As lieutenant-colonel of the *Musquetaires Noirs* you mustn't disappoint the ladies."

"Of course not!" laughs Raymond—his first real laugh since he recognized as galley slave his comrade of the Rhine.

Leaving the office of Monsieur d'Argenson, D'Arnac

hurries back to the Duc de Villars, and, telling him how the matter stands, thanks him for his advice.

Within an hour after that he has elbowed and fought his way through the Rue Quincampoix, which is now filled by trading brokers rending the air with wild bids and offers of stock.

Arrived at the Rue de Venise, Raymond is received by Lanty with open arms at the cabaret L'Epée du Bois. Here they make hurried arrangements for O'Brien's departure for Vienna, to which the Irish officer eagerly assents, remarking: "Faith, a few months' rest in the country will do me no harm."

Then D'Arnac, not thinking it wise to accompany him outside the gates, Dillon, shaking hands with him, mutters: "When I come back, I'll be my old self, Raymond, me comrade!—and THEN—!" His eyes complete the awful sense.

A moment after, as the wild cries of the excited crowd float up to them in the little cabaret from the neighboring Quincampoix, the Irishman sneers: "Bedad, Uncle Johnny's stockbrokers are making a fine howling outside, but from what you tell me of Monsieur d'Argenson, I imagine this grand stock speculation is making a good many enemies for the man who has despoiled me of wife and fortune. Keep that in mind, Raymond, my boy."

So with a parting clasp of the hand O'Brien leaves his friend, and with a well supplied purse furnished by D'Arnac, and two or three servants and flunkies, Comte Dillon, notwithstanding the awful ordeal he has gone through, makes a very pleasant and rapid journey to the Austrian capital.

———

CHAPTER IV.

THE BROTHERS PARIS.

THIS remark of Dillon's, about Uncle Johnny's stock speculations making him enemies, leaves so much of an impression upon Raymond's mind, that going away from the cabaret L'Epée du Bois, he gets to speculating upon Monsieur d'Argenson's curious change of position, from a seeming friend, to at least a secret foe of Monseigneur Law.

A remark that he catches from one broker to another, as they are refreshing themselves in the cabaret, would elucidate it, if D'Arnac had had data enough to solve the problem.

"*Parbleu!*" remarks this speculator. "Do you know it is rumored that the Regent is going to give to the India Company the sole collection of the taxes of France? If so, the stock will double in value in less than a month."

"*Mon Dieu!*" replies the man addressed, "how the Brothers Paris will writhe!" and goes into side-splitting laughter.

The affair they alluded to was the reason of D'Argenson's change of front, if Raymond had but guessed it.

A few years before this, four very worthy financiers of Avignon had come to the capital, and under the name of the Brothers Paris had made great sums of money in various speculations; chiefly in buying and selling Government securities that were very much depreciated at that time. They had finally obtained from the Regent of France a contract consolidating the old *Fermiers Généraux* of Louis XIV., each of whom collected the taxes of a certain province, into one great company called the new *Fermiers Généraux*, the profits of which had been very great.

This concern, for a certain percentage, undertaking the entire charge of the tax business of the country, and making returns to the royal treasury of all its collections under the law.

On this very profitable enterprise Uncle Johnny had cast longing eyes, and was at this very moment making arrangements, by means of his favor with the Regent, to withdraw the same from the Brothers Paris, and put it in the maw of the all-grabbing—all-devouring India Company.

His reasons for this were very far-seeing. Monseigneur Law (called generally, for some unknown and inexplicable reason by the people of France, Lass) had determined to have *no other stock* in France in which

the public could invest their money, save that of the
all-pervading India Company.

When this has been accomplished, he is then prepared
to make the boldest, the most astonishing, and the most
audacious proposition any single individual ever made
to the government of any great country; but until he
has destroyed every other floating investment in the
realm, he cannot move in this colossal scheme.
Therefore he has been putting out his lines, and laying his
plans for this great financial *coup d'etat*; the practical
annihilation of the new *Fermiers Généraux* being
his present objective point.

Now these Brothers Paris were four very diplomatic
and very shrewd gentlemen of the Hebrew persuasion,
who are not generally very much at fault when it comes
to business matters pertaining to gold and shekels.
And they were struggling with all their might and main
and intrigue, to prevent the astute Scotchman from
shearing the children of Israel.

The youngest brother, Monsieur Reuben, was a most
bizarre and avaricious speculator, and had made considerable money out of his enemy already by adroit
speculations in the stocks of the India Company.   But
he did not propose that his own pet concern should be
absolutely wiped from the face of the street.   To avoid
this he was gaining all the friends that were possible,
and had approached Monsieur d'Argenson (whom he
had known in his wily mind to be always lukewarm in
his friendship for Law) with such magnificent financial
offers that the Lieutenant-General of Police has fallen
under his bribes.

Together they are scheming to get with them the
blustering, devil-may-care De Conti, and have been
assisted in this by Monsieur Charles de Moncrief, who
has a grudge both against the policeman and the prince
for the atrocious merriment in which they indulged
upon his appearance as a senile cupid at the first *Bal
de l'Opera* ever given in Paris.

For Cousin Charlie never forgives, and he has determined in his acute yet narrow mind that Monseigneur
Lass is destined to be the great power of the nation,
and that the Regent of France is going to be forever
his backer and friend, and that anyone whom he can put

into active opposition to them must perforce go to the wall—no matter their power—no matter their blood—even if they are as strong as Marc René, Marquis d'Argenson and Louis Armand de Bourbon, Prince of the blood.

To do this Cousin Charlie has, with his unscrupulous tongue, very frequently dropped hints in the presence both of D'Argenson and De Conti of rather sneering remarks Monseigneur Lass has made with regard to them, which would have caused the gentleman to whom he attributes them to open his eyes in astonishment, as they are simply atrocious lies. For instance, such suggestions as these: "We have many silver *marcs* in France, but only one copper one—*Marc* René d'Argenson!" and: "What is the use of my trying to put money in the bank when De Conti shovels it out at the other end upon his hundred mistresses?"

"Did Lass say that?" cries that Prince on this coming to his ears. "Did he say that, De Moncrief? Egad! I'll live up to my reputation."

Acting upon this view, De Conti soon afterwards makes his compact with D'Argenson, Leblanc, the stockbroker, and the Brothers Paris, and they form a company called "The *Anti*-System," in contradistinction to the "System" of Monseigneur Law—the main object of which is to destroy the Scotchman's power and success by any means at hand—chiefly by withdrawing all the money possible from the royal bank, of which Law is director-in-chief.

To this partnership they furnish the following capital:

D'Argenson, the police intrigues and low spying.

De Conti, the blustering, brow-beating, savage assaults, and, if necessary, a little killing and murdering by his Italian bravos.

Leblanc, the wily intriguing, the insidious lying, the putting forth of disparaging rumors upon the street, and the "bearing" of the stock of the India Company, whenever possible, by false quotations and any other foul means in his power.

The four Brothers Paris, the power of Israel in the enormous capital that they can bring to assist the affair, with whatever additional sly digs and pushes they can inflict upon the credit of the India Company.

But all this time *outwardly*, these gentlemen are the great friends of Monseigneur Law, for they fear mightily the power of the edicts of France, that they know he can obtain for the asking from Philippe, Duc d'Orleans, Regent of the realm.

This it is that has prevented any great trouble coming from D'Argenson upon Raymond d'Arnac for his robbery of the galleys of France, and O'Brien Dillon for taking French leave of the oar.

The Minister of Police wishes to use the friendship of the Commander of Troops in Paris, and the undying hatred he knows must fill the persecuted Irishman for the great financier.

During this time Cousin Charlie is apparently a very great friend to both parties, and rubs his hands together, and thinks, in his narrow way, that he has destroyed both D'Argenson and De Conti, by causing them to knock their heads against a stone wall that will never fall at their butting, but forgets what a broader mind would have instantly perceived, that if they ever do bowl over Monseigneur Lass, they will probably destroy Charles de Moncrief also, his fortune at this time being utterly dependent on the financier for whom he is manufacturing enemies.

But, oblivious of this, the Procureur du Roy placidly goes on feathering his nest, taking advantage of his being one of the directors of the Bank Royal to engage in some very questionable stock speculations, in which he employs the broker named Papillon.

It is upon this business he has called to see his agent on the day in question, at Papillon's apartments at Lanty's tavern, with such lamentable results to his nervous system.

The effect upon De Moncrief's nerves is so great that, after seeing the sleeping *forçat*, and being revived in the café of the Turk's Head, he is driven to his rooms feeling his sixty odd years a greater weight than he has ever felt them before.

It is full three hours before he recovers sufficiently to visit the office of the Lieutenant of Police and beg him to take instant measures for arresting an escaped galley slave at present at the auberge on the corner of the Rue St. Denis and the Rue de Petit Lion.

But this request is received in a very off-hand and supercilious manner by Monsieur d'Argenson : " My dear De Moncrief," he purrs, " it is impossible for any-one to escape from the galleys, and still more impossible for a fugitive *forçat* to enter Paris without my knowing it. Your remarks are an insinuation upon the police, and as such upon me. But to satisfy you I will send to the inn you speak of and prove to you you are mistaken. Wait and see the result ! "

This Monsieur de Moncrief does, though very nervously.

Within half an hour the messenger returns and says shortly: " The apartments of Monsieur Papillon are still occupied by that stockbroker. They have never been vacated by Monsieur Papillon."

" Impossible ! " cries the Procureur.

" Go with my agent and see."

Thus commanded, Cousin Charlie, taking a couple of stout police officers with him for his protection, tremblingly makes a return visit to the Turk's Head Inn, and there finds in his rooms Monsieur Papillon, who astounds him by reiterating that he has never given up the occupancy of them; though his landlord had raised the rent upon him, he has still kept them.

This has come about in this way: Lanty, as soon as he had transported O'Brien Dillon to his cabaret in the Rue de Venise, had immediately destroyed any trace of the Irishman's occupancy, and the stockbroker, after a fruitless inquiry for equally convenient apartments at a less rent, had returned, walked into his rooms, and never dreamed anybody had been in them during the few hours of his search for other lodgings.

" You are sure, my dear Papillon," says De Moncrief, after the policemen have gone away, " that no one else has ever been in these rooms ? "

" Of course not ! No one would dare to occupy them."

To this Cousin Charlie suddenly cries: " But you never smoke," and sniffs the air dubiously, for there is still upon the hangings of the room a faint odor of O'Brien Dillon's constant pipe. Whereupon De Moncrief becomes so nervous that he is unable to discuss with Papillon the rather shady financial operations in which the two are engaged.

On going home he ponders over the matter, and chancing to hear from his valet that Raymond has returned to Paris from Toulon, where a number of the galleys had been stationed, a sudden flash of thought starts him for the Hôtel de Chateaubrien, in which Raymond has taken temporary headquarters with his sister, to see if he can worm out some hint of the matter from him. This sudden thought has been, that if anyone in the world would assist the escape of O'Brien Dillon from the galleys of France—that man is his old comrade of the Rhine campaign—Raymond le Comte d'Arnac, lieutenant general in the army of France.

So, looking much the worse for wear, the agitation of the last few hours having moved him a year or two along the book of time, Charles de Moncrief is ushered into the bright *salon* of Mme. de Chateaubrien, very eager to discover, but very much frightened as to what may be disclosed to him.

He is received very affably by la Marquise; for her brother had just told her of the successful manner in which he has finished the O'Brien Dillon affair, and the two have decided it will be unwise to show open distrust of their cousin.

Their ease and light spirits indicate that neither of them have the fortunes of an escaped *forçat* upon their shoulders.

Notwithstanding this Cousin Charlie goes to pumping in his deft legal way, asking Raymond for a description of the great water *fête* at Marseilles, saying how much he would have liked to have been there, but his old bones feared the journey.

"A little rheumaticky, eh?" remarks the young officer, and volunteers a graphic description of the festivities at the commercial port; perhaps rather incautiously describing the galleys that have taken the semi-regal party to their fête on the Island Pomègue.

D'Arnac's frank manner during the whole narration almost forces the lawyer to throw away his suspicions.

Moncrief becomes easier in mind and chuckles: "You look well, my young general! The cares of office do not seem to oppress you."

"No," laughs Mimi, "I don't think Raymond would feel unhappy if they even made him a maréchal; though," says the young lady contemplatively, "I think I made that remark to Aunt Clothilde some half-hour ago."

"Ah, the Comtesse de Crevecœur—she is well, I suppose?"

"She has quite recovered from her bereavement, - —but not from her poverty," replies la Marquise, quite seriously.

"Poverty—how is that?" asks Raymond, suddenly. "My uncle's government investments should have left her rich. They're up to par. When I last spoke to poor Henri they were seventy-five per cent. discount."

"Alas, he sold them when they were seventy-five per cent. discount!" replies Mimi. · "It was the fearful shock of their going up to par that probably put Henri on his deathbed."

"*Parbleu!* He was very foolish and very obstinate. I advised him not to," remarks De Moncrief, contentedly. Though he is quietly chuckling to himself. For it was really his insidious suggestions about the uncertainty of *Billets d'Etat* that had induced the invalid Comte to sell all his government securities, when they were seventy-five per cent. below par. All of these had been deftly purchased by Monsieur Papillon, the agent of Charles de Moncrief, who was very well aware that they must soon be worth their face value, under a certain little stimulus about to be put into them by his friend, Monseigneur Law, who has the touch of Midas."

"You astonish me, Mimi!" says Raymond, very seriously. "You really think the Comtesse is poor?"

"Poor, not exactly. Though she thinks she is, which is to her perhaps the same. Clothilde declares she is going to speculate on the street to regain the money of which she assumes she has been robbed."

"Speculate—buy stock—*one of our family!* I'll see Clothilde to-morrow. Perhaps I had better visit her to-night."

"Nonsense—they all speculate now—the Regent's edict says no noble shall suffer in rank or prestige by buying or selling scrip of the Bank or Mississippi Company—even the Princes of the blood are taking their fling in the street. Besides, I have another errand for you this evening," remarks his sister. "Mademoiselle Quinault has sent to you a little letter. You must see the child to-night, Raymond; otherwise you would break her——" Here Mimi suddenly bites her lips, and thinks "Why did I say that? One would imagine I was trying to produce the effect that I fear upon my brother."

But this remark about Mademoiselle Jeanne delights De Moncrief, and he pats Raymond on the back and chuckles: "It is a great thing to be the guardian of the pet of Paris," then looks wise and whispers: "But there are rumors about."

"What rumors?" cries D'Arnac, savagely.

To this the Procureur rises and says, with the ease of the gossiper: "Ah, dear boy, you will discover in time enough," and would go away quite happy, for D'Arnac's face is very expressive.

But as De Moncrief says adieu to Mimi this young lady, remembering Lanty's story, gets to laughing in her mind at Cousin Charlie's adventure at the Turk's Head Inn. She says carelessly: "You don't look well this evening, poor old boy."

"*Poor* OLD boy—*rich* YOUNG boy! Never better in my life!"

"I am delighted to hear that," remarks Mimi, with incautious rapidity. "I had heard that you fainted four times to-day in the café of one Mr. Lanigan. I—" then suddenly checks herself with a gasp, for Raymond has a warning look, and the old gentleman, in the very act of bowing to her, has literally staggered from the room as this careless young lady cuts short her words.

But they are enough! She has done the business! Charles de Moncrief knows that some one must have brought quick report to the Hôtel de Chateaubrien of this morning's adventures. Why? Because there was one for whose welfare they were anxious at the inn of Mr. Lanty Lanigan.

"Raymond returned from Toulon this morning," he gasps to himself. "My ghost arrived this morning. It is no ghost." And he trembles with shivers. "It is O'Brien Dillon!"

Staggering to his carriage De Moncrief orders: "Monseigneur Law—Place Louis le Grand—like lightning!"

Entering the magnificent residence of the financier, he begs to be announced at once, but does not receive audience, intimate though he is, for an hour, for a great crowd of people are there, imploring to see the financial dictator.

Finally getting entrance, Law looks at him, astonished at his appearance, and cries: "What's the matter?"

"Your life and mine!" whispers De Moncrief.

"How?"

"O'Brien Dillon has escaped!"

"From the galleys? Impossible!"

"Raymond d'Arnac brought him into Paris with him this morning."

At this there is a fearful imprecation from the great Scotchman, who, though he has had many matters on his mind, has not forgotten his terror of the Irishman, whom he has twice ruined and betrayed.

"You are sure?"

"No and yes! It is a conjecture, yet it is a certainty." And De Moncrief gives Monseigneur Law all the information in his power.

"It must be looked to at once," replies the financier. "Still, I think I have nothing to fear *personally*—just at present."

"No!" cries De Moncrief, desperately. "The Regent has given you a guard of honor. You have eighteen sentries every night to protect you. He can't get in and murder you in your bed—but God help me! I have no one to protect me, save a trembling Swiss valet and the old *concierge* who keeps the door below! Mother of Heaven! what shall I do this awful night? D'Argenson won't believe Dillon has escaped. Perhaps the policeman will stir himself when he hears I'm dead in my bed to-morrow morning." And Cousin Charlie wrings his hands in a helpless, despairing kind of way.

"For that reason," says the financier, struggling with an uneasy smile, "you will be very apt to follow my advice carefully."

And he gives De Moncrief such instructions that, if they are carefully followed, will certainly in a little time disclose the whole facts of the affair.

Together they go to work and instantly put spies and emissaries hunting all over Paris for the supposed escaped galley slave, and send dispatches by quick riders to trusted agents in Marseilles and Toulon to see what has happened to *forçat* number 1392, convicted under the name of Paul Casanova of sorcery—is he alive or dead?—if living, his whereabouts?

These men are to make reports to De Moncrief.

"I have too many other irons in the fire at present," remarks Monseigneur Lass. "Besides, it is a little more immediately connected with your personal safety than mine."

But as Cousin Charlie takes leave of Uncle Johnny his nervous apprehensions are by no means lessened by seeing the financier giving very careful and pertinent directions to the officer of the guard, that has been so fortunately placed over his safety some few days before this, by order of the Regent of France.

For the Duc d'Orleans is commencing to regard Monseigneur Law as his financial Santa Claus who gives him all of the money he wishes to throw away upon his sycophants and mistresses. He takes every care of payment off easy-going D'Orleans' mind, who has but to spend. Through his agency the taxes upon wine, oil and salt and other necessaries have just been removed, and the Parisian people worship the financier and the Regent who made him.

But the precautions that Uncle Johnny takes make Cousin Charlie very anxious.

"*Mon Dieu!*" he mutters to himself, "I have no guard—I am unprotected against that desperate miscreant! *Tonnerre de Dieu!* I will be the first to feel his vengeance. His awful eyes turned to me as they put the chains upon him. He will come straight to my apartments. To-night I am a dead man!"

Then a new idea darts into his shivering soul. He drives straight for his rooms, makes up hastily by the aid of his valet a little valise of clothes and immediate toilette necessaries, and, taking these in his hand, he says to Lavalle, his Swiss flunkey: "I am going into the country for a few weeks—no matter where—a lady—you understand!" (emphasizing this with a diabolical grin) "so you need not come with me."

With this he takes his departure from his magnificent suite of apartments in the Rue de Nevers, in search of a temporary abiding place in Paris, and hunts the town

over without success, the capital has become so filled
with speculators from the world at large, who have
come to try for fortune in this financial Mecca, that it
is almost impossible to find a present resting place for
one's head in the taverns and inns of Paris, though
additional buildings are going up at the rate of one
hundred per week.

Even the power of money will not obtain for Charles
de Moncrief a proper lodging, and he is compelled to
pass an awful night amid the fleas of a disreputable
cabaret of the butchers' quarter, where he dreams the
stings of these insects are O'Brien Dillon's knife
wounds.

In the morning he makes another attempt for better
accommodations; but in the midst of this he stops
going about from tavern to auberge—from cheap lodgings to furnished rooms, for this sudden thought has
made him quake.

"What if I meet him on the street?"

He cries hurriedly to his coachman: "Drive to
the Hôtel de Crevecœur!" Then mutters to himself: "That is safest! He will never look for me
there! Besides, I can have fine apartments with my
Aunt Clothilde, without even the paying for them."

Being driven to the house of the Comtesse de Crevecœur in the Rue St. André, he there takes up his
quarters in the very rooms that D'Arnac had occupied
some few years before, on his return from the Rhine to
Paris.

While there in semi-hiding, Charlie de Moncrief, who
is never idle, devotes himself to his own self-glorification
in the eyes of his Aunt Clothilde de Crevecœur, explaining
to that avaricious widow the enormous fortune he is making upon the Rue Quincampoix. Then having filled her
heart with envy and her eyes with astonishment at the
prodigious riches he talks about, he asks her does she
not think he could better support the dignity of the
House of Crevecœur with his enormous wealth, than
his cousin, Raymond d'Arnac.

"Not at all," says the fat Clothilde, ingenuously.

"Indeed—why not?"

"Because, Monsieur Charles, you would not be
nearly as generous to the widow of the Comte de Creve-

cœur, with all your wealth, as Raymond, who is liber-
ality itself !"   For D'Arnac's purse has always been
open at his aunt's bequest.

"Ah ha! Then it is settled, I suppose, that Raymond marries the little Julie, under the provisions of
Henri's will !" mutters the Procureur, attempting
mirth.

"Oh! That is a matter of the future!" says the
Countess, airily—for she is mortally afraid of Cousin
Charlie's thwarting the affair."

"You fat liar!" mutters De Moncrief to himself,
grinning at the prevaricating Clothilde.   "Raymond
d'Arnac signed the marriage contract ten months ago,
but the estates shall yet be mine."

For Henri, Comte de Crevecœur, under the suggestions of the Procureur, during the absence of Raymond in Marseilles, had made upon his deathbed a
very curious last will and testament—one over which
Cousin Charlie has often rubbed his hands and
chuckled.

Apart from Clothilde, after a little consideration,
Cousin Charlie goes to rubbing his hands and chuckling
again, muttering: "D'Arnac was jealous! Now,
under the allurements of pretty little Quinault, who has
all the pride of a *grande dame*, and all the enchantments
of the pet actress of Paris, Raymond, who has the
enthusiasm of a boy and the stupid principles of a
moralist, instead of the conscience of a man of the
world in affairs of the heart—may *not* keep his contract
to Mademoiselle Julie de Beaumont; and this beautiful
house, and the magnificent country estates of Henri de
Crevecœur will come to me.   With the millions I have
made in stock speculations, I will become one of the
great nobles of the land, and it will be De Moncrief—not
D'Arnac—who will be the head of the house of Crevecœur !"

Under these rosy imaginings Cousin Charlie becomes
quite sanguine; but his boastings of his successful stock
operations on the Rue Quincampoix have put an avaricious devil in the fat Clothilde's heart that will not
down, and some of her efforts to become a female
Crœsus bring great danger to Monsieur le Procureur's
dreams of exalted rank and grand seignorial rights.

CHAPTER V.

THE NAUGHTY QUINAULT.

IN HIS designs Monsieur De Moncrief has a very potent ally—the natural jealousy of man toward man.

This mental force commences to work upon the impetuous Raymond almost directly after the agitated exit of the Procureur du Roy, upon the night of his galley slave episode.

D'Arnac turns to his sister and mutters : "Mimi, how could you be so rash ?"

"I could not help it! And didn't my shot go home? Besides," she says airily, "what have we to fear with D'Argenson our friend, and O'Brien Dillon never even condemned ?"

Then she ejaculates with clenched hands and beaming eyes: "How I hated and despised Cousin Charlie as I thought of the miserable wrongs he had heaped upon the brave Irish soldier, plotting his very destruction as he broke bread with him at your board that day, when Dillon had come back happy and rich from the conquest of the Turks. And when I recollected the dangers he had placed upon your life through the agency of that scoundrel Gaston Lenoir, in the Rhine campaign, I could not help giving Monsieur Charles de Moncrief one pang of fright and terror."

A moment after she says falteringly : "Perhaps Monsieur Lenoir will have another grudge against you. He——" then checks herself suddenly.

"Another grudge against me—how ?"

"Ah—of course—how ?" stammers the lady. "How ?" Then she twists her idea suddenly, murmuring : "Why might not Cousin Charlie work upon Lenoir's avaricious mind again ?" and suddenly starts, grows pale, and cries out : "That awful will ! Uncle Henri was an idiot to make it !"

"You are referring to the little Comtesse Julie de Beaumont," returns D'Arnac. "That will is not so curious. It was my father's wish as well as my uncle's, that I should marry the Comtesse Julie. I might as well marry her as any other heiress. The house of D'Arnac must not be allowed to die, my sister. I have already signed the marriage contract, as I promised my dead father years ago."

"Then the sooner you fulfill your marriage contract, the better," cries Mimi excitedly.

"Pooh! there's no hurry."

"No hurry—when my uncle's will decreed that in case you should not marry the Comtesse Julie de Beaumont on her eighteenth birthday, that the estates should all go to Charles de Moncrief?"

"*Pardi!* Julie's birthday is a long way off—next December, I believe."

"Yes, the 15th of December," replies Mimi; "but I pray you to make it as soon as possible," she goes on agitatedly.

"Why?"

"Because it will take a danger from your life."

"How?"

"Do you not think, my brother," she answers, her eyes full of apprehension, "that the man who placed your life in jeopardy on the Rhine, to get these estates, will not place it in danger in Paris—will not do anything his brilliant yet ignoble mind suggests, to prevent that wedding by any means, fair or foul, and in his power? May not he work upon Lenoir, that cruel duelist?"

"Of that I must take my chances as other men."

"But he is so fatal—only yesterday morning his skill murdered young De Provens!"

"Don't let that trouble you, dear Mimi," replies D'Arnac shortly, "I have defended my life before—I can do so again." Then, as if anxious to dispel the affair from his mind, he suggests lightly: "And now give me the note from little Quinault!"

"Here, take it," replies Mimi, and hands him a letter; then, as if terrified as to being consulted in regard to its contents, she falters: "The excitement of to-day—your return, and the danger I feared was on you, have been too much for a woman's nerves. Good-bye for this evening."

So the sister leaves the brother engaged in opening a peculiar epistle, which reads as follows:

MON SEIGNEUR:

A bird has whispered in my ear that you are now Lieutenant-

Colonel of the *Musquetaires Noirs*, and in Paris.

At this I should be frightened were I not so anxious to see you, for Mimi, your sister, tells me I am very naughty—because—guess why?

No, I think I'll postpone my confession till I see my guardian general. Oo—oh! won't you utter very wise words when you hear of the affair! I am trembling, though still

Your obedient ward and vassal,

JEANNE FRANÇOISE QUINAULT,
SOCIETAIRE *Comedie Française.*

P. S.—It is *not* an actor this time, so you needn't frown and tear your hair. I have underlined *Societaire* three times, to inform you I have been elected *once*, which is very good, I think, for precocious nineteen. Old Gabriel, who is *pension-naire*, though she is seventy, wept when she heard of my good fortune. JEANNE.

N. B.—I would make this longer, but I am going to the last rehearsal of "Jaloux Desabusé," in which I hope to make you laugh to-night. For, of course, you will come and see me this evening at the theatre. Afterwards you know I have a *petit salon.* J. F. Q.

Au revoir.

" It is not an actor," remarks D'Arnac to himself, very savagely, chewing his moustache. "*Diable !* Is it some one worse?" and strides rapidly to the theatres in his heart the feelings of the dog who won't eat the bone himself and won't let other dogs eat it either.

In this very comfortable state of mind Monsieur d'Arnac pays his money and forces his way into the Theatre Français, but does not see much of the performance.

He is hardly aware whether it is comedy or tragedy. All he knows is that there is a beautiful creature on the stage, even more lovely than the one he left in Paris a year ago; that her graceful figure is a little more rounded in the curves of beauty—and her eyes are even brighter, for there is a wondrous expectancy in them—and her laugh is perchance merrier—and her ideality and sentiment more exquisite than even when last he saw dear little Quinault on the boards.

But from around him float to his ear remarks that make D'Arnac want to fight and slay; though after a little he changes his mind about this, as he can't fight and slay nearly half the people about him.

"Isn't she exquisite," says a beautiful comtesse to another lady sitting beside her. " How *some one* must love her! "

" I should think so," returns this lady's companion, a vivacious lady-in-waiting at the Court. "*He* adores her."

Then she whispers into the ear of the Comtesse, at which the other gives a startled cry and says: "*Mon Dieu!* do you really mean it ? What a happy fellow!"

At which Raymond grinds his teeth, and would give his head to know the happy fellow's name, so that he could make him unhappy.

A little later the conversation of an old gallant and a younger beau reaches him from his right:

"*Mon Dieu!*" says the juvenile, "Quinault will put one or two more on her list to-night. Doesn't she enjoy making them love her and rejecting them ? Poor De Sartimes even now smiles sadly, though he was stabbed six months ago."

"*Parbleu!* have you not heard the *bon mot* she gave him ? He told her he loved her, and she said (for she is a quaint little *diablesse* and always assumes that she inspires the love of the church, not the love of the theatre): 'Monsieur de Sartimes, I shall only wed in my own rank. I will *try* to become your wife if you will *try* to become an actor.'"

"*Morbleu!* this to a son of the old marquis!" mutters the other. "She will soon be suggesting to Monsieur d'Orleans that he aspire to the crown of Molière."

"And then have you heard about De Guiche?" chuckles the younger dandy.

"Only that he adores her."

"Well, what do you think she said to his suit ? 'Please repeat your offer to my guardian, Monsieur le Comte d'Arnac. If he desires me, I am an obedient ward, and will sign the marriage contract!'"

"*Diable!* Did she expect a *marriage* love—," cries the other, "from the son of the Duc de Guiche, one of the grandees of France—an actress—oh, ho! he! he! to what villain ideas are we coming ?"

These remarks drive Raymond away from the theatre to the Café Procopé opposite; he fears he will suddenly wring somebody's nose, or slap somebody's face; though these speeches are made utterly unconscious of his presence, as he has been away from Paris for over a year, and his appearance is quite unknown to most of the gallants of the town.

Sitting down at one of the tables, D'Arnac tries to bring common sense to bear upon the matter, and reflects that any action he may take would only bring his *protegée's* name more prominently upon the lips of men and women. He has heard every actress on the Parisian stage spoken about something after the same manner, and has never thought until now it is anything but the regulation thing; though Mademoiselle Jeanne's charms being greater, the gossip about her is probably more pronounced than that in regard to less attractive goddesses of the stage.

Even as the young man cogitates, disquieting words come to him, as the café is full of people chatting and laughing, it being an *entr'acte.*

A gentleman sitting at the table next to him remarks to another: "They say little Quinault carries on her *rôle* of *comedienne* off the stage. That a certain young literary *quill* named Arouet, who is ashamed of his name since he returned from the Bastille for writing scandalous verses about our last King, and has adopted the *nom de plume* of Voltaire, invents brilliant lines for her, which she recites to her various adorers, with admirable but most cutting sarcasm. You know, of course, about Lenoir?"

"No," says the other, "what was it?"

"Well, Lenoir, who has become one of the moths, burning their wings at the candle of little Quinault, hinted to her a few days ago that he loved her, and she replied: 'Monsieur Lenoir, I have had already twenty chances to change my name to one beginning with "*de.*" When you have succeeded in acquiring the prefix of nobility perchance I may consider your application.' At this Lenoir, who is of Spanish birth, though I believe of good family, gnashing his teeth fled before the witty actress."

As the two get up and leave their table, Raymond looking after them meditates: "This is what Mimi referred to," and grows very savage not only with Lenoir and all the other gentlemen pursuing her, but also with his *protegée*, and makes up his mind to be very stern and severe with that young lady at the first opportunity.

He soon finds the pretext he is seeking.

This comes from the old actor Baron, who strides into the café and, recognizing Raymond, takes off his hat and makes his politest and lowest bow, congratulating him upon his promotion and honor; then remarks: "I am glad that your new rank has not made you forget the young lady for whose artistic success *we* have both done so much. This is your first evening in Paris; I presume you have been at the theatre."

"Yes, from which I have been driven by the remarks about Jeanne's numerous adorers," returns Raymond gloomily.

"Ah, doesn't she fascinate every one?" babbles the actor. "But you need not fear the courtiers, my boy. *Pardieu!* I think she turns a pleasanter eye upon the financiers."

"Financiers!" ejaculates Raymond. "Not *stock-brokers?*"

"One, the King's Stockbroker."

"Lass?"

"Yes, the one who makes every one rich. I believe she has asked him to make speculation for her on the Rue Quincampoix. I am afraid she needs the money."

"For what?"

"Oh, the expenses of an actress. She has a *petit salon* that is growing very fashionable among *littérateurs* —Monsieur Voltaire—Monsieur Campistron, the author of the piece you listened to this evening—myself—and other celebrities—," replies Baron modestly. "This is expensive. I am afraid Mademoiselle Jeanne has been going in debt."

"In debt?" cries D'Arnac, very savagely, but very delightedly. For he has got the subject upon which he can lecture Mademoiselle Jeanne for all her other faults under the head of "extravagance."

And Baron leaving him, he meditates gloomily upon this till the theatre is over.

So the greenroom not exactly being the place for his guardian effusions, giving the young lady time to arrive at her handsome apartments on the Rue de Condé, Monsieur d'Arnac strides toward them very full of his stern precepts and good advice.

He mutters to himself: "Wait till she hears from

me!" and seems to imagine he will pose in his rôle of guardian exceedingly well, but does not know he is going to encounter a young lady who has grown in wit if not in wisdom, since he last listened to her charming voice.

The pretty *salon* of Mademoiselle Quinault, brilliantly lighted by candelabra filled with wax tapers, and adorned very admirably in regard to furniture, delicate *bric-à-brac* and exquisite but expensive trifles of art, looks very bright this evening.

Beyond is a little dining-room, in which a gourmand supper is being served, with ten covers; though only nine places are occupied, that at the head of the board being vacant.

At this table are seated several of the celebrities of Paris, among them Monsieur François Marie Arouêt, who is just becoming noted under the name of Voltaire, and is at the right of his hostess, indulging a very good appetite.

The place at her left is occupied by Campistron, the author of the play of the night, who hates and envies the rising young *littérateur* opposite him. The actor Baron and the adolescent Comte de Guiche, who still sighs for the bright eyes of the young lady at the foot of the table, make up the gentlemen of the party.

The ladies are a mixture of those of the stage and those of the *grand monde.* Pretty Mademoiselle Seine of the *Français*, and old Desmares, representing the theatre. The old and literary Madame de Caylor, who is the duenna who watches over Jeanne, does *les convenances* for the party, while the vivacious Marquise de Prie gives to it the lustre of the aristocracy.

They are all chatting very merrily and happily; wit is flowing about with the wine; when into this bright gathering, like a bull in a china shop, comes Raymond le Comte d'Arnac, full of righteous indignation against the world in general, and one or two of the gentlemen here present in particular; also with a long lecture in his mind to read the exquisite lady who rises, her eyes beaming with happiness, to salute him as he is announced.

Suddenly, to the astonishment of all the guests except

old Baron and her duenna, who have seen her perform this act before, Mademoiselle Jeanne makes
obeisance to the entering general, gorgeous in his uniform of the *Musquetaires Noirs*, and, kissing his hand,
murmurs: "*Mon Seigneur!*" as she did in the old days,
before she had floated into the galaxy of fame.

And how is this obeisance greeted?

Young De Guiche, who would give his eyes for a
similar salutation, stares in envy, then starts in astonishment, as D'Arnac after uttering the usual form of con-
ventional greeting to the lady bending before him, and
being introduced to those of the guests he does not
know, suddenly catching sight of the vacant chair at
the head of the table, remarks very sternly: "Jeanne,
what gentleman do you place at the head of your board,
as if he had a right there? For whom was that place
intended?"

At this, little Quinault, who has gazed at him for one
moment with disappointed, and perhaps affrighted eyes,
suddenly emits a little snicker and says: "For you, *mon
Seigneur!*" favoring him with mocking courtesy.

"F-for me?" stammers Raymond embarrassed.

"Certainly! I had expected you at the theatre!
In proof that this place was intended for you"—here
she gives another little giggle, in which two or three
of her guests join, she leads D'Arnac to the head
of the table, and points to a cake fort in frosted sugar,
in front of his chair, upon which is placarded in red
candy letters: "To the Hero of Friburg!" then
laughs mockingly, "Fight with him as much as you
like—only please postpone it until after you have
carried him away from the feast! Take your chair,
hungry general!"

And he being compelled for very shame to take instant
occupation of it, she courtesies to him again and
murmurs: "What are my fierce lord's orders? I will wait
on him myself—he would be savage with the varlets
this evening."

"Pooh! nonsense!" stammers Raymond; for the rest
of the party are grinning.

"It is to beauty to attend on valor!" ejaculates
Baron pompously, quoting from an old play.

Upon this, noting D'Arnac's manner, Monsieur

Voltaire suddenly sneers: "Are *young* generals always savage?"

"Of course," answers Raymond, grinding his teeth. "It is our business, as it is with you gentlemen of the pen to be always witty—though sometimes neither of us succeed!"

The laugh that greets this (for people are generally more ready to applaud at the *bon mots* of the man of rank than the good things of the aspiring knight of the plume), making D'Arnac think himself very witty, brings good humor to him.

So he settles down between vivacious Madame de Prie and pretty Mademoiselle Seine, and enjoys a very pleasant little supper. Jeanne, her face covered with happiness, sitting at the foot of the table, and playing the fairy of the feast, with her bright eyes, façile tongue, brilliant intellect, and exquisite spirit.

She is dressed—heaven and her *modiste* only know how! But her toilet has in it effects that make her beauty as vivacious, sparkling, and intoxicating to the senses of man as the champagne that froths in her glass as she proposes the health "of the hero of Friburg!"

So much so that it appeals even to her own sex. De Prie whispers enthusiastically to Raymond: "She's as lovely as De Sabran herself!" then cries out, perhaps a little maliciously: "You are very fortunate, Monsieur d'Arnac—BOTH?" and smiles the smile of one who could say more, but does not dare for prudence sake.

"Both?" laughs Jeanne, who overhears only the last—"both what?"

"Both *ladies*, of course," remarks Voltaire. "Who but your sex, Mademoiselle Quinault, make the fortune of man—good or evil?"

"Since you are all guessing," replies De Prie, between sips of her champagne, "I make my remark a riddle! A prize to the one who solves it! General d'Arnac of course barred, for he, I imagine, *knows.*"

"Very well," says De Guiche, who has been looking on Raymond with jealous eyes, and hopes perchance to do a bad turn to this very much favored gentleman's affairs of the heart. "I will have my trial for Madame de Prie's rebus. By 'both' she refers to the lovely De Sabran and our charming young hostess. By 'fortunate' she means that Monsieur le General, at the *fête* of the Island Pomègue, was the favored gallant of the beautiful Hilda; while here he is the honored guardian and mentor of the exquisite Quinault, to whom we all fill our glasses with champagne, and our hearts with ———!"

He looks the rest at the young lady he toasts, who, as De Guiche speaks, grows for one second very white and pale, even to her ivory shoulders, and then becomes blushing as the rose.

"*Couleur au natural!*" laughs Monsieur Voltaire, gazing at her flashing blue eyes and changing emotions.

"The prize is yours, my astute Comte!" cries la Marquise, at which Mademoiselle Quinault grows pale once more.

As for Raymond, he can't be quite sure whether it is De Guiche's ardent glances or malicious information that causes Jeanne's blushes and embarrassment. Whichever it is he hates him for it.

Then, struggling to play the courtier, he says, squeezing out a laugh: "If Madame de Prie meant all you say, Comte, she must indeed have thought me fortunate. But at present my happiness depends on only *one* of the ladies!" And he gives the blushing Quinault a glance that makes her grow wondrously joyous for the moment.

"Of course," sneers Voltaire, "that refers to the *nearest* charmer. Perchance you made on the Island Pomègue the same remark to the other!"

This puts the dagger into little Quinault again; whereupon, seeing its effect (for this great writer is a man of immense brain but little soul), he adds: "Your honeyed words, General d'Arnac, must have had an effect on la Sabran also. I saw her carriage in front of the barracks on the Charenton road to-day as you first paraded *Les Musquetaires Noirs!*" thus turning the knife in poor Jeanne's gaping wound.

But this young lady has a soul that conquers any exhibitions of anguish to delight her tormentor. She cries: "Of course, Monsieur Voltaire. All women adore heroes. Why not the hero of Friburg? Is he so poor a hero that he has but *one* heroine? Naturally, I appreciate Madame De Sabran's emotions!"

Then she forces a stage laugh that has the merry ring of spontaneity, though she feels very surly towards her guardian, and intends to show it on convenient opportunity, which comes quite shortly.

As they rise from the supper table, perceiving De Guiche has hardly found favor in Raymond's eyes, his rebellious ward inveigles the young Comte into a *tête-a-tête*, and in this young gentleman's attentions becomes curiously oblivious to every one else in the room, not even noticing the hero of Friburg, although he has on his new and gorgeous uniform and commanding airs as lieutenant-general.

Under the apparent spell of De Guiche's insipid compliments she seems to go into a trance, vouchsafing to Raymond's brightest speeches only monosyllables, and devoting her shell-like ears, tripping tongue and brilliant eyes to placing her *tête-a-tête* in paradise.

From his ward's inattention, Monsieur d'Arnac turns ferociously to Mademoiselle Jeanne's duenna, Madame de Caylor, who, being generally deserted on account of her many years and few charms, welcomes the gentleman to her side with much effusion as regards both gratitude and interest.

- It is to his sister she owes her present position as chaperon of the young actress, which is an easy one. As a matter of fact, it is Raymond who pays her salary.

But D'Arnac's address does not give this old hanger-on of the court of France and ancient dabbler in poetry any great comfort this evening.

He remarks gloomily to her; "My dear Madame de Caylor, you, I fear, are too handsome!"

"Oh, General!"

"Yes, I fear you are too beautiful to make your position effective. I told Madame de Chateaubrien that when she requested you to accept the post. You are not dragon enough!"

"Oh, I'll be anything you wish," replies Madame de Caylor, anxiously. Then she throws poetic eyes about, and languishes them on Raymond, murmuring: "Whom shall I sting?"

. "You see Monsieur Popinjay talking to Miss Butter-fly?"

"Y-e-s!"

"Do you always remain in the *salon* when he favors this establishment with a call?"

"Unless I have some other duties."

"Very well. I hope you will have no other duties when De Guiche calls. Devote yourself entirely to him."

"And when any other of the young courtiers call?"

"The same. Make them all think they are visiting Madame de Caylor and not Mademoiselle Quinault," adds Raymond, savagely, thinking that will curb their coming if anything will.

" Ah, I understand," remarks the Baroness. And D'Arnac leaving her, she decides to be a very faithful dragon, because the dragon's quarters are very pleasant, and the dragon's remuneration is liberal.

Mademoiselle Jeanne, whose bright eyes have observed Raymond's conversation with her duenna, imagines that he has been pumping Madame de Caylor on the subject of her epistle.

Chancing to be near him, as the guests are rising to go, she whispers: "You received my note?"

"Yes," replies D'Arnac, "and brought my lecture." Then he says moodily turning evil eyes on the young Comte de Guiche, "is *that* your confession? It was not an actor this time, I believe. "

This remark seems to give la Quinault, for some unaccountable reason, inexplicable yet decided joy.

She gasps: "Why, you are——" then checks herself, for Raymond is bursting out again, and whispers: "Don't scold me before them all; I shall feel like a baby! Wait till they go, then play the wise and experienced guardian, *Mon Seigneur*, and I will perform as the naughty ward and disobedient vassal."

And her joyous vivacity would disarm any one but this young gentleman, who, however, contrives to bridle his temper, and daudles about the room with a rather surly air until the other guests have taken their leave, and he finds himself facing Mademoiselle Quinault and her duenna.

"Now sit down, guardy, and lecture me!" remarks Jeanne, giving him a happy smile. "Put your gloomy face into words."

On this Madame de Caylor rises and says: "I shall leave you now, with your permission, Monsieur le General, as I presume you have some private communication to make to your ward."

And this lady departing, D'Arnac would open his batteries upon the young lady standing before him in exquisite beauty and mocking grace, did she not fire off his cannon for him.

She says airily: "You look at me as if I were a culprit. Why?"

"Why? You yourself know. Your letter confessed a fault."

"Oh, I only wrote that to tease you," giggles Mademoiselle. "True, Mimi did say I was naughty—but she has said that *so many times.*"

"With reason, I presume," remarks Raymond severely.

"Sometimes. But this time it was only because I said a few saucy words to a gentleman I do not approve, Monsieur Lenoir. She feared they would make him feel revengeful towards me. But I have lots of enemies," continues the young lady, nonchalantly; "half the actresses in the theatre detest me, and most of the critics have dipped their pens in my blood."

"Humph! I had presumed it was the Comte de Guiche to whom you referred."

"Oh! I have no further interest in poor De Guiche," cries Jeanne merrily. "His affair was six months ago. *He has not succeeded in becoming an actor.*"

"Ah, ha! You have had other admirers *since?*"

"Lots of them. But the list is a long one and might fatigue you. I will give you samples!" laughs Mademoiselle Quinault. "Monsieur Voltaire, who writes sonnets to me. Monsieur Baron, who says he made my fame. Màréchal de Villars, who kisses my cheek whenever he meets me, and murmurs 'pride of the army' and 'good little girl' (which is more than you have ever said about me); Monsieur de Sartimes, who, I am informed, is still very unhappy about me; Le Comte de Horn, who looks so pale and interesting."

"Le Comte de Horn? *Diable*! You permit the admiration of such as he?" mutters D'Arnac aghast, for Jeanne has named the most reckless *roué* of the day.

"Why, he has the royal blood of the Netherlands in his veins. He is slightly related to the Regent."

"But the most dissipated and wicked speculator on the street, and the most unfortunate, I am told. Speaking of this, I am reminded," continues Raymond, "that *you* are extravagant—that you are in debt!"

"*Was* in debt, my guardian general!" corrects the young lady, lightly.

"You—you don't mean to say that your profits as *societaire* have paid for this luxury?" queries D'Arnac, gazing astounded about the apartment, which is a marvel of expensive good taste.

"Of course not! That is the Rue Quincampoix and Monsieur Lass, who has been very kind to me!" returns Mademoiselle Quinault. "Debt is a thing of the past with me."

"Ah, ha! Speculating!"

"And why shouldn't I?" cries Mademoiselle, defiantly. "Hasn't the Regent made public edict that no noble will lose his rank by buying stocks—don't the princesses of the blood beg Lass for shares—why should not I have my fling also? I've got a thousand shares of the old India stock—the ORIGINAL stock—'the mother'—and that has given me the right to buy two hundred and fifty of the second issue, 'the daughters!' I got them through the kindness of Monsieur Lass. Lanty took my order and fought his way through the crowd—and I stood looking at him outside. People were crushed half to death! It was so terrible—so exciting! Every 'daughter' is worth seven hundred *livres* now per share. They say they are going to be worth one thousand—perhaps two thousand—perhaps three thousand—perhaps more! The more 'mothers' you have—the more 'daughters' you can get—and soon they are going to issue the 'grand-daughters'—and the more 'daughters' you have the more 'grand-daughters' you can get. Monsieur Voltaire says I'm not only getting rich, but a family," chirps the young lady, blushing a little at the joke. Then she cries enthusiastically:

"Oh! It pays to be the pet actress of the Parisian stage!"

"Too well!" cries D'Arnac, savagely, for the richer she gets, the less he thinks she will be indebted to him; and casting angry eyes about they light upon the magnificent diamonds gleaming upon Mademoiselle Naughty's fair neck and arms, and he mutters viciously: "Did you buy those from the profits of your stock speculations?"

"What—sell a share of my stock NOW?" cries the little speculator. "Never! It's going to be worth ten times its present value. I have had private information from Monseigneur Lass."

"Then who gave you that diamond necklace?" cries D'Arnac, his voice as stern and his eye as severe as looking at a mutineer.

At this aspect of her guardian, Jeanne suddenly emits a suppressed snicker; next assuming a childish pout, commences to devour the little lace handkerchief she has in her hands, and mutters: "I—I shan't tell you!"

"You must!"

"I—I *won't!*" and Miss Defiant stamps indignant slipper.

"You shall—he shall answer to me!" And D'Arnac, taking Mademoiselle Rebel sternly by both her pretty shoulders, holds her so her blue eyes look into his, and says: "His name!"

At this she gives a shriek of laughter right into his savage eyes, and cries: "Mimi!" then gives forth two alluring, mocking giggles.

"My sister?" stammers Raymond, growing confused and overcome.

But the laugh goes out of Jeanne's eyes, and fire flames in them, and turning on him she whispers, with white lips: "Who do you think gave it to me? My Heaven!—you thought! What did you think of me— *what?* Answer! It is I that command now!" And the *comedienne* has changed into a *tragedienne* of wild eyes and terrible mien, and cries: "Answer! What did you DARE to think!"

"I——I merely demanded what, as your guardian, I have a right to know!" stammers D'Arnac,

forcing himself to calmness. "The greater your popularity—the more I have a right to inquire! The
greater the number of your admirers, the richer they
are, the higher rank they have—the more it is my duty
to ask! You are not twenty yet—for five years more,
according to the law of France, I, as your guardian,
have the right to direct you and the power to require
you to answer my questions."

"That was before I became a *societaire* of the Français," replies Jeanne, with haughty voice. "When I
became that I became dedicated by the law of France
to the public."

"The public will doubtless be a more agreeable
guardian to you than I am—it will not ask so many
questions," sneers D'Arnac. Then he mutters in a
choked voice, for she has wounded him greatly: "I—
I believe you are right. Even a ballet girl placing her
foot on the boards at the Opera becomes the ward of the
state. I—I shall trouble you with my authority no
more. If you need a guardian for any legal purposes
connected with your property, I—I have no doubt Monsieur de Villars will be pleased to act for you! Permit
me to take my leave!" and he makes her the bow of
adieu; though with a heavy heart, for it is not a pleasant thing to relinquish the control of a being whose
spirit and beauty have conquered the world.

And with this he wins his battle.

For as he turns to go—in fact is half-way to the
door—a pair of pretty, but desperate, hands seize
upon him, and teary blue eyes are gazing piteously into
his, and a pathetic voice is crying wildly to him:
"Don't go! I said it released me from your guardianship, but I didn't say it absolved me from my oath of
vassalage to you—one I took on the cross when I was a
child. Don't go!—I'll get you my bank stock—sell it
—throw it away—do anything—don't go! You shall
scold me as much as you please. You shall be as cross
with me as you like—don't go! You shall read the love
letters that are written to me—don't go! You shall
lock me up in a convent—don't go! Come—lecture me
as much as you like—be as angry with me as you like—
punish me if I deserve it—only, guardy—*don't go!*
Mon Seigneur—DON'T GO!"

And she kisses his hand, and gives him the obeisance she has been accustomed to since the night he saved her in the street fight at Friburg.

Under such entreaties, from such a ward, what guardian could refuse her charge?

Then she murmurs: "I—I don't think you—you had better scold me this evening—I'm crying now. Keep that till to-morrow—come at two and you'll find an obedient vassal. But you're—you're not angry *now*, are you, general guardian—you're not savage now with your little Jeanne, are you, *Mon Seigneur?*" and sends Monsieur Raymond d'Arnac away from her very proud of his conquest over his rebel ward.

For as he strides away the lieutenant-general has the proud bearing of a maréchal of France, and says to himself, very contentedly: "*Pardi!* what a victory! but I brought the audacious chit to terms—in short order!"

But it is a victory that has the elements of danger and defeat to the conqueror as well as the vanquished.

In fact, the vanquished goes tripping to her chamber and smiles at her own fair reflection in the glass and shakes a playful finger at her piquant self and laughs through her tears. "Is he—is he jealous of me? Oh, you naughty little Quinault!"

CHAPTER VI.

PARIS THE BUCKET-SHOP OF THE WORLD.

SELF-GLORIFICATION has not left D'Arnac the next morning; he comes down to meet his sister at breakfast, very much pleased with himself, and therefore very much pleased with everybody else.

Noting this, Madame la Marquise remarks: "A pleasant supper last evening, I imagine?"

"The supper was well enough," replies Raymond nonchalantly; "Jeanne was as *spirituelle* and sprightly as a fairy, but——," here Raymond meditatively attacks a cutlet with knife and fork.

"Well—but?"

"She likes to be too popular and too rich."

"Both very natural," answers Mimi laughingly.

"She would not be a success on the stage were she
not the first, and she could not gratify her artistic
ideas were she not the second."

"Oh, I don't object to admiration across the foot-
lights," says Raymond, giving his cutlet a more savage
stab, "it's the generality of the attentions she permits—everything is fish that comes to her net, from
the son of a duke to a jobbing stockbroker."

"Oh, Monseigneur Lass; Jeanne simply bows
to his financial greatness, as nearly every one in
France does—countesses, duchesses and princesses be-
seeching him for shares," remarks Mimi airily.

"Then I shall stop Mademoiselle Jeanne," cries
D'Arnac determinedly.

"Then you'll have a very pretty battle on your
hands, *mon general!*" laughs his sister.

"*Sapristi!* one I have already conquered," laughs
Raymond. "In ten minutes I routed Miss Rebel,
horse, foot and dragoons, and, *voila!* the triumphant
guardian."

This success alarms his sister. She opens a subject
that has been upon her mind the evening before. Affecting a laugh, she suggests: "Don't you think you
are rather juvenile to play the guardian to such a
charming young lady?"

"*Diable!* I was younger when I undertook the task
by six years," replies D'Arnac confidently. "And I
think I have made very good work of it."

"Ah, yes, but she is *older*," dissents Madame de
Chateaubrien.

Whereupon her brother gets very red in the face,
and a curious gleam comes into his eyes that gives his
sister a shiver.

But this also makes her more determined to press a
project she has reflected on overnight. She says sug-
gestively: "Don't you think that you ought to
visit your *fiancée?* Melun is not so very distant from
Paris."

Her brother's answer astounds her. "Oh, that
chit!" he replies as if the thought was not entirely a
pleasant one, "I can visit her in a month or so! There
is plenty of time. I suppose Julie has grown into
quite a slip of a girl by this time." Next he says con-

templatively, " I wonder what she looks like. She was ugly at ten."

"She is beautiful at seventeen," Mimi cries enthusiastically, "and very anxious to get out of a convent."

"Of course, anxious to get from under the rod of mother superior !"

"What makes you jeer," answers la Marquise savagely. "Don't you think you had better arrange for the wedding ceremony ? You are bound to Julie by the marriage contract, and a great deal financially depends upon the ceremony being performed in proper time."

"And I shall make the proper time the limit," remarks D'Arnac nonchalantly. "I'll have my whack at gay bachelorhood as long as it lasts. Have you anything further to suggest?"

' No—only——"

"Only what?"

"Only—" falters Mimi, "don't forget in having a ward that you have also a *fiancée.*"

"*Diable !*" cries her brother, getting very red in the face, "what do you mean to insinuate ? Remember, my sister, that your brother is a man of honor."

"'Then," says Mimi, standing to her guns, "remember that you are a man of honor, and remember also, that every day you postpone your marriage, gives the man you now know as your enemy, another chance at your happiness—perhaps another chance at your life !"

"Which chance I will take for the pleasure of six months' more gay bachelorhood !" laughs D'Arnac. Then he cries savagely, perhaps desperately: "*Ma foi!* would you mate me with that chit before my time ? I have promised to wed her by the 15th of next December. On that day I give my hand as I gave my word, but until then—' Gay Paris, gay Paris !' and he bursts into a little gay *chanson* indicative of the delights of the gallants of the French capital.

With this, breakfast being over, Raymond takes hasty leave of Madame la Marquise, laughing: "Don't look so pensive, Mimi. I have a review at the *Musquetaires* this morning," and his horse being ready, rides off towards the Port St. Antoine and the barracks of that crack regiment, leaving his sister wondering how this affair will culminate.

She knows the customs of the time, and the prejudice of the nobility would make it a greater dishonor to his family for Raymond d'Arnac to marry the brightest luminary in the theatrical world, than if he embezzled from the military chest of his regiment; that the players of her day are considered a class apart from other people; that though Louis XIV. made a special edict decreeing they were to be regarded as other people, and invited Monsieur Molière to dinner with him, to the disgust of his courtiers; that the edict has changed neither court nor church, and that the ladies of the stage are considered to have no right to matrimonial ideas outside of their own class; that they may give their hearts, souls and bodies to the nobles, but not their hands.

Thinking of this as she rises from the table, Mimi sighs: "Poor little Jeanne!"

But Raymond, as he rides from the review to the pretty apartments of Mademoiselle Quinault, has no sighs in his heart. He is enthusiastic, curiously happy. He comes up with military tread to her apartments, and is ushered into her little *salon* by Madelon, her pert maid servant, who has a grin on her comely yet peasant features as she says: "Mademoiselle is at home to *you*, Monsieur"—for Madelon is a naughty little soubrette and has been maid to Mademoiselle Seine and some other actresses who have had love affairs with gentlemen of the *grand monde*, and, acting according to her lights, she already regards the handsome young general as the proprietor of the establishment, pretty little Jeanne included.

Striding into the exquisite room, Monsieur d'Arnac gives a gasp of astonishment.

For it is not the fascinating actress of the Français who rises to receive him, but the business woman of the Rue Quincampoix.

Behind a pile of her stocks, flanked by rolls of securities, stands Jeanne, who cries: "Behold! here they are, guardian general. Here are the 'mothers' and the 'daughters.' I place my fortune entirely in the hands of the gentleman who has looked so well after my interests in the six years he has taken charge of me. Now, shall I burn them, *Mon Seigneur.*

"No!" mutters Raymond

"Shall I sell them? They have gone up one hundred *livres* a share to-day."

"Perhaps you had better not even do that," replies D'Arnac, who has reflected that he has no right, whatever his personal feelings may be, to injure the fortune of the young lady standing before him. "Only," he says, "I do not care for you to associate with financiers and brokers."

"Very well, handle the mothers and daughters for me. I bow to your superior judgment. You are a general—generals are always such excellent men of affairs," says Jeanne archly.

With this little sarcasm at Raymond, who handles his money in the free and easy manner of a soldier, Mademoiselle Quinault puts the bonds aside, laughing: "*You* shall speculate for me, guardian, but *I* will obtain the information, eh?"

"As you please," remarks D'Arnac. "*Diable!* Who could refuse you anything?"—for he has been looking at Mademoiselle, who is more coquettish perhaps in her toilette of the morning than she was in her robe of the evening before.

"Then, if the autocrat is mollified, we will have an afternoon of it. You shall tell me of Marseilles, and I will gossip to you of the theatre. Have a seat, savage general. Oh! not so far away—there's room on the sofa, by me," chirrups la Quinault.

So, after a pleasant half hour's conversation, Jeanne suggests dinner, saying: "Horseback exercise at the review develops a soldier's appetite, eh, *mon brave?*"

And Raymond admitting the truth of this, they go into the little dining-room, where Madame de Caylor joins them, and in her company they have a very pleasant meal, the duenna making herself very agreeable to the dashing young general, for his conversation with her of the evening before has put a curious idea into this romantic poetess' head.

This notion that has crept into Madame de Caylor's Sappho-like brain is presently added to by D'Arnac himself.

Raymond gets into the habit of dropping into the Français about the end of the performance, and loung-

ing about the greenroom (after the custom of that day)
and escorting Miss Jeanne and her duenna home,
thus warding off the attentions of gentlemen whom he
considers dangerous, and making a good many enemies
for himself by his exploits in this line.

And these gentlemen, filled with the malice of dis-
dained attentions and defeated hopes, in the course of
a little time, set rumors afloat which are not greatly to
Raymond's credit, nor conducive to the fair fame of
Mademoiselle Quinault.

Naturally these reports reach last the ears of those
most affected by them; especially as the generality of
the world consider such little affairs as are hinted at by
the disappointed suitors of the *comedienne*, as *de régle*
between a gentleman who is a general in the army and
count of France, and a colonel of a regiment of the
Garde, and a lady, no matter how fascinating, no matter how *spirituelle*, no matter how GOOD—who is an
actress—even though she be the greatest on the stage.

These rumors floating about in the air eventually
find their way to the ears of another lady who has, since
her return from Marseilles, been devoting a good deal
of time, a good deal of savage longing, and a good deal
of jealous apprehension—mingled with some fearful
spasms of rage toward the dashing young general of the
army. For her very helplessness at the slights of Raymond d'Arnac makes De Sabran all the more vindictive.

Three times the mistress of the Regent has seen this
man she had thought her very own in Marseilles, ride
through the streets of Paris, and following at a safe
distance, admiring his graceful horsemanship, his
debonnair manners; and three times she has seen him
dismount and toss his bridle to his orderly, on the Rue de
Condé, immediately before the apartments which she
knows are occupied by Mademoiselle Quinault.

On coming home from these abortive attempts at interview with the young officer, without even a smile or a bow
from him, her maid servants and attendant women who
have fallen upon troublous times, have wondered what
is coming over the wayward temper of the beauty, upon
whose loveliness they wait.

"*Mon Dieu!*" cries her first lady-in-waiting, "she'll
be boxing my ears next. She did that to one of the

maids to-day.   Is she losing her money in stocks? But
no, that is impossible!"

"Has the Regent been unkind?" wonders another.

But they know D'Orleans is as devoted as ever. Then
one of them says with a grin to her companions:
"*Pardi!* I've guessed it—she's having. her *first* love
affair."

At which the abigails put up a sudden titter, which
dies into a discreet silence as Hilda de Sabran, gleaming with the diamonds of the Turk, passes through the
apartment *en route* for some court *fête* or sybaritic
supper party, upon which some gentleman will spend in
curious entertainment or bizarre *menu* for the surprise
of his guests. what would have been considered the fortune of an heiress in the preceding reign.

For Paris is growing richer—*richer*—RICHER!

Monseigneur Law has made it the financial Mecca of
the world.   Boyards are coming from Moscow and St.
Petersburg to speculate on the Rue Quincampoix.
Italian nobles are flocking from Turin and Rome.
The Armenians and Greeks of Constantinople and
the money-changers of Vienna are thronging to the
capital of France.   The diamond dealers of Holland
and the merchants of England, together with the Jews
of the whole world, are crowding here—by carriage, by
diligence, by private conveyance, on foot, on horseback—any way on earth to get to Paris, to insert their
fingers in this great financial pie that is now being
baked very deftly and well browned, with a fine crust
of stealing and cheating upon the Rue Quincampoix.

For Monseigneur Law has by this time obtained from
the Regent the decree taking from the *Fermiers Généreaux* and the Brothers Paris the collection of all taxes
in France and transferring their tremendous privileges
to the India Company, which will increase its revenues
a hundred of millions a year.

And now, having destroyed the *Fermiers Généreaux*
and every other stock in which the floating money of
the country can be invested, one day in September,
John Law, of Lauriston (commonly called Monseigneur
Lass, of France), has made the most audacious and yet
the most far-sighted proposition that ever financier
made to any of the great governments of the world.

He has said: "With your permission, Monsieur le
Regent, I WILL PAY THE NATIONAL DEBT OF FRANCE."

"You—will do it?" cries D'Orleans, his eyes beaming, for it has been his one thought to get rid of this
crushing weight upon the government finances.
"*Diable!* it is impossible! Seventeen hundred millions—you—a private individual!"

"Within one month, Sire, I, on my own security,
guarantee to pay the national debt of France—seventeen hundred million *livres*. Give me the edict. On
my head be it! Within a month I'll pay it all."

"You shall have the edict—on your head be it. If
you do it, you will be a god!" cries D'Orleans.

"Then worship me," laughs Lass, easily, and sends
the Regent away laughingly to squander a few more
millions on his mistresses and sycophants, though in
Philippe's mind there is one thought: "*Mon Dieu!*
How will he do it? If he does, Law is the greatest
man the world has ever seen."

But this audacious tender of Monseigneur Lass is the
wisest, the most far-sighted move he has ever made in
his whole life, and furthermore is simple as paying out
money from one pocket into the other—for that is literally his proposition.

He has destroyed every commercial company—every
stock jobbing concern in which floating capital can be
invested. When he announces that in one month he
will liquidate the public debt of France—seventeen
hundred millions—what will become of the seventeen
hundred millions that he pays over?

It must seek re-investment.

What investment is there?

Only the stocks of the India Company, OF WHICH MON-
SEIGNEUR LAW HAS FULL CONTROL!

This announcement being made by edict of the
Regent, the holders of government securities for a few
days are delighted. They rush to the royal bank to
have them liquidated.

Then their pockets full of money—what will they do
with it? How invest it—how hide it—how make it even
secure?

BUT ONE INVESTMENT IS OPEN TO THEM! THE
STOCKS OF THE INDIA COMPANY!

They rush to the Rue Quincampoix and buy the securities of that concern.

Up its debentures go—higher and higher!

Another payment is advertised of government securities. More money must go into the stock of the India Company. Higher still it goes!

The holders of government bonds receiving their money at the Bank Royal (Law's bank) rush to the Rue Quincampoix, and deposit it in the India Company (Law's). From there it is carted back to the royal bank, and again paid out.

Up go the securities of the India Company once more!

And all the time, what is the result of the Scotchman's audacious but masterly financiering?

The entire money of the country is simply changed from an investment in the funds of France, to an investment in the funds of a company controlled by a private individual—and that man, Monseigneur John Law, the financial dictator of the commercial world.

Higher and higher, in this financial battle, mount the securities of the India Company, and greater—greater becomes the wealth made by the lucky speculators in Mississippi securities. And with sudden riches comes startling luxury, delirious extravagance! The prices paid for even the necessaries of life double, triple and quadruple.

The streets are crowded with the richest of equipages. Real estate mounts in value one thousand per cent.!

On the Rue Quincampoix, shops that rented for one thousand *livres* jump to sixty thousand a year.

Pandemonium reigns supreme! The crowds are so great they squeeze each other to death on that little street, fighting for bargains in stocks. The speculation is of the most bizarre kind. The selling of "daughters" and "mothers" is shrieked by struggling stockbrokers, who are almost torn to pieces in their efforts to bull and bear the market.

Quasimodo Junior, the hunchback of the Café Procopé, transferring his scene of usefulness, hires out his hump to stockbrokers to write contracts upon, in the crowded street, and makes one hundred and fifty thousand *livres.*

The methods of robbery invented by stockbrokers to do their clients would put the modern promoter to shame. The schemes of reprisal of their clients would make railroad magnates blush with envy and hang their heads at their own puerility.

More government bonds are paid off, and more money seeks investment in the India stocks—and higher go the securities again.

And over all this seething cauldron of profligacy, of extravagance, of gambling in everything on earth— from the loves of women to the lives of men—one man reigns supreme.

PARIS, THE BUCKETSHOP OF THE WORLD—MONSEIG- NEUR LAW CHALKING UP THE QUOTATIONS ON THE BLACKBOARD!

BOOK II.

THE RAID OF THE POLICE.

CHAPTER VII.

ROBBING THE OLD WORLD.

THIS whirligig of excitement, luxury, and extravagance of course has its influence upon Raymond, his sister, and Mademoiselle Quinault.

D'Arnac finds his income from his estates and his official appointments, which had been generous, become in proportion to his expenses more and more limited.

Little Jeanne, on the contrary, grows richer and richer, for her stocks that were originally worth five hundred *livres* are now worth six or seven thousand a share, and a third issue is promised to be called the "granddaughters" that will greatly increase her fortune.

Somehow, her fortune inspires her with a curious hope:—her eyes that had been wistful as they turned towards her *seigneur* have now in them beams of a new happiness.

As for Cousin Charlie, in his riches he has forgotten his terror of the ghost of O'Brien Dillon. It has never reappeared to him, but the agents of Monseigneur Law at Marseilles have sent him such reports that he shivers as he thinks of the Irishman he has injured; for they make certain to his analytic mind that *forçat* number 1392 has not been drowned from the galley *La Sylphide*, but has, through the agency of D'Arnac, in some way escaped.

In gaining these details he also receives sufficient information to be very well satisfied that De Sabran loves once more the old comrade of her husband, and had an assignation with him that very night on the Isle Pomègue, which Raymond's sudden discovery of O'Brien Dillon had postponed.   For to Charles de Moncrief's mind no man could refuse to look upon Hilda's wondrous beauty, *if she loved him.*

Then he has said to himself: "Why can she not love *me*?" and has gnashed his teeth in impotent desire, for in his heart of hearts Cousin Charlie still has one project that he feels will make him really and truly a boy again—and that is the conquest of the magnificent beauty of the Mistress of the Regent of France.

This information about the escaped galley slave, being brought to Monseigneur Law, makes that gentleman look very serious.   He says to himself: "Not that I fear O'Brien Dillon, *immediately*, but by it I learn something else.   It proves to me in this galley slave entering Paris and leaving it unreported that I have lost the friendship of Marc René d'Argenson, Lieutenant-General of Police!"

And he is very right in this—only instead of losing the friendship of the Lieutenant of Police—he has gained his active hatred.

For envy has entered the soul of D'Argenson, as he has seen the tremendous success of this man he had once coolly ordered out of Paris, as he would a common vagabond and wayfarer.   For the glory of Monseigneur Law is now beyond the glory of any other man in France—even D'Orleans himself—for he has that charm which gives the greatest popularity on this earth— the power of making other men rich—and women also.

He is besieged by countesses, duchesses and princesses, begging him for shares in these securities, which go up day by day, and even night by night; as the crowd of speculators under the smoking oil lamps of the Rue Quincampoix shout and battle, bearing and bulling the quotations of the various stocks of the India Company.

Even the Church has beamed upon his glory, and has appointed an abbé to convert the financial dictator, which has been very easily accomplished—Monseigneur Law subscribing, with the ease of a man of the world, to the religion of the country he lives in.

The *beau monde* has taken him also to her heart; the
world of fashion throngs to the grand *fêtes* at his
great house on the Place Louis le Grand, and court
beauties petition and beg and humble themselves for
invitations, for all seek the favor of this man whose
touch is that of Aladdin upon the lamp, and who
can summon the genius of riches at his bidding.

But among the court ladies who are most persist-
ent in bothering the comptroller of finance for shares of
stock in the India Company, none equal Clothilde, the
Comtesse de Crevecœur, who has become a perfect
fiend upon the Rue Quincampoix, and struggles and
jostles the stockbrokers, and haggles with dealers in
securities, in the varying struggle for fortune; for the
joy of the speculator has entered her fat soul, and will
not be appeased save by the misery of the speculator—
which may come afterwards.

This panjandrum of enormous speculation, inflated
fortunes, and their attendant luxury and debauchery
produces wondrous complications and bizarre crimes.
Many of these are the indirect product of Monseigneur
Law's financial operations.

That gentleman, with the wisdom of a great speculator, has determined to build up his financial fabric on
the solid basis of the successful colonization and development of the great valley of the Mississippi, now open
to the hand of France.

The year before he has founded the city of New
Orleans, which to-day remains to his honor—a lasting
monument of what this man would have done for
France, had France but permitted him.

To obtain emigrants to the new land every induce-
ment has been offered by means of flaming placards
and announcements. He has made the populace
believe the new town on the banks of the Mississippi a
city of palaces, when it is but a village of log cabins.

These allurements, not meeting a sufficiently ready
public ear, emigration has been slow. To build up his
colony he must have men and women in quantities to
suit; and Lass is not the man to want a thing and not
obtain it.

He has consequently within the preceding year
bought from a German petty potentate twelve thousand

stout and hearty male peasants of the Palatinate; four thousand of whom have already arrived in the new colony.

For these peasants wives must be procured. Consequently Monseigneur Law some ten months previous had received an edict from the Regent, permitting him to export vagabonds of both sexes to Louisiana, and under the then friendly police administration of D'Argenson this had been done.

This first shipment of rogues, vagabonds, criminals and women of the town had been received with open arms; but the ladies exported, not turning out of the greatest domestic value, Monseigneur Law about this time, finding further necessity of female emigration, had obtained another edict from the Regent of France, authorizing him to export the daughters of very poor families to the land of the West.

Filled with this project, he is about to rob the Old World of its peasant girls, to give population to the New.

When this edict is brought to D'Argenson for his police to carry out, the smile of the devil runs over his gloomy face, and he says to himself: "This order I will execute so as to bring the shrieks of an outraged people upon this financier, whom I hate."

Taking counsel with De Conti, they prepare the grandest—the most extravagant police raid on record.

"In it," cries De Conti, "my dear D'Argenson, we must abduct those who are loved, so that those left behind will curse our friend Lass till their cries go up to heaven. *Burgeoisie* who have adored mistresses must despair at their loss. Doting fathers of poor daughters must be bereft of their offspring. Of course, with the rich and *noblesse* it must be hands off, but the others, how they will damn the Scotch *emigré.*

Acting on this idea, these worthies give secret notice to their adherents throughout France, and one bright night, on the 1st of October, they inaugurate an official and police raid upon the inhabitants of both Paris and the surrounding country, that makes a wail and shriek such as the Israelites of Egypt sent up to heaven on the loss of their first born.

On that dread night D'Argenson, with his myrmidons;

De Conti, with his bravos, to whom he offers fifteen francs per head, and the local officials of the surrounding villages, who have had their instructions, steal forth and make a foray on the beauty and youth of the poorer classes—on all not under official protection, or so high in rank they are beyond them.

That night the prettiest peasant girls in over two hundred *communes* disappear. Most of the loveliest of the *demi-monde* flit as if by magic from Paris. Eight vessel loads of them are taken to Louisiana to become brides to colonists, adventurers, Indians, anyone who will take them—to make New Orleans more populous.

The screams and imprecations of the bereft fill the air, and for one short week Paris is compelled to virtue.

But within seven days there are even more beautiful women on the streets of the city than there had been before the blighting ruin had come over its courtesans; and in the rising tide of stocks on the Rue Quincampoix the public forgot it, though it left many vacant places by peasant firesides, and many a gay young student sighed for the bright eyes that even as he grieved were filled with tears in the log cabin of some settler of the Mississippi.

But, oh, what delicious opportunities for audacious private revenge this affair offers to the initiated! What chances to pay off personal grudges and feuds that have been put at interest, not only to commoners, but to the *noblesse*, for on that dread night many young ladies of quality disappeared.

Private information of this projected raid having been brought to Madame de Sabran and Charles de Moncrief it has placed in both their wicked heads very curious ideas.

The lady has cried: "Now I have her! She is mine! Raymond shall never again see this woman for whom he has slighted me."

The gentleman has laughed: "*Pardi!* if I can but arrange a little plan, the bride may be wanting that may one day deprive me of my hope of the estates of Crevecœur."

So for this affair both had hired private bands of bravos and ruffians for their special purposes.

This intended raid is officially made known to

Raymond d'Arnac on the morning of the day on which it takes place.

D'Argenson (who for his advice in the O'Brien Dillon matter, perchance thinks he has some claim to the lieutenant-general's good offices) sends for him, and after showing him the Regent's order remarks: "We make our raid to-night. Would you kindly see, my dear D'Arnac, that the regiments under your immediate command are so disposed that no chance broil may take place between individual members of them and the police? Also will you give us all aid in your power?"

"I, of course, will not move the troops under my command," replies D'Arnac very civilly, for he feels some obligation to D'Argenson, "unless ordered by the Regent, or Monsieur le Duc de Villars, commander-in-chief of the garrison of Paris. As to the regiments immediately under my control, I shall issue orders that will keep them in their barracks this evening, for it is a soldier's nature to respond to the cries and entreaties of any pretty woman. As to the *Musquetaires*, they have certain privileges. Those on leave will not be recalled, but the bulk of the command I shall keep in their barracks. Those that are in the city probably will not trouble you or your policemen. They are gentlemen," remarks Raymond proudly.

For this corps possesses among its ranks many volunteers of the highest name, family and fortune; a great many gentlemen volunteering to act as privates until they receive their promotion as officers of the general army. Dukes have carried muskets in it, and many a maréchal of France has marched as a volunteer under its banner in the preceding reigns, and the custom has not altogether died out.

"I am much obliged to you, general, for your action," replies D'Argenson. "It may prevent many broils between my men and the soldiers about Paris."

"Very well," answers Raymond, "I shall take the steps that I have outlined to you, as effectively as possible, and if military support is needed, I shall be at your service, Monsieur D'Argenson, as soon as I receive command from the Maréchal de Villars, or the Regent."

This meeting passing off pleasantly enough, Raymond, in the course of the day, does as he has promised, and finds himself busy getting the various regiments of his command into their barracks, and issuing such orders as will curtail as much as possible the number of *Musquetaires* in the city during the coming night.

Occupied with these duties, he is at the barracks outside the Port St. Antoine until about seven in the evening, when, riding into town and feeling hungry, it occurs to him, as he comes down the Rue St. Denis, to stop at the café of the Turk's Head and kill two birds with one stone—that is—discover from Lanty if he has had any communication from O'Brien Dillon and get a pleasant supper as well.

On making inquiry for "mine host," Mr. Lanty surprises him by making his appearance *a la* brigand with a huge pair of bell-mouthed blunderbusses buckled to his side, a slashing cavalry sabre swinging behind him, and the excitement of coming battle in his Irish eyes. Though bloodthirsty in his equipment, there is mystery in his manner.

He leads Raymond to a quiet corner of his house and whispers: "Bedad! Monsieur General, I've little toime to talk to ye; I'm goin' to do a little of the old business to-night—just to freshen me hand."

"'Of the old business'—what do you mean?" laughs D'Arnac.

"Fighting! I'm one of the raiders this evenin' that'll make Paris howl. There'll be many a pleasant jostle and riot in the affair, and the pay is very good. I am one of a special band of ruffians hired by your cousin, De Moncrief, to do some social diviltry to-night on the great police raid."

"Hired by Charles de Moncrief! Were you engaged by him in person?" says D'Arnac inquisitively.

"Oh, no! Geronimo, the Corsican, is making up the band. Ye see, I've got quite a reputation as a fighter on the street. I've chased three or four swindling stockbrokers out of it at the end of me sword, and they think there's no such bully on the Quincampoix as your humble servant. That's what made them engage me. It's a special band of fighting men they're getting up. It's not for business in Paris, I'm told, as I've a horse to ride."

"You are sure Cousin Charlie has a hand in the matter?" queries Raymond wonderingly.

"Sure as that angels have wings. Didn't I hang back saying the police would get hold of me and didn't Geronimo say I was to be a policeman to-night myself—that his orders came direct from the Procureur du Roy?"

"Oh, ho! I presume Cousin Charlie is taking advantage of this police raid to abduct a ballet girl."

"Be jabbers! then I think it's a curious place he's getting her from. Be me soul! this is the first time I heard of ballet girls being abducted out of convents!" laughs the Irishman.

"Out of convents—what makes you think that?" whispers D'Arnac.

"On account of the rendezvous. We're told to meet together by midnight, outside the walls of *Les Filles de la Vierge!* in the village Villeneuve. That's about ten miles out, I take it?"

"And you are going on such an errand for Charles de Moncrief?" ejaculates Raymond astounded.

"Bedad, I'm goin' to spoil it!" returns the Irishman, and astonishes D'Arnac more.

"Spoil it!" cries Raymond. "May you not get spoiled yourself?"

"Begob! if it's any divil's game, I am going to try to spoil it! I don't love Cousin Charlie. Besides, I think I will be safe enough doing it. Two of the band are men I bring with me from this hotel—the butcher and the underscullion. They're both at me beck an' call, and good fighters, having been soldiers in the Army of the Rhine, when knocks were plenty. I don't guess the whole band will amount to more than seven or eight; I'm good for three myself, and I think the butcher will make meat of a couple of the Italians—he's so accustomed to slaughtering cattle."

"Well, take care of yourself," says D'Arnac. "Comte Dillon wouldn't like to come back and find no Lanty."

"Be the Powers! he'd cry his eyes out, as I did over him," answers Lanty. "Besides, there's a little girl up the street that would do some weepin' also. I've told Marie to keep close in the house this evenin'. Heiresses may be in demand," adds the Irishman, with a twinkle in his eyes.

"You have no news from O'Brien?" asks Raymond as he rises to say good-bye.

"No, only this, which came by the courier yesterday. It simply says (the Comte is not much at writing ye know): 'Tell D'Arnac I have succeeded in Vienna, and am on my way back after—.' He didn't put the rest into words but I know what he means. He said also outside of Paris he would notify me from the Auberge *Le Cerf du Bois*—it's down the Melun way. I was tryin' to foind ye, this mornin', to deliver it, but ye were out of town, I'm thinkin'."

"Yes, at the barracks," replies Raymond, and goes on his way, giving little heed to the matter, except that he imagines it may give Lanty a funny story to tell him. The Irishman is like a cat, with his nine lives, and pretty certain to fall on his feet from any distance less than balloon height.

As Raymond rides, a smile of expectation comes upon his face; he remembers a promise to escort his pretty ward and her duenna from the Theatre Français this evening. His spur quickens his charger's gait and he dashes rapidly up to the Hôtel de Chateaubrien to change his military garb for evening attire.

Going to his apartments, this is very easily done, with the aid of his valet, and looking at his watch, D'Arnac notes that it is nine o'clock, and hastens his steps.

As he is passing through the main hall of the building, the voice of Mimi, who is singing some little *chanson* of Mouret's, comes to him from an adjoining *salon*. A moment after apparently hearing his step, she appears at the door crying: "*Voila!* how do you like me, *en fête*, my brother?"

"Ah, going out for the first time since Uncle Henri's death?" remarks Raymond, noting that Madame la Marquise is in very gorgeous evening toilette.

"Yes, a little *concert de salon* at the Comtesse d'Isle Adam's. I thought I would get your opinion," remarks Mimi. Then she says archly: "How do I look?"

"Like the prettiest widow in France," whispers D'Arnac, giving her blushing cheek a kiss.

"You will not come with me? I have an invitation for you," suggests Madame la Marquise, looking at him inquiringly.

"I am sorry—another engagement."

"Ah, yes; the usual one," she says, "at the Français." This last with a little sigh.

A moment after she remarks, forcing herself to smile, for her brother's eternal Français business is not at all to his sister's liking: "If you will go, I have an errand for you. You can return Mademoiselle Jeanne her scent bottle and handkerchief. She left them here this afternoon. She came to tell me of the new part she is going to play in Monsieur de Voltaire's tragedy of *Artémire*, which *entre nous* little Jeanne has given me her private opinion, will be—," she whispers into Raymond's ear, "by the critics."

"The scent bottle is pretty—perfume delicious—," remarks Raymond lightly. "Have a sniff, Madame la Marquise," and, opening the bottle, he throws some on the handkerchief and places it under his sister's dainty nostrils.

"What an extravagant little wretch la Quinault has grown to be!" cries his sister.

"Why?"

"Why this scent bottle is of gold and Venetian glass of the most exquisite workmanship. Look at it! The bauble cost perhaps twenty *louis*. And this handkerchief—nothing but *point de Venise*, with Jeanne's initials in its little center."

"Twenty *louis* more, I suppose," laughs D'Arnac. "She is an extravagant little puss, but then she's a rich little puss also, I can tell you! As her guardian I can announce Mademoiselle Jeanne is worth a million."

"A million—good gracious!" gasps la Marquise, growing pale, for the richer Jeanne gets, the more frightened she is of her charms and fascinations upon the young gentleman standing opposite her.

Then she says suddenly and seriously: "But you will have to give this Français business up. Some day you must call upon your *fiancée*. You can't postpone it much longer on account of the distance. They have brought Julie from Melun to another convent nearer

Paris—just within easy ride—Monsieur laggard in mat-
rimony."

"*Diable!*" mutters Raymond between his teeth.
"I'm sorry for that!" Then he cries angrily: "Why
do they try to thrust this child down my throat? If I
have to take my medicine, don't let them force it upon
me, so as to make the dose more bitter."

"Don't talk that way to me," says la Marquise, quite
haughtily. "Keep your contract like a gentleman,
with closed lips. Don't be so ungallant as to sneer at
a young lady you have not even seen for seven years.
She's a beauty, I can tell you!"

"You have seen her?"

"Yes; I rode out to-day with her aunt to Villeneuve."

"Villeneuve!" says Raymond, suddenly. "Villeneuve—has anyone else been talking to me about
Villeneuve?" Then he suddenly cries: "Lanty—by
heaven!"

Next greatly astonishes his sister, for he says quite
anxiously: "What convent did you say my affianced is
placed in?"

"There is only one in the village—*Les Filles de la
Vierge*," answers la Marquise.

"*Les Filles de la Vierge?*" gasps D'Arnac, a dazed
but horrified look flying into his face.

"Yes; *Les Filles de la Vierge*," repeats Mimi. "But
what do you mean?" for the eagerness with which
Raymond has put this question has astounded his sister."

"I mean I am no more the laggard in love!" he replies, forcing a laugh. "I am going to ride out this
evening and see my *fiancée*."

"To-night—you won't get in. It's after nine
o'clock. Don't you know all convents close at
eight?"

"Yes, yes; I'd forgotten," remarks Raymond. "But
for all that I shall ride out very shortly!"

And with these ambiguous words he leaves his sister
astonished—his manner hints more than his words.

Into D'Arnac's mind has suddenly sprung a strange
suspicion of Charles de Moncrief's intentions this evening—one that he thinks just as well not to mention to
his sister, for it would alarm her, and he does not care

that a lady's name which is to be connected with his in marriage should become the talk of Paris as that of the heroine of a great adventure.

As he strides away he suddenly thinks of the other convent—the Carthusian—the one he visited nearly seven years before, when he encountered almost the anathema of the church, to bear little Jeanne into Friburg the night before the assault, to save the lives of O'Brien Dillon and his regiment.

This makes him feel very tender towards Mademoiselle Quinault. She would feel wounded if he forgot his appointment with her. He will excuse himself to her, tell her to take a cab and go home with her duenna, as she has often done before.

With this in his mind he hurries to the theatre, enters the greenroom of the Français (of which he is a privileged visitor) and, fortunately, seeing the actress off the stage, gives her the little handkerchief and scent bottle his sister has charged him with.

"I've half a mind to keep the 'kerchief as a souvenir," he suggests.

"Oh! not that one," she cries. "Not the one with the red initials; it is a present."

"From whom?" mutters D'Arnac in awful voice.

"From Monsieur le Duc de Villars," she laughs. "You don't count your old chief among the prohibited ones, do you?"

"Of course not," answers Raymond; and presenting his excuses would leave her pouting at his desertion did not little Jeanne have a bright and pleasant spirit and charming temper.

She places her little hand upon his as he is going away and says: "I forgive you, *mon seigneur*. I see you have business of importance this evening." Then she laughs: "Whoever it is with I pity them, from the appearance of your countenance," for D'Arnac's eyes have a curious gleam in them, as he is thinking of his Cousin Charlie.

With this Jeanne flits away, for the call boy is after her, to prevent a stage wait. And D'Arnac, who has been pondering over what he has to do, suddenly goes out of the stage entrance, hardly noticing in his haste that there are more hangers on about the portals of Thespius than he has ever seen before. Outside, he marches to the front of the theatre· and looks carefully through the audience to see if he can find any *Musquetaires* on leave about the Français.

Fortunately he meets two—the Chevalier D'Aubigné, a volunteer of the regiment, and De Soubise, one of its lieutenants, and an old friend of Raymond's former days in Paris.

"Do you want an adventure ?" he whispers to the young men.

"Yes, anything for a lark!" replies D'Aubigné, a young fellow of about eighteen, with bright eyes, sunny hair and sunny smile.

"I am with you always," answers Soubise ; then laughs : "Do you remember how we drew swords to save the great man of France that night after la Quinault's *début?* "

"Very well!" replies D'Arnac. "Rendezvous in one hour with me at the Pont áux Tripes, with fresh horses and accoutrements; fully armed, but not in uniform. Make yourselves look as much like brigands as possible for gentlemen to do."

"Oh, oh! General Knight Errant!" laughs D'Aubigné.

"Who is she ?" whispers De Soubise.

"I'll explain later—time is everything!" returns Raymond. "I will make arrangements for your leave of absence. Both of you put plenty of ammunition in your pouches and plenty of money in your pockets, for which I will reimburse you on my return. Now good-bye for an hour!"

And he leaves the two young men gazing after him in astonishment, and calling a fiacre makes the man fly through the streets to the Hôtel de Chateaubrien, where, fortunately, finding his valet, he gives him some hurried orders ; drives off to the house of De Villars, and thanks God that he finds the Maréchal at home enjoying a pipe, and in very comfortable humor. His interview lasts scarce two minutes; he simply asks for leave of absence for a day or two, for personal, perhaps grave family reasons—saying that it is important that he take De Soubise and D'Aubigné with him.

"Ho, ho! an adventure—a lady?" laughs the Maréchal.

"Yes!" replies Raymond, with military candor—though he does not mention his suspicions. Under any condition he does not wish Julie's name made the talk of Paris.

"Very well! I authorize your leave of absence, together with that of De Soubise and D'Aubigné. See that you come out better off in this fight than you did with De Conti's ruffians the last time, *mon Bayard!*" grins the old gentleman.

Getting back to the Rue St. Honoré, Raymond finds his valet with a rig that gives him an appearance somewhat between that of an escaped jail bird and a gentleman farmer.

Putting a pair of excellent flint lock pistols into his belt, making sure he has lots of ammunition for them, and girding on his cavalry sabre, D'Arnac mounts a fresh horse that is ready for him.

Arriving at the Pont aux Tripes, he finds D'Aubigné and De Soubise waiting for him, having the look of cutthroats and marauders, for D'Aubigné, who has appeared in private theatricals at court *fêtes*, has rigged himself up *a la* brigand, with Sicilian hat and jack boots, red sash and Italian stiletto, as well as the usual arms of a cavalryman. De Soubise, who is always the gallant, appears more like a gentleman bandit than the other.

"Now," says Raymond, "let's get under way. We must ride as rapidly as we can without tiring our horses."

"Which way?" says De Soubise.

"To Villeneuve!"

"Oh! down the Fontainbleau road," replies D'Aubigné.

"No! Villeneuve is on the opposite bank of the Seine," remarks De Soubise.

"You're mistaken, I think. It's this side," dissents the Chevalier.

On this Raymond's two companions go into a discussion, D'Arnac gazing at them, disconcerted, for he isn't sure which is right.

Finally, De Soubise says: "I know it is on the east bank!"

"Why?" asks Raymond, suddenly entering into the conversation.

" Because I've been there," replies his lieutenant.

This settles the matter.

"How shall we get there?" D'Arnac hurriedly asks.

" It's perhaps twelve miles by the road from where we stand," is the answer. "We must cross the river by one of the town bridges and then take the Charenton route."

CHAPTER VIII.

THE AMBUSH IN THE SENART FOREST.

" LET us ride at once!" cries Raymond. "While we are talking they may be carrying her off."

"Her! Oh, ho! She is a woman!" laughs D'Aubigné.

" If we are to act with discretion under you," whispers De Soubise, " give us some idea of the foray."

" I will, as we journey."

Whereupon the gentlemen, turning their horses, make for the eastern part of the city, crossing the Seine hurriedly by the bridges of the Ile St. Louis, thus getting back into the more settled portion of Paris.

As they ride towards the Port St. Antoine, the first signs of commotion and the noise of the police raid that is taking place in the center of the city come to their ears.

"*Diable!* listen," whispers D'Aubigné. "D'Argenson and his myrmidons are at it."

"*Pardi!* but they will make a hole in the courtesans of Paris this evening," laughs De Soubise.

For Raymond, in explaining his suspicions of De Moncrief, has been compelled to give his companions information of the business the police are doing this night.

He, however, does not reply. He is turning over in his mind rapidly the best plan of action; but, to his chagrin, finds himself unable to come to any absolute determination as to what his course should be; he knows so little of the locality in which this affair must take place.

Riding rapidly they leave Paris, and passing the Port St. Antoine, on the road just outside the gates, which is bordered chiefly by sheds and hucksters' booths, they overtake a carriage that has apparently left the town just before them, probably conveying some party to one of the neighboring country villas.

The coachman whips up his horses as Raymond and his comrades come clattering behind him, but as they pass him becomes suddenly sleepy and stupid; so much so that he does not answer D'Aubigné's question, if he knows whether there is a convent at Villeneuve?

But they have no time to pause to arouse the driver, and ride hurriedly on.

A moment after they are near the barracks of the *Musquetaires Noirs*. As they pass, Raymond for a moment debates whether he shall order a few files of the regiment to accompany him; but his time is getting short now. Besides, if the affair turns out to be nothing, it would make him the laughter of his command. If it is really as serious as he suspects, he does not wish the Comtesse Julie's name to be mentioned in the barracks of Paris.

With Lanty and his butcher and under-scullion, and the two gentlemen spurring by his side, his party (including himself) will amount to six—enough, he thinks, to do what he wants successfully. A greater number might even embarrass him.

He quickens his pace; they reach Charenton, and crossing the bridge over the Marne turn their horses' heads up the valley; the Seine flowing on their right hand as they gallop along the road to Villeneuve.

Getting into the open country, D'Arnac looking at his watch says: "We have time enough to reach the place without exhausting our chargers."

Slackening their gait he gives his companions some further details of what he fears is his Cousin Charlie's design.

At which D'Aubigné, throwing back the fair curls from his boyish forehead, laughs: "How I will fight for your little comtesse, my colonel!"

And De Soubise, who is a man of comparatively few words, cantering beside Raymond, simply grips his commander's hand.

D'Arnac feels very sure he has two gentlemen with him who will do their *devoirs* for his lady's sake as gallantly as knights of old.

Then Raymond throwing off the commander, and both gentlemen being of the *noblesse*, they chat as comrades as they hurry along the country road, passing through the hamlets of Maisons and Valenton.

So communing contentedly together, their ride seems a short one, as they find themselves in Villeneuve, which is a quiet village situated on the Seine near where the pretty little Yeres river runs into it.

Here, after looking about for a few minutes without discovering the convent, and being saluted by the welcoming voices of some hundred dogs, they finally come upon a little inn.

D'Aubigné, jumping off his horse, awakens, after some trouble, the innkeeper, who comes out in a very sleepy and disturbed state of mind. Noting the appearance of the horsemen, the moonlight falling upon brigand accoutrements and ominous arms, mine host gives a little shriek of terror, and bolts back into his house, closing and locking the door behind him.

But D'Aubigné is battering upon the portals again, crying: "Come out—we won't hurt you! Come out, trembler—give us what we want, and we will pay you well. If you open the door, you will find a *louis* right under it."

This the man cautiously does, and discovering the gold piece, takes heart again, and reappears saying: "Gentlemen—what will you have—refreshments—supper?"

"No—information!" replies D'Aubigné. "Quick information!"

"Is there a convent in the town?" asks Raymond sharply.

"Yes, Monsieur."

"Ah, what is its name?"

"*Les Filles de Notre Dame!*"

"That is not the one I want," replies D'Arnac. "There is another!"

"Not within three miles on this bank of the river,"

"This is Villeneuve?"

"Yes,"

"Then there is another."

"Yes! of course there's *another* Villeneuve!" answers the man.

This astounds De Soubise; makes D'Aubigné mutter, "I was right!" and horrifies Raymond.

"*Another* Villeneuve!" he gasps.   —

"Of course there is—Villeneuve le Roy, just across the river!" replies the innkeeper. "This is Villeneuve St. Georges."

"*Diable!* You know the other place?"

"Yes," says the man, "sometimes I go across to buy carrots there. They're cheaper than on this side."

"Is there a convent there?"

"Yes, sir."

"What is its name?"

"I am not quite sure, but I think it is called *Les Filles de la Vierge.*"

"That's the place," cries Raymond. "How can we get across?" disappointment in his tones, for he has wasted an hour coming to this wrong place on the wrong side of the river.

"There is no ferry here."

"*Morbleu!*"

"If you will go a little further up the river there is one near Ablon."

"How can we get to Ablon?"

"You can't get to Ablon. It's on the other side of the river."

"*Nom de Dieu!* Don't joke, fellow. How can we get to the ferry?"

"Oh, pardon!" stammers the innkeeper. "Cross the Yeres. There is a little bridge a hundred yards from here. Then go up the bank of the Seine for a mile and you are at the *bac!*"

"Do you know any of the country beyond?" asks Raymond, who thinks he might as well get the topography of the vicinity properly in his head this time.

"Oh, yes, back of the ferry on this side is the forest of Senart. There is a fine chateau there—though I ———"

"Well!"

"I don't think they have much money!" ejaculates the innkeeper, hesitatingly, who can't seem to get out of his head that he is talking to bandits; an opinion that is enforced by the incautious remark of D'Aubigné, who cries: "If they cross the river the forest would be the best place to waylay them!"

At which the Boniface flies into the house again, and they can hear him double bolt his doors. And though D'Aubigné assaults it again, for they wish to ask him a few more questions, he is obdurate and prays them for the sake of the Virgin to go away and leave him alive.

"Come!" cries Raymond, "we have no more time to waste on innkeepers!" and looking at his watch, he finds it is after twelve o'clock.

With this, spurring their horses, they canter over the rustic bridge that crosses the Yeres, flowing between its high banks covered with vines and lined with poplars. A moment after they are on the side of the Seine, which runs rippling on their right.

On their left the ground slopes up gradually to the high table land of Brie. Before them they can see heavy woodland, casting shadows in the moonlight, about a mile away. They ride up the bank of the Seine, and in the course of perhaps a quarter of an hour find themselves at a ferry—but the boat is not upon their side of the river.

It is apparently in use, for a woman is awake in the ferryhouse, and to their questions replies that the boat has been called to the opposite shore a few minutes before, but will undoubtedly soon return. It is large enough to carry six men and horses.

But as the woman speaks she suddenly utters a shrill "*Mon Dieu!* what is that?" and running out on the bank of the river, listens.

The three horsemen, who have dismounted, listen also, for to their ears comes the faint noise of combat from across the water. One or two pistol shots are heard, then a louder report and a few cries and screams.

"Jump in and swim our horses to the other side!" cries D'Aubigné, with the impatience of youth.

"No," replies Raymond, putting his hand upon the boy's shoulder, "we would have difficulty in landing in the face of an enemy. Besides, we would be swept down by the current, and land a mile below. Get

behind the ferryhouse, quick ! Conceal the horses—
my God ! they're coming ! "

" *Diable !* You are right ! " answers De Soubise, for
in the still night they can hear the sound of the ferry
barge as it crosses attached to a rope stretched high
above the river, from bank to bank.

Raymond, peering across, can see that the boat is
occupied by more than the ferryman.

He withdraws behind the cabin himself, and, looking
at his companions, finds they have prepared their arms
and are both ready with sword and pistol, for whatever
may come.

He hurriedly prepares himself also.

" If they are carrying off the comtesse, we will take
them as they land,' whispers D'Aubigné, for the boat
is almost on their side of the river.

But just at this moment there comes to Raymond's
ears words that make him start: " Be jabbers ! It's
lucky we've got the river between those murderin'
divils and ourselves, Butcher."

"It's the voice of a friend ! " cries D'Arnac, and
runs down to the river bank so incautiously that Lanty,
shouting " Bedad ! they're on this side of the river,
too ! God help us, Butcher! " springs out to attack him
with sabre and pistol.

But on the bank he gasps: " By the powers! it's
Giniral d'Arnac! " and a moment after adds: " Be
my soul ! I thought you were a bandit ! You look like
one, anyway! What other cut-throats have ye got with
ye? " and rolls his eyes upon D'Aubigné and De Soubise, who have hurriedly followed their commander's
steps.

" Two *Musquetaires*—I've no time to explain! " ·

" Neither have I. We must get away from this
place quick! They'll be comin' over soon themselves
with the girl."

" They have carried her off? "

" Aye! Bedad an' I tried to stop 'em. I'll tell ye
·about it as we get away from the ferryboat. For your
life don't try to cross—there's a round dozen of 'em—
fighting men. They're coming over *sure*. I know
their route! " whispers Lanty, laying detaining arm on
D'Arnac, who is about stepping into the boat. " Let's

lave in a hurry, or the ferryman may tell 'em that we are still on their track, as we are, ain't we, Butcher? Faix, I'm not the man to desert screaming beauty in distress. Fortunately the butcher and I saved our horses, though we left the poor under-scullion on the other side of the river, dead, if Italian knives will deaden anything."

While he is speaking, Lanty and his butcher, who is a swarthy, short, thickset man, lead their nags out of the boat. Then mounting his horse the Irishman shouts with all his lungs: "Fly for yer lives!"

"Fly—never!" cries D'Aubigné. "What does the coward mean?"

"Tell young spitfire it's a ruse," whispers Lanty to Raymond. "I am doing this for the benefit of the ferrymen, so they tell Geronimo and his band we're runnin' away." Then he yells again louder than ever: "Boys, hurry to Paris or they'll murder us!"

And the whole party clatter off as fast as their horses can take them, D'Aubigné by this time understanding what is required of him.

A quarter of a mile from the river Raymond reins in and says: "Now tell me all about it!—Quick!"

"Well, the short of a long story is, I thought I would spoil De Moncrief's little plan, and, as ye hinted, the old fox nearly spoilt me. I and the butcher and the under-scullion rode into Villeneuve le Roy on time, making rendezvous with three others, under the walls of the convent; Geronimo, leader of the party, and two gentlemen of the Italian persuasion, bein' the others. Begob! I thought that was all of 'em. Corsican Geronimo, who is a very gentlemanly mannered cut-throat, told us to draw back a little. Then, as the clock struck twelve up in the tower of the church, he rapped on a little portal of the convent wall, and it was opened suddenly, and the swatest voice in the world said: 'Is that you, Cousin Bon-bons, and is ugly Raymond with you?'"

"Raymond! She meant me!" whispers D'Arnac under his breath.

"Musha! I was afraid so at the time from the description," returns the Irishman with a dry chuckle.

"With that, before she could utter another word,

Geronimo, who understands these things, clapped a sudden hand over her mouth, and whisked her out of the convent into which she had made a feeble effort to retire, and, closing the door after him, he says: 'This is the girl, boys! Two hundred and fifty *livres* a piece for ivery one of ye!'

"And I said: 'Not for me!' and drew me sword. 'The girl is mine! I'll spoil yer-plans, ye murderin' villains!'

"And the butcher and the under-scullion stood by me. I thought it was only three to three and we had an easy thing.

"Bedad! I didn't know yer Cousin Charlie.

"With that, up springs a dozen more of them from the surrounding hedge. They had been put out of the way so as not to frighten the girl—too soon.

"I plucked the little lady out of Geronimo's arms—but I could not fight a dozen of them with one hand, so I had to drop her, the poor thing had fainted I think.

"A minute after I had to stop fighting and take to running. But by the blessing of God, I and the butcher got back to our horses again, for most of the others were occupied by their leader's directions about their captive, and though we were pursued we got down to the bank of the river, where I found the ferryboat, and here we are by the mercy of God, though I am afeard the poor under-scullion will never scour dishes again. He had two knives in him when last I saw him. But they're comin' over on this side. I know their plans enough for that, and I know this country very well, Mr. Raymond. They want to get on the main road. They're going to take her to Melun."

"Are you sure of that?"

"Certain! Fresh horses are there for 'em. They'll get her to Marseilles as quick as they can and on board ship for New Orleans and the Injins."

"Not while I live!" replies D'Arnac.

"Then we might attack them in the ferryboat, before they land!" suggests Lanty. "I've got a long gun here at me back that will shoot across the river," and he pats a very curious weapon that he has slung from his shoulder after the manner of a cavalryman.

"Impracticable! You might shoot *her!*" answers

Raymond. "Besides they would then keep on that side and we want them on this !"

After a moment's consultation with De Soubise, it is arranged that they retire from the river, and waylay the party as they pass along the road to Melun, the forest of Senart being the very place for this business.

So they wait where they are, resting their horses, with the exception of Lanty, who returns nearly to the ferryhouse again, to bring news of the crossing of Geronimo and his bravos with their captive.

But here there is so much delay that D'Arnac himself, after waiting two hours, goes to the side of the Irishman, and whispers : " If they do not cross soon, we must cross to them. If they have gone by the Fontainbleau road on the other side of the river they'll have two hours' start of us."

But even as he says this, the noise of the moving ferryboat comes to them, crossing to their bank of the river.

As well as they can distinguish in the darkness, for the moon has gone down, it is full of men and horses. Raymond would return to his command, but Lanty observes: " We have plenty of time yet. It will take two more loads to get 'em all across, and they won't bring the girl till the last trip. They'll be an hour more, and we'll have a little light by that time which'll help us."

This turns out as Lanty predicts. Four men with horses disembark. The boat goes back to the other side, moving very slowly, the ferrymen are tired and sleepy, and the rope damp with morning dew. Some time after it brings over four more horsemen. Then it goes back again, and in the first light of the morning they discover there are four more men in the boat, with their horses, and a figure that appears to Raymond like that of a woman.

" That's her! I recognize the dress of the convent!" whispers the Irishman. " Now, we'll go along the road ahead of 'em and work up a little surprise for the murderin' divils in the wood of Senart."

With this they return to their party, and Lanty leads the way along a dusty lane that runs to Montgeron, remarking parenthetically: " I know the country very well. I've been all over it for cabbages for my hotel, and spring lamb for the high livers."

After riding perhaps half a mile, they reach the direct Melun road, and taking their way along this towards the south, soon find themselves in the heavy woodlands of the forest, where Raymond selects a place for the ambuscade.

With the deftness of a man accustomed to attack and defense, he picks out a spot where the road, making a sharp turn, runs between a large rock on one side, and on the other a dense thicket, capable of perfect concealment for man and horse. Just opposite the rock there is a large oak tree with spreading branches, some of the larger of which extend nearly across the road, which narrows at this point on account of the limestone. In the thicket he places De Soubise and the butcher; on the other side just behind the rock he stations Lanty and D'Aubigné. Then he gives his directions.

As the escort turns the rock, the attack is to be made.

They are to use their pistols at once, being very careful to shoot at no one near the captive. After the volley they are to charge, sabre in hand.

"An' what will ye be doing?" says Lanty to D'Arnac, with the familiarity of an old acquaintance.

"I? I shall be waiting."

"What for?"

"To get the girl! And I'll have her," says Raymond. "Look after the men of the party; I'll get the girl."

"Ah, you always like nice things," laughs D'Aubigné. "But from where will you get Mademoiselle; not the middle of the road?"

"From the branch of that tree," answers D'Arnac, pointing to a big leafy limb that hangs over the center of the lane. "My signal for the attack shall be my spring upon the man as he rides under me carrying the comtesse."

"But they may see you too soon, and retreat?" dissents De Soubise.

"Hardly in that heavy foliage; but perhaps I'd better make sure," replies D'Arnac. Then turning to the butcher he says: "Your coat is green—give it to me and take mine."

"I never refuse good bargains," grins the cattle slayer, and does as he is bid, producing a fearful appearance in Raymond, as the garment is dirty, spotted with beef blood, and very much more disreputable than what the young general had sported for the raid, which is saying a good deal.

"Now, with your cap, my man, I don't think they'll notice me till they feel me."

And this further exchange giving Raymond the appearance of a slaughter-house tramp, he mounts hastily to his perch amid the laughter of D'Aubigné and the guffaws of Lanty.

A moment after D'Arnac, from his tree, whispers: "Quiet! prepare yourselves—they are coming!"

But it is a false alarm, and they wait and wait, Raymond with feverish impatience and anxiety, for he feels this danger has come upon the girl, not for her own sake, but for his—that this attack upon her safety has been made because she is his affianced wife.

Even as he thinks this, Lanty, who has gone down the road on foot, returns very hurriedly and, passing him, whispers: "They're coming, carelessly and disorderly—I think it will be a *fête champetre* for us."

Five minutes after the head of the party come into sight. They are riding slowly and carelessly, apparently fatigued from their night's efforts. More afraid of pursuit than attack in front, they are arranged in the following order:

Three men ride ahead. Just behind them comes their lieutenant, a very suave-looking gentleman of sweet Italian manners, who carries in his arms, in front of him on the saddle, the light, graceful figure of a girl of some sixteen or seventeen still robed in her convent uniform. She is perhaps fainting or under the influence of some drug, for she makes no outcries—she sheds no tears—only there is a fluttering of her white hands as she is borne along.

Two men ride behind some twenty paces; the others, the rear guard, six in number, are nearly two hundred yards in the rear. D'Arnac from his perch can see they expect their danger, if any, will come from Paris, for all of the cavalcade occasionally look searchingly behind them, and Geronimo, their captain, rides with the rear guard.

The first three men, carelessly laughing and chatting in an easy way, in bad French, pass under Raymond but do not see him. Some movement of the girl has attracted their attention, and the brute who carries her remarks savagely: "Curse you, Miss Baggage! Scream again and I'll slap your pretty ears. Won't even the Eastern drug stay your long tongue? But for the big reward, I'd cut your white throat and leave you in the road!"

This is a very unfortunate expression for the fellow—it curdles the last drop of pity in D'Arnac's heart. The Italian is just coming under the tree as he makes it. Glaring down upon his unconscious head, Raymond's eyes meet two hazel ones beaming, through despairing tears, towards heaven, imploring mercy that comes not from men—two appealing hands are clasped in prayer.

As her eyes meet D'Arnac's, the girl gives a sudden startled cry—the brute's hand is raised to fulfill his threat—at that moment Raymond springs and *strikes*, and the fellow thinks some wild animal has stung his vitals.

In Hades he informed inquiring devils that a bear had just sprung upon him from a tree and killed him.

Of the others left behind, two fall to pistol shots and one dies to the sharp crack of Lanty's long gun. The two remaining varlets fly for their lives towards their rear guard—leaving D'Arnac with an uninjured but fainting maiden in his arms, and grouped about him his party unscathed by combat.

CHAPTER IX.

THE EMPTY COACH ON THE MELUN ROAD.

"*Dieu merci!* this finishes the affair!" says D'Aubigné, gazing in boyish wonder at a dead ruffian he has killed.

But it doesn't!

The two flying bravos are now with the rear guard, making them eight in number, and these come on for vengeance and their promised reward—they cannot bear to be balked of the golden pieces they thought in their very hands but three short minutes before.

Their leader, Geronimo, the crafty Corsican, points out the small number of their enemies, who have only won a victory by surprise.

These ruffians bar D'Arnac's return to Paris, and the affair commences now to have an ugly aspect, for three or four of them carry carbines. These, under their leader's direction, they unsling, and commence to shoot.

Were Raymond unencumbered he would charge them, but, as he looks at the childish but beautiful face that —still unconscious—is turned up to his, and thinks this trouble has come upon her because she is his promised bride, he cannot bear to take any risk of injury to her, which may come through some chance shot in the *mélée*.

Therefore D'Arnac orders his party to retreat along the Melun road until they arrive at some farmhouse they can defend, or obtain assistance, or reach some crossroad by which they can return again to Paris, without fighting their way through the men who bar the road to the capital.

So they retire gradually, through the pleasant woodlands of Senart.

But this retreat makes their enemies more confident. They come nearer, and the fire from the carbines grows more galling, the butcher getting a slight wound in the leg.

"Ah! long bowls is yer game," says Lanty. "I can beat ye at it!"

He unslings his curious gun from his shoulder, and, deliberately dismounting and taking a rest, fires what his companions think is a marvelous shot, for he puts *hors de combat* a pursuing bravo.

"What kind of a gun is that?" asks Raymond, astonished.

"Bedad! It's one I bought at Nuremberg, in Germany. It's a curious thing—goes straight because it takes a twist. Faix! if I was a good marksman I could kill them all with it."

This makes their pursuers more cautious. They keep out of shot.

So they pass through the forest of Senart, and

coming to the more open country the sun, which is getting higher in the heavens, beams upon them so fiercely that D'Arnac fears the effect of the heat upon his charge, whose nervous system seems unequal to her first experience of life outside convent walls.

They have already seen some peasants going to their morning work in the fields; but these, noting their appearance, fly from them. They pass a little hamlet, the inhabitants of which bar their doors, despite D'Arnac's entreaties, who now wants aid, not for himself, but for the fainting maiden. Apparently she has been put under the influence of some sleeping potion, which has now partially passed from her, leaving her semi-sentient, with distracted mind and agitated nervous system.

"*Diable!* no wonder," remarks D'Aubigné, looking at Raymond's butcher coat. "You would frighten anything."

A moment after they see ahead of them, about a quarter of a mile, a cross lane, which comes in from the east.

"Do you know anything about it?" asks Raymond.

"Aye," says Lanty, "it goes to the other road leading from Paris by Brie."

"Very well; we will take it and return. Just give those fellows another shot," returns D'Arnac, quickening his horse's gait, which is languid, as the charger has been kept on the move all night and has grown sleepy.

Just before he arrives at the crossroads he hears a shot and the Irishman gallops up, crying exultingly: "Be jabers! I've wounded Geronimo. His crowd are in full flight."

"Very well! here's more good luck," replies Raymond, who has been greatly concerned about the state of the fainting girl in his arms. "Here's just the thing for the little comtesse."

He is looking at a closed carriage that is turning into the main road to Melun, from the crossway.

"Why," cries D'Aubigné, "it's the same coach that we passed going out of Paris. You remember it—the same sleepy driver."

By this time D'Arnac, riding hastily, is alongside of

the man, and the carriage being closed, he asks, "Is it empty?"

"Yes," growls the coachman, very sleepily, "empty—don't disturb me—I'm going to Melun."

"I engage your carriage," cries Raymond. "I hire it!"

Without more ado, he springs off his horse, bearing Julie in his arms, steps into the carriage with her, sits down, and as he closes the door of the coach finds occupying the vehicle with him two armed ruffians and a veiled female silent figure on the opposite side of the carriage.

The bravos glare at him in astonishment. Raymond does the same to them. Then one says, with a hoarse laugh, noting D'Arnac's captive and his disreputable appearance, "*Diable!* You're in the same business as we!"

"Yes!" gasps Raymond. Then sudden inspiration coming to him, he adds "Who's your captive and how much do you get a head?"

"More than you do," sneers the fellow, "though we don't wear quite so much blood on our clothes, and who invited you to join our company?"

"Myself!" answers Raymond, affecting the French of the poorer classes. "This coach I thought was empty, and this girl was fainting. My orders are to get her to Marseilles *alive.*"

"*Mordieu!* Your hirers are more considerate than ours. "They don't care whether our trollop dies or lives, so long as she disappears."

"You are on special service, I see?" says Raymond. "I am one of De Conti's bravos."

"So are we," returns the other man, and astonishes D'Arnac; "but I think our gold is from a woman's hand. The orders are so vindictive. But here comes our captain—you will have to talk to him."

Here D'Arnac receives another shock; the carriage is now surrounded by fifteen mounted men, who have come suddenly up from behind; riding some hundred yards in the rear of the carriage to prevent pursuit, they had been hidden by a turn in the cross-road from Raymond's eyes, as he came up to the coach.

"*Tonnerre de Dieu!* what are you doing here?"

blusters their leader, who is mounted on a curiously marked piebald horse of great speed and action.

"What you are doing," answers Raymond, "taking a girl to Marseilles. There's five hundred *louis* for this chick." At which Julie, who has partially revived, utters a shuddering moan and murmurs: "Spare me, assassin! I saw you kill him!" Which gives D'Arnac a very good footing with his fellow cut-throats at once.

"Then we'll help you," chuckles the leader, "and take half of the reward."

But before he can receive answer to this, a shot is heard behind them, from Geronimo's followers, who have taken heart again and come on.

At this the captain of the second band says: "We are pursued. I feared so! We must dodge them by crossing the river." Then he calls to Raymond, "Help us drive them back!"

And D'Arnac springs out of the coach, runs to De Soubise and whispers instructions in his ear; that gentleman and his companions having stood looking on with amazed faces, awaiting directions.

"Go back with them, my dear Soubise," he says; "help them drive back Geronimo's bravos. This crowd is too large for us to fight, besides Julie will get a rest in the coach. In her state I dare not put her on horseback. We can leave this party at our leisure. They're not particularly interested in us."

While he is speaking the veiled woman's figure in the coach has turned to him.

As D'Arnac had entered it, though her hands are bound and she can make no movement, a sudden nervous tremor has run with one quick quiver through her frame. Her head has been suddenly turned towards him as he sits scarcely a foot away, and two eyes gleaming with unutterable amazement, yet unutterable hope, have blazed upon him through all the heavy veiling wound round her head.

While D'Arnac is out of the coach giving his directions to De Soubise, one of the brutes, noting the veiled one's movement, has whispered in her ear: "Quiet, you jade. Try to escape and I'll cut your throat from ear to ear. Those are our orders."

Then Raymond returns and the coach goes hurriedly

on, shouts from the rear indicating that Geronimo and cut-throats *number one* are probably now getting their fill of fighting from cut-throats *number two*.

A moment after the coach turns hurriedly into another cross-road, making for the Seine, flowing some miles away; and, going down a gentle descent, after about half an hour they reach a pretty little inn upon the bank of the river. The house is of stone, two stories in height, solidly built, with stabling fifty yards away, near the river bank, also of stone.

Behind the building rises a high limestone cliff; the auberge being apparently built in some old quarry long since disused.

Just beyond the limestone the Seine flows deep and silent between poplars and willows. Floating upon it is a large barge used in crossing the stream at this point. It is not a regular ferry boat, but apparently constructed for the uses of the inn, and capable of carrying both men and horses.

D'Arnac notes these things as he springs out, for the carriage has stopped.

The leader rides up again and says: "We have driven them off for a time, thanks to your comrades—they're good fighters, my abductor with the bloody coat. How many murders did you achieve last night?"

"*Par Dieu!* only two. How many did you?" answers Raymond.

"None. But we may do one this morning, if this jade gives us any more trouble. We breakfast here, lads; then cross the river to the Fontainbleau road. We put her in a caravan of vagabonds at Fontainbleau. What do you do with yours?"

"The same thing," replies D'Arnac.

"Very well, you keep with us, and help us out on our fighting. We may have more-before night. By that time I guess we'll have got her mixed in with the rest of them. They took eight hundred out of Paris last night for Marseilles and Louisiana. But they're behind us. Besides, they've been gathering up peasant girls in quantities to suit. But come in. Leave a couple of your men on guard outside and make a merry meal."

"*Mon Dieu!* what shall we do with this?" says one

of the ruffians in the coach, touching the veiled one on the shoulder.

"Oh, bring her in and lock her up in the inn !"

"And if the innkeeper objects ?"

"The innkeeper won't object. *Maladetta !* let me see the innkeeper object," cries the head bravo.

With that two of the men lay hasty hands upon the veiled figure in the coach, and lifting her without much ceremony, half bear, half drag her into the inn.

"*Diable !* that's rather rough usage," remarks D'Aubigné, who with De Soubise and Lanty are standing by Raymond. "I wonder she didn't cry out !"

"By me soul ! she's gagged," says Lanty. "She's got the look of a rale lady, though wrapped up loike an odalisque."

"Why not rescue her ?" whispers D'Aubigné.

"Impossible !" says Raymond, "with the charge we now have. But I shall report the affair to the police in Paris." Then he says suddenly to De Soubise : "See— Julie's reviving. I will get her on my horse that the butcher leads, and we can leave those ruffians (he points to the inn), cross the Seine and return to Paris. Run into the house, D'Aubigné, and see if you can get some brandy—anything to revive my charge. Then we'll cross the river while the brutes breakfast."

But even as he speaks, D'Arnac, turning to the coach to lift out Julie, suddenly gives a stifled cry and picks up something from the floor of the carriage.

Then beads of perspiration gather upon his brow, his eyes become excited, his face grows pale, his lips tremble as he mutters : "My God !" as if astounded, for he is gazing on the little kerchief—that mass of Venetian point lace, with la Quinault's initials in the same red embroidery upon it, the one he had placed in the hands of little Jeanne the evening before at the *Comedie Française*. He falters, with knitted brows : "What does it mean ?"

Then something flies through his mind like lightning flash.

"Come," says De Soubise, "let's get under way at once !"

"Impossible !" whispers Raymond.

"Why not ? Your comtesse is reviving."

" We have now TWO to save ! "

" What other ? "

" MY WARD, POOR LITTLE JEANNE, OF THE FRAN-
ÇAISE ! "

CHAPTER X.

THE DEFENSE OF THE AUBERGE.

WITH this they call Lanty into consultation.

"Bedad ! An' if it's little Quinault, she saved my
life once, and she's welcome to it now ! " remarks the
Irishman.

After short discussion they decide there is but one
thing for them to do. That is, to take the comtesse
into the inn, revive her there, and while doing so, ascer-
tain without doubt who the veiled captive is. If it is as
they fear, their plans for Jeanne's rescue must be gov-
erned by the circumstances of the case.

"Anyway," remarks D'Aubigné, who has returned
from the inn with some spirits, " a little breakfast won't
do us any harm; the odor inside that dining-room is
delicious this morning."

So forcing some brandy down the girl's throat they
half carry, half support Mademoiselle Julie into the inn.
Apparently sentient, at present she says nothing—only
looks at them with frightened eyes, for their appearance
is not reassuring.

At the entrance they are met by the agitated wife
of the innkeeper who cries out: " God help us ! They're
bringing another beauty in ! These ruffians will be
abducting me next ! They've got one pretty one
upstairs, and here comes another ! "

This is emphasized by the master of the house staggering along the hall, his bottles clinking, his mugs
spilling their contents, his knees knocking together, and
his face ashen with tribulation and terror. He opens
the door of the dining-room from which oaths and
laughter come.

The leader of the party, seeing Raymond, calls out :
"Come and join us in a friendly glass ! "

" After I've secured my chicken upstairs, as you've
done yours ! " answers D'Arnac.

Then drawing the landlady aside, he whispers: "Take good care of this young lady; revive her at once; put her on a couch upstairs! Give her something to eat and drink, and blessings, not curses, will be your reward!" pressing a gold piece into the woman's hand.

Its touch seems to reassure her, though she still looks on D'Arnac's accoutrements and butcher coat with distrust as she replies: "I can't put her into the same room with the other. They've locked her in and have got the key. Two villains are on guard at her door, while the others are eating us out of house and home." Then she shudders, "Good heavens! they'll wake the comte, our best customer. He never gets up till nine."

"What comte?" says Raymond, hurriedly, for he knows any respectable citizen will be an aid to him in this crisis.

"The German-Irish comte," cries the woman, wringing her hands. "The one that pays ten *livres* a meal and drinks champagne three times a day. The one who arrived two days ago with two *valets de chambre*. The one who is good for one hundred *livres* a day."

"What's the name of your inn?" asks Lanty, a sudden wildness in his voice.

"Le Cerf du Bois."

"Bedad! it's the place!"

Here a door opens above, and a voice cries very savagely from the second story: "Madame Innkeeper —by the piper that played before Moses! what is the meaning of these varlets rousing a comte of the Empire from his morning slumber?"

To this D'Arnac gasps: "O'Brien Dillon!"

While Lanty shrieks: "Begorra! it's him!" then whispers, "I've been thinkin'—. For the love of God kape those ruffians here, and I'll fix ivery man of 'em!" Without waiting for more words he bolts out of the house, and speaking hurriedly to the butcher, who is taking care of their horses, the two men mount and hurriedly gallop off.

As they do this Raymond is turning to greet his old comrade of the Rhine.

But some one is before him!

With a scream and a shriek, Julie, to whom the brandy has brought renewed life, suddenly flies upstairs, and seizing the arm of a gentleman, who makes his appearance at the head of the stairs, sobs: "You're a comte—you're a noble—for the love of the Virgin protect me from those villains downstairs! Yes! that one in the green coat—the assassin with the blood on him—the one I saw murder a man half an hour ago."

"Stand back! ye divil!" says O'Brien, suddenly drawing ready rapier.

"You know me!" cries D'Arnac, running upstairs.

"I know ye for the bloodiest-looking cut-throat I've ever laid eyes on!" answers O'Brien. "Varlets, to my aid!"

A couple of stout German serving-men fly out to him.

And on the stairs is a very pretty impromptu tableau. Julie, with her light, graceful figure outlined by the robe of the convent, on her knees, with upraised hands imploring the protection of O'Brien Dillon, in shirt and trousers (for he has hastily arrayed himself); that gentleman turning very savage eyes upon D'Arnac, and confronting him with drawn rapier and upraised pistol! Raymond, with outstretched hands and beaming eye, and loving words—but damned as to appearance, by the butcher's awful coat.

"For God's sake give me a word!"

"Not till I've taken this lady away from yer sight. She trembles every time she puts her pretty eyes on ye!" answers the Irishman. "Don't take another step up the stairs, or there's a hole through every man of you!" for De Soubise and D'Aubigné have come hurriedly after Raymond, both laughing at the curious contre-temps.

With this, the Irish gentleman, bowing with the courtesy of the old school to Mademoiselle, says: "Permit me to introduce myself;" then whispers into Julie's pretty ear a few words that seem to vivify her; next remarks: "You trust me?"

"With my life! I am the Comtesse Julie de Beaumont, the affianced bride of Raymond, the Comte d'Arnac, stolen last night by these fiends from my convent."

"Madame," replies Dillon, "Raymond d'Arnac is the best friend I have on earth or in heaven. As his

affianced, you may count on me with my life and
my honor. Permit me to conduct you to a suitable
apartment."

And he escorts with great ceremony the little
comtesse to a neighboring room.   As he turns he
suddenly cries to his servant men: "Blow a hole
through him if he tries to come up the stairs;" for
Raymond has made another step, and Julie has given a
shudder.

Returning alone, O'Brien says hurriedly: "Now,
butcher and murderer, for the little comtesse calls you
that, and that's what ye look like, what do you want
with me?"

"Your friendship!" answers D'Arnac, who has been
pondering over his appearance, "Don't you recognize
me?" and he suddenly takes off the butcher's coat and
throws away the butcher's hat.

Then Dillon, with a scream of astounded joy and
love, takes his comrade to his heart.

"By my soul! who would have guessed you?   What
brought ye here?   What is the meaning of the little
girl's fear of ye, when she says she's going to wed ye?
Fear comes after marriage."

"For God's sake talk low.   Let me explain!   This
is De Soubise, of the *Musquetaires*—this the Chevalier
D'Aubigné.   Quick! where we can't be overheard."

"This way," whispers O'Brien.   "I know this inn
pretty well.   I've been here two days," and leads
Raymond to a balcony running in front of the second
story.

In going there, they pass the two bravos guarding the
door of the chamber in which the veiled one is confined.
A smothered moan coming faintly from its portals
makes Raymond hunger to fly at these men's throats—
but prudence compels patience.

So he follows O'Brien.   But the moan has banished
all pity from his heart.

Stepping on to the veranda, which is covered by a
large awning during the hot weather, made of heavy
canvas, and supported by rafters running from the
house, Dillon's lips form the word "Now!"

Then, in very cautious whispers D'Arnac tells briefly
but completely his adventures of the night.

"Bedad! another of Cousin Charlie's wicked devices, for which I've come back to repay him!" returns O'Brien.

"But how are you here? Are *you* safe?" queries D'Arnac.

"Safe? I'm in communication with D'Argenson himself. I am only awaiting the necessary papers from me master, the Emperor of Austria, who has been pleased to do me great honor in consideration of my sufferings." Here a shudder runs over O'Brien Dillon's bright face, but forcing it away, he mutters: "Soon I'll have a glory from my Emperor that will wipe it out. But I can't explain now. The courier bearing my first appointment lost the papers in an avalanche coming through the Alps. I've sent by the way of the Rhine to have duplicates forwarded to me. Until that time I'm remaining here quietly—happily—forgetting eighteen months of despair—but REMEMBERING WHAT CAUSED IT! —Now to your affair! You say you fear little Jeanne who saved our lives is a prisoner in that room?"

"Yes. What do you advise?"

"There are fifteen of those villains, all told?"

"Yes, thirteen below and two up here."

"Then we must take no chances."

"The odds are pretty long, but we will be reinforced in a few minutes. Lanty said he'd been thinking, —and rode off suddenly with the butcher," answers Raymond.

"Then God help us if Lanty's been thinking!" gasps O'Brien. "There's no telling what misery he may bring upon us! Look at the misfortune it brought on me! Look at the damn billiard shot! Ah! I won't think of it. Only one thing—we must rescue the veiled lady—Quinault or no Quinault."

So they sit waiting for the Irishman's return, Raymond dreamily noting the beauty of the scene. Behind them the river flowing swift and silent, between green banks broken on their side by a few limestone cliffs. To their left, down the bank, he sees the little village of Soisy; beyond, the wood of Senart; among the trees, the tower of its old chateau; above them, up the river on their side, Etiolle, and, further on, St. Germain; and, in the distance, the spires of Corbeil.

Suddenly, dreams give place to action. O'Brien Dillon, looking out of the balcony, whispers, hastily: "God help us all! What has that crazy fiend been doing?"

For just at this moment, Lanty rides up to the inn, bearing a shrieking girl, who is in bridal robes, followed by a woman, screaming and tearing her hair, and pursued at a distance by thirty or forty peasants.

Springing hurriedly off his horse, he brings the screaming girl into the inn; then flies upstairs and whispers in triumph to Raymond: "I've abducted a bride right out of her groom's arms. Faix! I'm afraid the butcher's cut off! There's two villages up for vengeance. They'll murder every bloody villain of 'em below!"

"They'll murder every bloody man of us also—idiot!" cries O'Brien Dillon. Then he says, suddenly: "There is but one way—we must separate ourselves from those ruffians downstairs at once!"

"What do you propose?" whispers Raymond.

"Knife the two cut-throats upstairs and throw them down the passageway. We've got the two girls up here. Then we must keep the stairway against the bravos while the peasants slaughter them below. After that perhaps we can make a parley with the villagers and obtain terms. There's a hundred of them coming now, and more'll follow. Lanty's raised up a hornet's nest for us as well as the bandits."

Without another word, acting with the promptitude and barbarism of the soldiers of that day, O'Brien Dillon and Lanty spring on the two ruffians on guard at the chamber of the veiled lady.

These men are easy victims. The arrival of the shrieking bride has created a commotion below which has attracted their attention.

In another second they are knifed and tossed down the stairway to their astonished comrades. Then one vigorous kick, and the door flies off its hinges to Raymond's foot.

Springing in, he finds, half swooning, with bound hands, and gagged mouth, hair dishevelled, and eyes which have in them the fear of death, poor little Jeanne. Upon locking her in the room, they have taken from her the veils about her head, that almost deprived her of the breath of life.

Despair flits from her fair face, drawn with the suffering of the awful night, and hope—divine hope—takes its place.   Her bruised lips struggle to utter words beneath their gag as Raymond plucks it from her mouth.   There are tears in his eyes as he unties the little wrists confined by cruel cords.

He thinks little Jeanne is trying to falter out thanks, for her tongue is so swollen she can hardly speak; but, womanlike, she is whispering: "Who is that girl? That girl you carried in your arms?"

Here O'Brien cries suddenly: "Quick! Raymond, fight! No time for love—*fight!*"

In a flash D'Arnac is at the head of the stairway. Jeanne would follow, but reaching the door, the sight before her eyes makes her pause.

The ruffians below are crowding up the stairway with hoarse cries of vengeance for their slain comrades.

At its head stand De Soubise, Raymond and D'Aubigné—the boy a little in front—more eager; his coat thrown off, his right arm naked as his sabre, the joy of battle in his youthful eyes; Lanty and O'Brien leaning over the balustrade prepared to battle from the side.

As they see Jeanne, they greet her with a cheer— the boy crying: "I've seen you play comedy, little Quinault, now see me play tragedy!"

Then with a rush the bravos come on.   D'Aubigné, giving point with his sabre, spits the foremost. Others fall by the pistols of O'Brien and his comrades.

At the discharge, the leading ruffians fall back, and D'Aubigné, laughing in their faces, puts his foot against the body of the wretch he has spitted, and kicks him off into the face of the crowd that now rush up with another and more hideous yell.

So they come on—come on—never cease coming on —though some are killed and others wounded.   They will win by very force of numbers, for though the leading files are slain, the others press up and over them.   Soon there may be but *few* bravos left, but there will be *none* of O'Brien Dillon and his party.   Soubise, fighting like a tiger, has already been struck down insensible, and D'Aubigné slightly wounded.

Out of the *mélee* Raymond and Dillon drag Soubise into Jeanne's room. Then go back to fight again. While she, bending over him, gives to this man who has risked his life for her safety, the tender care of woman's nursing.

Then the crisis is upon them. The two German serving-men, having fired off their blunderbusses, suddenly lose heart and jump off the balcony into the garden below, to be captured and knifed by the peasants of the surrounding country that are now flocking into the grounds of the place, uttering savage cries of vengeance.

O'Brien Dillon has followed his two flunkies to the balcony, calling to them: "Cowards! don't disgrace my liveries!"

On the veranda a sudden idea comes to him. He seizes one of the beams that project from the house, supporting the awning, and with the strength born of his mighty travail in the galleys, the tremendous development of arm and shoulder that comes with that awful toil—he has wrenched it from the building.

With this long spar, he comes to the side of the stairway where their opponents are even now making a lodgment, and leaning over the balustrade commences to wave it about—to send it through the air—with the same giant force he had given to the oar of the galley. Each stroke sweeps down the bravos that are crowding up, crushing their heads and breaking their limbs.

One yells: "My God! he's got the strength of a galley slave!"

This recollection for one moment unnerves Dillon, and perhaps would be fatal to them, for the bravos crowded up again.

But at this moment there is a wild yell below. The peasants have entered, armed with knives, sickles, and scythes, a few of their leaders having swords.

They have fallen upon the bravos below and are massacring them and knifing them, man by man urged on by the sobbing bride in her wedding array, and the screams of her mother, who cries wildly for Lanty's blood, though she can't find him.

CHAPTER XI.

LANTY THINKS HE'S FIGHTING THE TURKS.

THIS gives respite to Raymond and O'Brien. No longer bothered by the attacks of the bravos, who have turned to meet the slaughter in their rear, they strengthen their defenses.

The little landing at the head of the stairway they barricade with heavy furniture grabbed *ad libitum* from the adjoining rooms. In Dillon's parlor they get a pathetic glimpse of the Comtèss Julie on her knees before a crucifix, telling her beads and saying her prayers with the faith of a child. Tears come into Raymond's eyes as he turns from her, thinking "this peril and this terror are upon her on account of me."

"Where's that divil Lanigan?" asks O'Brien. "Is he wounded? Where's Lanty?" he raises his voice anxiously.

"Coming, yer honor," cries the Irishman, and makes his appearance from O'Brien Dillon's chamber, carrying two small stone jars.

"My heavens! The baste's been getting drunk on me best Italian wine!" cries the Irish count angrily.

"Divil a bit! I drank the wine as a military necessity; these two bottles are now *bombs!* They're filled with poor Soubise's unused cartridges, and those I could spare from me belt, with powder sprinkled between, their fuses are two lamp wicks rubbed with powder. It 'll be God's own blessing if they don't blow us up when we touch 'em off in case of necessity!" says the Irishman, placing his two implements of war convenient to his hand.

While doing so there is a yell of joy from the peasants below, who have just finished the last of the bandits, and wild cries from the mother of the bride, who has espied Lanty on the second story. She is screaming: "There's the villain! there's the abductor that stole my Annette from the bridegroom's arms!"

"Keep yer tongue quiet, ye old hag!" whispers Lanty from the head of the stairs.

"Hag!" shrieks the woman, "Hag! *Ravisher!*"

"Five girls were stolen from our village last night,

and now we'll have your blood!" cries the bridegroom.

This is greeted with a short, deep howl of approval
from the peasants crowding around him. They have
wetted their Jacques Bonhomme fangs with blood;
they want more of it.

"Listen to me! I am a lieutenant-general of
France!" beseeches Raymond over the balustrade.

"A lieutenant-general of France! Oh, ho! butcher
of the bloody coat!" screams out the man, a horrible
shriek of derision answering his words, as the peasants
charge the barricade.

"Faith, nothing but killing will cure them, and,
please God, we'll give 'em enough of that!" remarks
O'Brien, grimly.

As Raymond, D'Aubigné and Lanty meet the crowd,
fighting behind the barricade, cutting over it and
lunging through it with their sabres, and firing their
pistols as opportunity offers, Dillon plies again from over
the balustrade his awful beam, clotted now with blood,
and smashes the heads of peasants against a heavy
bureau, part of the barricade at the landing.

The stairway becomes so obstructed with dead and
wounded that the others cannot get past them. They
give back suddenly, dragging their wounded away, and
go into consultation out of reach of the weapons of the
defenders of the upper story.

Then, in this breathing space, D'Arnac and O'Brien
examine the rear of the inn for chances of escape.

Immediately at the back of the auberge is a high, over-
hanging limestone cliff that runs down to the Seine,
only fifty yards away. Behind this D'Arnac knows is
the ferryboat. The inn is apparently built on the site
of some old and disused quarry, one white limestone
cliff coming close to its rear windows, but rising above
them some dozen feet.

From that cliff they could retreat to the boat and
place the Seine between them and the blood avengers
below. But between the inn and safety is a gap some
eight feet wide, the limestone rising straight and sheer
above the window—below a fall of thirty feet upon the
rocks.

To gain the top of the cliff from that window or low

roof is not the leap of an athlete, but the flight of a bird.

Two brick chimneys rise, one on each side of the window, but stop three feet below the level of the cliff. One probably comes from the guest room below; the other from the kitchen of the inn. These, near their top, are connected by two strong iron rods, to give them greater stability and brace against the wind, which sometimes sweeps quite strongly down the Seine.

Looking at this prospect, D'Arnac shakes his head; no chance there. A fact of which the leaders of the rabble are so sure none of their men are on this side of the inn, though the mob occupy the lower story entirely and each minute brings reinforcements to them.

There are at least one hundred of them now, and with a low savage roar they prepare to charge the stairs once more, to avenge their slaughtered yokel friends.

"We can't kill them all," mutters O'Brien gloomily.

"Hear me!" shouts Raymond. "There are women above with us. To give them safety we will surrender if you bring your village priest, and he will make oath that you will deliver us to the commandant or civil authorities at Melun."

"Yes," cry the crowd grimly, "we will make oath to deliver your corpses there."

With this the fight recommences, but grows so desperate that at last Lanty whispers: "Dodge the bomb!" And lighting the wick of one of the stone jars he tosses it into the crowd below.

As Raymond and his comrades throw themselves upon the floor of the hallway a great red glare, fearful explosion and stifling smoke come all about them. But over the deafening din rise groans of despair and moans of agony and shrieks of torture from the wounded. The lower hallway that was crowded with peasants but a moment before is deserted save by the dead and dying.

Another breathing spell for the defenders!

But reinforcements arrive again. The peasants know some time they'll have the blood of these men above who have destroyed so many of their *commune*. It will be soon now.

"Ah, what a beautiful bomb!" cries Lanty enthusi-astically; then whispers grimly: "By me soul! unless troops come soon little Marie will be weeping for me to-morrow."

To this the others answer nothing, for the fate of O'Brien's serving men has shown them the mercy they will get.

"By Heaven! we must escape!" mutters Raymond, growing desperate at the thought of what may come to Jeanne and the little comtesse; for the Jacquerie have never been merciful to youth, beauty nor innocence in ladies from the days when Captal de Bouch and Gaston de Foix, three centuries before, had to butcher them by the thousands to save the honor of the beauties of the French Court, crowded together in Mieux for safety from these peasants as they ravished the country side.

"The idea of gentlemen being butchered by these *canaille!*" snarls O'Brien, and he looks again for some safe exit from the inn, D'Arnac going with him. But turn where they will they see no chance.

Despairingly they even look again at the window and the limestone cliff above it. Lanty coming behind them and following their eyes, which have been scanning once more the chimneys, suddenly whispers: "I've been thinkin'!"

"Hang your thinking!" mutters Dillon. "See what it's brought us to."

"Bedad! I've been thinkin' about them chimneys. The way ye used that beam ye must have the strongest arms and shoulders in the world. Couldn't ye climb up on to the chimneys and those iron bars that hold them together and sling one of us on to the cliff—the lightest one—young D'Aubigné? There's some bushes up there he could get a grip on. One of us there, this rope ladder I've been making of bed cords and bed slats at odd times in the fight will take up the rest—even that senseless Soubise."

"Sling a man there! How shall I sling him? What footing have I on those chimneys?"

"Hang down from the nearest of those iron cross bars, by your knees. Then get your feet under the one further from the cliff. That will hold ye. Then bend over after the manner of the soldiers' exercise of the

Roman Cross. Take young 'D'Aubigné in your hands and wave him about like ye did the beam—like the oar in the galleys—No! I won't talk of that to ye, because that always unmans ye, Gineral! But sling him so that his hands grip the bushes on the other side."

"*Pardi!* I'll try it," mutters O'Brien determinedly, "if D'Aubigné will take the risk."

With this, Raymond, taking the place of the young man, who is on guard at the landing, and the affair being explained to D'Aubigné, he cries: "I'd take the risk a dozen times rather than those knives that are waiting for me below! I only weigh one hundred and thirty-five and am agile as a cat. Give me one grip on the shrubbery and I'm up to the top of the cliff."

"Then, for God's sake, quick," mutters O'Brien.

Climbing out of the window, he ascends one of the chimneys, his strong hands gripping desperately its sides. The shrill voice of the innkeeper's wife coming to him from below makes him hurry. She is crying: "Holy Virgin! they're setting fire to my house!"

"Keep 'em back!" whispers Dillon to Raymond, talking very low.

Then D'Arnac hurries to the stairway, and as the crowd charge Lanty gives them the other bomb, which produces even greater havoc, for the peasants are more numerous and crowded together. The newcomers, who have not learned of the slaughter, have pressed to the front, confident and reckless.

This explosion sickens them. Once more they give back.

But while Raymond and Lanty are holding the stairs, the feat of a Hercules is being performed at the back of the inn.

Hanging by his knees from one of the bars running between the two chimneys near their top, the bar that is nearest to the cliff, Dillon catches with his feet the other iron rod, which stretches some eighteen inches behind it and parallel to it, holding the two chimneys together. Thus hanging, head down in the air, he whispers: "Give me a pillow or folded blanket, something to put under my knees to keep the iron bar from cutting into them!"

And D'Aubigné, passing a blanket up, a moment after hears O'Brien's voice saying: "Are you ready?"

"Yes," answers D'Aubigné, and clambering out, the boy swings himself up to the Irishman, who lifts him in his arms, and, turning him head downwards, catches him firmly by each ankle.

Then Dillon commences to sway D'Aubigné about, his strong arms and shoulders working by the power given to him by the awful exercise of the galleys— backward and forward—a longer sweep each time—till the young man's head flies in the window, and he has to grip the sill to keep from being struck against it.

Finally, O'Brien gasps "Now!" between clenched teeth, and with every sinew and every muscle doing its all, and a little more, he swings the boy straight out towards the cliff above, lifting him by very force of muscle above his level, and D'Aubigné's quick arms, clutching wildly, grab a strong bush growing on the limestone, and he whispers, strengthening his grip upon a stouter branch above, "Let go!"

Released, he clings to the cliff, and getting footing upon it, clambers to its top in two seconds more, with a panting "Thank God!"

By this time O'Brien Dillon is at Raymond's side, whispering : "We've done the trick ! D'Aubigné is on the rock. Back to the room !—Get the ladder !— I'll guard now and nurse my legs that are nearly broken."

Acting quickly, D'Arnac throws the ladder, which is about twenty feet long and has been hastily improvised by Lanty from bed-cords and the rounds of chairs; D'Aubigné secures the end he catches to two small trees growing near the surface of the cliff, and Raymond fastens his end securely to a heavy bedstead he drags near the window of the room.

As he does this, Dillon appears carrying Soubise, and followed by the two girls. "Bedad, I've got my best coat, money and papers. The *canaille* may have the rest !—Now—quick—it's your only way !" he says hastily to the ladies, who hesitate, looking at the height. "The Jacquerie give no mercy to ladies." Then he cries: " D'Arnac, fly back and guard the stairs ! Good God ! they're coming again !"

This Raymond does, and by happy inspiration throws an empty wine-jug into the crowd as they charge the stairway. Thinking it another bomb, they retreat in horror from it.

A moment after he is touched on the shoulder by Lanty, who whispers : "They're all on the cliff. You and I now !".

Running to the window, they clamber up the rope ladder, and are assisted to the height above by the ready arms of D'Aubigné and O'Brien.

"Faith ! we're just in time. Those divils have set the house on fire !" mutters Lanty. As he comes up the rope, smoke issues from the window.

"Quick, to the boat before they discover us !" whispers Raymond.

Urged by their fears, they make short work of the descent to the river, which is not very steep, O'Brien assisting the little comtesse down, who seems to have regained some of her spirits in the sunshine.

But Jeanne declines Raymond's proffered aid, saying briskly: "Give your hand to the *other* lady—she needs more your assistance !" and trips down the incline with light feet, though there is a set look in her blue eyes.

A minute after they are all in the boat, which crosses the river attached to a rope that is stretched from one bank to the other. It is padlocked to the landing-place, but O'Brien smashes the fastening with an iron wrench that is used on some of the machinery of the boat.

"Bejabers ! that *was* a scorcher !" says Lanty, wiping the perspiration from his brow and gazing at the inn, which is now blazing. "By all the divils outside St. Peter, I havn't had such a pleasant morning since the battle of Belgrade. It was as good as fightin' the Turks —barrin' the plunder."

Then he suggests: "Couldn't we get some of the horses in the stable? They're only ten yards away; those divils are all occupied with the fire. Just a little plunder to finish up the fun.'"

Raymond would check him, but O'Brien says: "Without horses what would we do for our wounded man and the ladies on the other side ?"

Thus encouraged, Lanty sneaks up to the stables and shortly comes down, leading four nags that belonged to the bravos killed in the inn above; conspicuous among them, the piebald steed that had been the property of their leader.

"Begob!" remarks the Irishman, "our own beasts were impossible. They were tied in front of the auberge and are surrounded by half a hundred yelling carrot-pickers. I'll have a try for two more horses any way!"

He would go back again—but now there is a cry from the peasants about the inn. They have discovered that their prey has escaped them, and looking about have noted the party in the ferry-boat.

As they run down the hill, O'Brien, with one vigorous shove, gives the barge impetus into the stream, and D'Arnac, Lanty and D'Aubigné, working for their lives, pull the boat out upon the rope towards the opposite bank.

They have not much time to spare, for they're just in deep water as their pursuers reach the bank.

Lanty, unslinging his gun, which he still carries at his back, would fire upon them, but Dillon stops him, muttering: "We've blood enough on our hands now!"

Then with a sudden cry of triumph, the peasants cut the ferry rope leading across the river, and reasoning with bucolic brains, think they have bagged their prey.

"By my soul," chuckles O'Brien, "if it was the rope on the other side, they'd have us! As it is, the current will sweep us across to the bank to which we're hitched."

To assist this, Lanty and D'Aubigné put over oars and row now quite sturdily.

So they drift in silence, broken only by the shouts of disappointed vengeance from their pursuers; none of the party saying a word, save Jeanne, who whispers anxiously to Raymond: "Is there a revolution in Paris? What is the meaning of all this fighting?"

"Don't you know?" says D'Arnac.

"I know nothing—simply that I was carried off."

"How?"

"Madame de Caylor and myself, after the performance, as you suggested, sent out for a carriage. It came, driven by old François, who has taken me in safety to and from the theatre a hundred times. There was some noise in the streets as we drove along. I thought but little of it. At my own door, suddenly the carriage was surrounded. François was struck from the box. Madame de Caylor was seized and put out on the pavement. Two men sprang into the carriage. I screamed—oh, how I screamed! But there were other cries and commotion in the street. I was not heard.

"'Then I screamed no more. The two ruffians had bound me, gagged me, and wound a veil about my head. And then came the long journey in which I despaired, until—to my astonishment—you stepped into the carriage bearing that girl." She turns unpleasant eyes upon Julie, who is sitting saying nothing, but probably meditating upon the wonders of life outside the convent.

Then Jeanne continues: "Then that awful fight! The despair—the bloodshed of the last hour. That man is Colonel Dillon, is he not? The one who commanded at Friburg. I recognize him, I think, though his hair is slightly gray—the friend you have spoken of so often—the one who disappeared from Paris so mysteriously."

"Yes," whispers D'Arnac, "but no word of this. That is still a secret even from you."

"Is she still a secret—even from me?" whispers Jeanne, again looking at Julie, who has commenced to play abstractedly with her little hand in the water speeding by.

But answer is prevented by Lanty crying: "Bedad! here we are, thank God! with the river between us and the murdering brutes who treat inoffensive citizens so cruelly."

They have reached the other bank of the Seine, just the distance below the ferry landing of the rope that swings them in to the green shore bordered with willows and blessed by safety.

CHAPTER XII.

"WHICH WOMAN?"

PUTTING over a plank they make a landing in the garden of a farmer, who, attracted by the blazing inn and commotion on the other bank, has been watching the party in excitement and fear.

But they assuaging his fears by a piece of gold, he shows them a path leading through his little orchard to a neighboring road. The horses being landed, they place the ladies upon two of them, little Jeanne being perched upon the piebald steed of the leader of the ruffians who abducted her. Soubise, wounded, but just recovering consciousness, upon another, Lanty walking by his side and steadying him upon his saddle.

Raymond leads the horse of Jeanne, and O'Brien does the same to the nag of the little comtesse, who, safe among the trees and pleasant hedge rows, the bright sun shining on her, commences to laugh at her picturesque but unconventional appearance, without side-saddle, and exhibits an astounding mixture of youthful vivacity, convent naiveté, and innocence of the world.

D'Aubigné follows after, riding the other horse, and singing merry *chansons;* his boyish debonair voice sometimes trembling, and his lips growing pale, as he thinks how near this day has come to snuffing out his young life.

Jeanne rides on in silence, her tongue still painful from the effects of the brutal gag. Perchance, too, her heart is heavy as she gazes at the piquant little lady riding ahead of her, and making a very pretty picture in her convent uniform.

Raymond trudges gloomily beside her, not saying a word; partly because he is very hungry—partly because he has a furtive fear in his heart about this meeting of his *fiancée* and ward.

Just here the *fiancée's* voice comes to him from the front, laughing merrily, and O'Brien Dillon is laughing with her, for she has just given him a rare touch of convent *gaucherie.*

"What a *marvelous* number of men about here!" she has babbled to O'Brien. "I never thought there were so many in the world!" and opens her eyes in innocent amazement.

"Not quite so many after our morning's work," answers Dillon grimly.

"Ah, won't that make the Mother Superior glad,"

cries Julie enthusiastically. "She says a man is the worst thing in nature—but I don't agree with her. I think an abbess is," and she gives him a little smiling pout, as O'Brien bursts into laughter.

Gazing on this picture D'Arnac thinks: "She is beautiful now; a little knowledge of the world and she is fascinating."

Then Jeanne's voice, so full of laughter at times, so full of music always—comes to him, and brings with it recollection. He is as the bird between two ripe red cherries—not knowing which one to pick.

But la Quinault is saying: "What is that ahead of us?" and a curious yet melancholy sight dispels introspection.

They have just come to where the country lane runs into the Fontainbleau road. Along its dusty path is creeping a caravan of wagons filled with women. These are surrounded by police and guarded by mounted *gendarmes*.

Traveling very slowly, the train has apparently left Paris that morning.

Upon it both Jeanne and Julie gaze in astonishment —perchance horror—for some of the women, clothed in the gaudy robes of their trade, are singing ribald songs. A few of them—peasant girls and daughters of poorer artisans—have a sad look of despair upon their faces.

One cries to them as they pass: "For the Virgin save me! They're taking me from the man I love to that far-away land where I'll die of despair!"

Another moans: "Mercy! Exiled for the crime of being poor!"

But the police close around them, and the sorrowful caravan passes on unmolested; some of the wayfarers to commit suicide in despair at leaving their homes, their friends, their France—some to die of exile in the swamps and bayous of Louisiana, some to grace the cabins of New Orleans—*none to return!*

Gazing at this D'Aubigné puts his hand to his sword, but O'Brien Dillon stops him, saying: "Young fire-fly, havn't you got fighting enough? We've all we can take care of without a brush with the police. And the sooner we move the sooner we'll get to dinner."

Then taking the bridle of Julie's horse, he remarks,

with a tear in his eyes: "Bedad! that's where ye would have been, little comtesse, if ye'd not been picked up in the nick of time."

Catching these words, Jeanne again puts question to Raymond: "Who is she?"

And he answers: "I'll show you!"

Leading the steed of the actress beside that of the *elève* of the convent, D'Arnac raises his voice, and taking off his-butcher cap and making his best bow, remarks: "Mademoiselle Jeanne Quinault, permit me to introduce you to the Comtesse Julie——"

But he gets no further, for the convent school girl, turning eyes upon him suddenly, shudders and mutters: "Keep away! Assassin! I saw you murder a man last night as they seized me at the convent gate! I recognized you in the moonlight—you and that other ruffian with the Irish face and long gun—the one who is laughing now!" for Lanty, hearing this, has burst into a guffaw.

"You are mistaken!" mutters Raymond, savagely.

"Mistaken? Shall I ever forget that awful green coat!"

"Bedad!" remarks Lanty to himself, "she's got her future husband and the butcher mixed up. Faix! when she steps up to the altar with the Comte d'Arnac she'll be thinkin' she's marryin' the butcher 'Jacques of the tripes,' who, I'm afraid, by this time is food for the crows over yonder!" And he looks toward the Seine.

But Julie, turning suddenly to Dillon, cries: "Keep him from me! I appeal to you as a nobleman, again. If he approaches, I shall die with fear! I like men *generally*—but this man—this awful butcher—this man who stole me from the convent—keep *him* away!"

To introduce Jeanne under these circumstances is an impossibility, and Raymond grimly drops back with his charge, reflecting rather contentedly that these two ladies will not make each other's acquaintance for the present.

So they pass along the dusty road, Raymond and Jeanne saying little; though Dillon and Julie, some fifty yards ahead, chat quite confidentially. The Irish general's soft voice and genial manner wins the confidence of the little comtesse, which, she confesses to him, has been much shaken in man by preceding events.

"You know," she remarks complaisantly, "I thought *all* men nice before last night—even cousin *Bon-bons*."

"Bedad ! who's Bon-bons ?" asks O'Brien, a smile rippling his face.

"Cousin Charlie—Monsieur de Moncrief—the Procureur du Roy, who comes to visit me quite often at the convent to ask me when I will be married, and if I have seen Raymond, and always brings me *bon-bons*. And once he wished to kiss me. But O-ough ! I only took the *sweets*."

"So Cousin Charlie is very much interested in you ?"

"Oh, greatly so, and in my wedding, which he says should not be over soon. But I don't like that ; the sooner I am wed, the sooner I have fun—the sooner I am out of the convent. Ten years I have been there, and in all that time I have seen but *one* boy—Raymond ; and *one* man, Cousin Charlie. The boy was ugly and the man was old," she adds, with a little, plaintive sigh.

Just here they pass a pretty wayside auberge. Dillon would stop for dinner, but Julie implores him piteously: "The longer I am from the convent, the worse for me ! The abbess will be crazy now."

"Sure !" says O'Brien laughingly, " you'd better make a good meal now. It may be bread and water you'll be getting when you return."

Here Julie astounds him. She says suddenly : "*What?* Bread and water for going to my aunt ?"

"Going to your aunt ?" ejaculates Dillon.

"Yes! Cousin Charlie was to bring Cousin Raymond and take me to aunt Clothilde last night at twelve. You know her, perhaps. She boxed my ears when I was young, because I said Raymond was ugly. And so he was—almost as ugly as that butcher there ! "

At which O'Brien, stifling a laugh, mutters : " You —you thought you would go to your aunt's at twelve o'clock at *night?*"

"Indeed I knew it. This letter proved it," and Julie puts her hand to her pocket; then says suddenly : " It must have been taken from me when they

seized me at the convent gate.   But it would make the
matter clear to you."

"You remember what it said?"

"Of course I do.   It was my *first* love letter!—and
said that Cousin Raymond could not come for me till
twelve o'clock at night, as he had military duties to
perform ; but if I would meet him and Cousin Charlie,
they would take me to my aunt's, where I could live in
luxury and ease until the wedding. *It said my wedding
dress was ready for me.*   Ah, that was joyous news!
and was signed 'Yours till death! Raymond.'"

"And you believed this peculiar document?"

"Of course I did.   Don't girls always believe their
first love letter?" prattles Julie.

To this wisdom O'Brien answers nothing, and, thinking the matter over, concludes it is just as well for
Cousin Charlie, and probably by his instructions the
comtesse has been robbed of her precious first love
letter, which he little doubts has come from Charles
de Moncrief.

Soon, chatting on, they arrive where the road
branches, and after some inquiry, learn one is a cross
lane leading to Villeneuve le Roy, which is scarce a
mile away.

"Oh, I can see its church spire through the trees,"
cries Julie.   Then the corners of her mouth droop,
terror comes upon her, and she gasps: "The Mother
Superior! Heaven help me! She'll think I've eloped."

"Bedad! that's what ye did, didn't ye?   I'll go and
explain your case, little comtesse, and beg ye off if I
can.   An Irishman's tongue is very smooth, and
perchance a little blarney will mollify the lady abbess."

"Oh, will you—will you—kind sir?" says Julie,
archly, "a comte's word will go a great way with her.
She believes in the nobility."

So O'Brien, taking Raymond apart, explains to him
what Julie has told him.

"Very well," answers D'Arnac, "you and Lanty
take Julie to the convent.   But what are *you* going to
de now without baggage—without servants?"

"But with money enough in my pocket," answers
O'Brien. "I shall take quarters in the inn at Villeneuve.
It's a pretty place, and as pleasant for me to wait as on

the other bank of the river. Give D'Argenson my compliments. Tell him where I am, and Lanty will go into town for me, and fit me out again."

"Begob, as to money," remarks Lanty, complaisantly, "I could fit him out if he was a grand duke. I'm worth half a million if I haven't lost it this morning. I'm a speculator in the Rue Quincampoix, I am."

"The deuce you say," mutters Dillon. "Half a million is a very pretty sum. It beats fighting the Turks." Then he turns to Raymond and questions: "And you —what will you do?"

"I see an inn near by, on this very road. We will dine there — Jeanne, I and D'Aubigné, and put Soubise to bed. I shall leave D'Aubigné in care of his wounded officer, and take Jeanne into town this evening. We have horses enough for that."

So they bid each other good bye, Mademoiselle Quinault thanking Comte Dillon for the great service he has rendered her—not only with her tongue, but with her eyes, which makes Raymond wince, for she has hardly been so kind to him as yet.

Then Lanty and O'Brien move away with the little comtesse.

But as Julie disappears better spirits seem to come to Jeanne. She suddenly asks once more: "Who is she?"

"A distant cousin of mine," answers D'Arnac, shortly. "A cousin, though she doesn't know me. I rescued her, as I did you, by accident—and received excellent usage from you both. She thinks me an assassin, and you imagined I abducted her, eh, Jeanne?"

' I—I don't know exactly what I thought," she stammers. "Perhaps I did think you an abductor—you were in very bad company, you know, and your appearance now would not acquit you before a judge."

With this she laughs a little blushing laugh—Mademoiselle Quinault's first laugh since Raymond d'Arnac rescued her this morning.

A few minutes after they find themselves at a pretty wayside inn, nestled in a garden, protected from the dusty road by a straight row of poplar trees.

They have plenty of money, which means hearty welcome and quick and effective service.

Soubise is put to bed, a neighboring doctor sent for, and D'Aubigné, Raymond and Mademoiselle Quinault make a pleasant meal of it, at a little table placed under the trees; for though tremendously fatigued and very sleepy, they have all immense appetites, and even Jeanne has now good spirits.

"I wonder who it is has caused your adventure, Mademoiselle Quinault," remarks D'Aubigné towards the close of the meal.   Then he asks curiously: "Who can hate *you* ?"

"Ah," cries Jeanne suddenly, "Perchance it is that Duclos, my rival!   I got four recalls the other night, and she but two.   If she has conspired at my kidnapping, I'll denounce her in the greenroom," and clenches her little fist so savagely that her companions spill their wine through laughing.

"*Parbleu!*   Stranger things have happened," giggles D'Aubigné.

But Raymond says no word.   He goes to thinking the matter over.   But think as much as he likes his mind brings no suspicion to him—not even a guess; though he means to question his ward further on the subject when they are alone, which they are very shortly, as they both set out to Paris together, leaving D'Aubigné with his wounded officer.

For the purpose of this journey, D'Arnac procuring for Jeanne, with some trouble, a side saddle and a riding skirt, places her upon the charger D'Aubigné has relinquished.   He, himself, mounts the piebald steed of the leader of la Quinault's abductors, which has too much spirit for a lady's use, unless controlled by man's hand upon its bridle.

Though Paris is but eight miles away, they ride slowly, for both are very tired, and it is almost dusk as they enter the city by the Rue St. Jacques, and passing along the streets St. Hyacinte and De Vaugirard come into the Rue de Condé, and pause in front of Jeanne's apartments.

Within the house they are met by copious tears and astonished exclamations from Madame de Caylor.   She says: "I feared you were murdered!   I did not know what to think.   I notified the police, but they could tell me nothing.   Since then I have cried!"

"What did the ruffians do to *you*?" asks Jeanne.

"Those assassins! those murderers! those abductors!" cries the duenna. "Nothing, except to look me in the face and say 'the pretty one is our game;' then throw me off on the sidewalk, and tell me to go into the house or they would cut my throat. I went in!" says the old lady.

"You have no hint or guess," asks Raymond anxiously of Jeanne, "as to who could have instigated this outrage?"

"No," replies his ward. Then she opens her eyes suddenly and gasps: "Perhaps it was Lenoir! He loves me—I mean hates me."

"Bah!" returns Raymond, "Lenoir could not have afforded it. This little adventure of yours has cost somebody a good deal of money. Fifteen armed bullies do not take their lives in their hands for nothing." Then he goes on grimly: "If it is a case of payment AFTER the affair, we have made it a cheap one; none will come back to demand their wages. I will think over the matter. Steps must be taken to thoroughly protect you."

Here Madame de Caylor brings astonishment upon them both. She says impressively: "Jeanne, you have another gentleman working to that end—one most powerful!"

"Who—De Villars?" asks D'Arnac eagerly.

"No, Monsieur de Moncrief. This morning I went with the affair to him to ask his aid."

"Ah, you told others?" mutters Raymond, very much annoyed, for he does not care that this adventure should make Jeanne's name more prominent than it already is on gossips' tongues.

"Only to him," replies the duenna. "He is such a friend of Jeanne's, and as Procureur du Roy might have an inkling of any wickedness going on. He thinks it is a woman!"

"Ah! what did he say?"

"When Monsieur de Moncrief heard of Jeanne's abduction, he commenced to cry out that it was some enemy of *his*—he takes so much interest in her, admires her beauty, and says she is the grandest actress on the stage, and should marry a noble, and Jeanne is always so happy after he says this last to her."

"Yes, Monsieur de Moncrief is always very compli-
mentary," interjects la Quinault; her eyes that had been
languid with fatigue, growing very bright, as she has
caught the last few words.

"Humph!" remarks Raymond grimly, "what makes
you think it is a woman? Did Monsieur de Moncrief
with the vanity of age imagine one of his ballet girls
was jealous of la Quinault?" and he bursts out laughing
at Jeanne's blushes and indignation—for she pouts:
"That horrible old coxcomb!"

"Oh, what a wondrous guesser you are, Monsieur le
General!" giggles Madame de Caylor, opening her
poetic eyes. "It might have been, for when I told him
he seemed stunned—then muttered almost to himself:
'God curse her! Her infernal jealousy will ruin me yet!'
But after a moment's pause he said in his impressive
way: 'Say nothing to any one. I will make inquiries.
Talk might prevent my investigation. Be assured I will
do my best to restore Mademoiselle la Quinault to the
home she graces and the theatre that she honors, my
dear Madame de Caylor;' and kissing my hand in his gallant way, Charles de Moncrief escorted me to the door
of his office."

"Indeed?" mutters Raymond, and would perhaps
question further, but he notes the fatigue in Jeanne's
eyes and attitude, and remembers how much she has
passed through this day.

And he turns to leave, but Jeanne puts her little
hands upon his arm, saying: "I have not thanked *you*
yet. You risked your life for me to-day. You are
always doing something for me, that I repay, I am
afraid, very badly. But I—" here she hesitated and
pauses.

"You," laughs D'Arnac, "you did not like the other
young lady; you wanted to be rescued by yourself
alone."

"P-p-p-erhaps," stammers Jeanne, growing red.
Then she suddenly cries with feminine solicitude: "But
you must have a wrap. The night is growing very cold,
and your butcher's coat, though picturesque, is not over
thick."

"*Pardi!*" answers Raymond, "a woman's mantle
over a butcher's coat; how the boys in the street would

enjoy me ! But I think I'll do very well. There is a cloak of some kind or other strapped behind the saddle on my horse. You have stabling near here. Send your man to see the nag you rode is taken care of. These horses may give us the clue to their riders—knowing the ruffians we may discover their employer."

So, coming down to the street again, he unstraps from behind the saddle of the piebald nag a long Spanish cloak, which thrown about him, makes D'Arnac very comfortable.

Then mounting the piebald steed, he rides off towards his apartments in his sister's great hotel on the St. Honoré, and imagines his day's adventure over.

CHAPTER XIII.

THE GAMEKEEPER D'ARNAC.

BUT THIS day has not yet finished with D'Arnac!

Jostled in the throng of the Rue Dauphin, he thinks he will avoid the Pont Neuf, which is crowded at this time of the evening with its hucksters, its charlatans, and its troops of promenaders. The Pont Royal will be almost as direct, and much less crowded. Besides, his appearance is now so brigand-like, it excites jeering comment from the *garçons* of the street.

So he turns on to the more quiet Quai de Conti, making towards the Pont Royal, and thus passes the little open triangle in front of the great hotel of Prince de Conti. In it lounge a number of lackeys, hangers-on, and the class of followers that bizarre prince with Italian habits always keeps about him.

As D'Arnac jostles his way through the crowd one of these who has been apparently watching, coming suddenly beside him, whispers in his ear: "You got back early! Come with me at once. She sent me here to await your return and bring you to her. She would hear all about it from your own lips."

Then ideas fly through Raymond's brain. In a flash he remembers the remark of the ruffian guarding Jeanne in the carriage, how a woman's gold will pay for this. Then he recollects he is riding the horse of the leader,

a curiously marked piebald steed; that he wears the
leader's Spanish cloak—that the night is dark.

Will Providence in this weird way give him the
knowledge of the enemy of Jeanne that he may protect
her?

As this goes through his mind, not daring to answer,
for the man may doubt his voice, he gives a gesture of
assent; and the fellow, making through the crowd, he
follows him, and passing along the quai they reach the
Pont Royal. Crossing the Seine, they soon find themselves on the Rue St. Honoré, and going through one
of the streets leading past the Palais Royal, they come
to the side entrance of a large house.

Here, after some bandying of words between his
guide and one or two attendant flunkies, D'Arnac's
horse is placed in charge of one of them, and the man
who has acted as his conductor so far, turning Raymond
over to the care of a pert lady's maid, he is ushered
through a long corridor, narrow and dark, at the end
of which is a doorway heavily curtained.

The soubrette says: "Wait here, Spaniard," and
steps in.

A moment after he hears a voice that makes him
start. "Show the man in, Rosalie. Let me know all
from his own lips."

These tones, though harsh with cruelty now, when
last they came to Raymond's ears, were soft with
love.

Almost unnerved by the revelation that now is his,
D'Arnac, throwing aside the curtains, finds himself in
a room made graceful by art, and glorified by decoration worthy of a palace, and in the presence of a woman
whom he once thought the most beautiful on earth;
and who, in spite of his conscience, in spite of his
fears, he still sees is as lovely as Cleopatra on her barge,
or Venus rising from the sea, or fairy dancing on the
lawn; for Hilda de Sabran is a mixture of the three.

She is evidently expecting some one—not a bravo—
some one more intimate. Her robe indicates this, for
it is a toilette containing every trick of modiste to give
her beauty its full display and charm. It is some black
robe of gauze, with sparkling glint of golden tinsel,
from out which arms, neck and bosom gleam as ivory.

In it, to some she would look an angel; to Raymond, knowing her now as she is—she seems a spirit of the night, whose loveliness is made for man's destruction—and woman's, too.

As D'Arnac gazes, she speaks. Half reclining upon a low couch, without turning to give more than a passing look, she says, an awful longing in her voice: "Have you succeeded?"

"Yes," mutters Raymond, very short of his words for fear she may recognize his voice.

But successful malice is too high in her heart for her to heed aught else. And Hilda breaks forth in a mocking laugh and sneering bitterness: "Then *adieu*, my Quinault. You are on your way to another land! You shall never see your Paris more—you shall never see your lover more!"

Then suddenly checking herself, she utters shortly, as if she wished to terminate the interview: "There is your money—the promised reward I have made double!" waving one fair hand towards a little table, where, among its ornaments, is a little sack of gold.

But even as she speaks, an eager longing to indulge her cruel joy in the history of the agony of the woman she deems her rival, comes to her and will not down.

She utters softly, coaxingly: "Tell me—all about it! Tell me—did she suffer—did she cry out in despair? Whose name did she murmur when her destiny came upon her—and she knew there was no hope?"

Getting no answer, she rises, suspicion coming on her, and looking at the table, her face grows pale as she murmurs: "Bravo, you do not take the gold. Why not?"

But the ruffian in the Spanish cloak says nothing.

Then she bursts out, gasping as if in fear, panting as if dismayed: "You do not speak—my God!—you did not succeed! Answer, lackey! Tell me, coward! You missed your aim—you did not succeed!"

And she in unbridled rage would perchance foolishly assault with her white, delicate hands the fighting bravo that her gold has hired. But suddenly the creature that she flaunts, flaunts her.

The ruffian in the Spanish mantle throws it off, and doffing the hat that has been pulled down over his face, cries: "I did succeed!"

And she gasps: "You—RAYMOND?" her eyes growing big with astonishment, perchance with terror.

And he says to her: "I did succeed! Jeanne is safe from your vile arts. Safe in Paris!"

With a low gasping cry Hilda covers her face with her hands, and sinks upon the ottoman, as he, bending over her, whispers: "Why have you done this? Has she ever injured you?" next pleads: "Could you not leave one innocent life alone?"

"No," she answers desperately. Then her white arms would clasp him, and her eyes, with all their potent charms, would allure him, as she murmurs: "Because—because you love her!"

"I?"

"You love her! Don't mock me. You visit her every day. At the theatre you warn off other gallants? Who but a lover would do this?"

"A guardian?" answers D'Arnac. "She is my ward."

"Your ward—your mis——"

"Not that word," commands Raymond, in awful voice. "Mademoiselle Quinault saved my life, and I have given to her the care of gratitude."

"Then prove it!"

"How?"

"By loving *me!*" And her voice grows soft with living hope and her eyes tender with subtle charm; for in the presence of this man she always thinks she loves him *better* than the others.

She murmurs, a caress in every tone: "When you have looked me face to face and eye to eye you have returned my love. Three times I would have had you to my heart, but first De Contj's ruffians—then the treachery of Charles de Moncrief—then the subtlety of Monseigneur Law—came between us, to rob me." This last in bitter voice and emphasized by wringing hands. But pathos comes to her again; she sighs: "Prove to me you love me, and I will spare her!"

"You *shall* spare her!" whispers D'Arnac sternly, "for I *will* protect her—protect her as I did to-day from your hired bullies—by killing *them!*"

"By killing *them!*" she murmurs. "By killing them!

That's how you have their leader's cloak—that's why they brought you to me."

Then her eyes grow luminous with admiration and her voice becomes strident, as if she triumphed even in his victory, though it has defeated her, and she laughs: "Gods! What a fighter you are! I saw you fight once—for *me!* Have you forgotten that day, as you have your love?" Next she astounds D'Arnac, crying: " To-night I am glad you conquered, for it has brought you face to face with me. My eyes again look in yours to make you love me!"

And to her witchery of beauty, she adds that charm of manner that makes men forget all but her loveliness, and pleads as for her very life, sighing : "You are always kind to me when you are near. Look into my eyes—and tell me that you love me—as you did that blessed day—that day I dream of now—that day by the blue waters at the island near Marseilles—that day you kissed me and said I should be yours—your very own ! Dost thou remember, Raymond ?"

There are blushes on her cheeks, and radiance in her eyes, and eagerness in her heart, and invitation in her gesture.

Heaven knows what wondrous trick her beauty might still play, DID HE NOT REMEMBER ALSO. For he replies in tones that for one moment give her hope : "I do remember. "

"Ah! God be thanked. "

"I *do* remember the fate you brought upon my comrade. Be you assured—I shall see no like despair comes upon my ward."

Throwing the Spanish cloak about him, and pulling his hat over his eyes, D'Arnac pushes the draperies aside, and giving her the bow of ceremony, passes into the long hallway.

She looks after him, in her face unutterable longing, but dominant even over this, intense surprise—it is the first time in all her life her charms have not been omnipotent over men.

Even now she can't believe it. The next second there is the quick swish of silk and laces, and a flash of beauty, as she flies through the apartment, and running after this man who has left her with defiance in his voice, and scorn in his manner, she tosses away her pride of beauty—even her pride of womanhood. For overtaking him just as he reaches the little side door opening on the street, she clasps her fair white arms around him, their delicate flesh made strong by the agony of despairing passion, and sobs: "Raymond, you shall not go—my love of loves—you shall not leave me! Have I not beauty to give you for which men sigh as for their joy of life?"

"I do not want it now. Remove your arms!"

"Have I not power to make you, young as you are, a maréchal of France!" she whispers hoarsely. "Love me, if not from love, from ambition. Give me your love—or feel my hate. I can degrade as well as elevate!"

"I fear not the first, and I reject the last! Take your arms from me!"

But this she will not do, and goes to begging him for his love, for this she cannot have seems dearer to her now than all the world. And she implores him to forgive her; if she has done wrong it has been for the sake of him; that she has loved him ever since he pressed her to his heart that day at Mieux, and cries out: "You did not think of your friend's fate *then*—why think of it now when I am in your arms?"

Perchance Hilda would do her entreating with less vehemence and her begging with lower voice did she but know that in a neighboring alcove, unnoticed in the dark, sits Charles de Moncrief, waiting to obtain audience with her. He is listening to her wild words, the smile of triumph on his senile face—ineffable joy in his abject soul, his ferret eyes blazing with some unholy glow.

Into his bizarre mind has come one thought: "This is my victory! The victory of Cupid over Venus! Venus belongs to Cupid now!"

But even as he chuckles he grows pale and mutters to himself : "If the Regent discovers NOW, I lose my trick!"

For, as he has been thinking, the outer door of the house has been unlocked and opened briskly by someone who has a key, and Hilda de Sabran has started back with a low, warning cry.

It is Philippe d'Orleans who enters, unattended, save by Monseigneur Law.

As the Regent comes in, Raymond passes out, jostling against him in the doorway.

"Who the deuce is this ruffian?" says Philippe, casting eyes after D'Arnac.

"Oh! the gamekeeper on my new estate," cries Hilda, who has an agile tongue for fibs.

"*Pardieu!* he looked more like a poacher!" laughs D'Orleans, who, having seen Raymond but once or twice, on official ceremonies and in the full uniform of a general of France, does not recognize him in his butcher coat and Spanish mantle.

"Oh, he is very honest, I am told," laughs Hilda. "He would not steal so much as a partridge."

"Perhaps *not a partridge*," thinks Uncle Johnny, who has the eyes of a hawk and has made no mistake in his man. Then he gives a shudder, cogitating: "If this infernal love affair of Hilda's come to the Regent's eyes—if he ever knows a young gallant stood before him instead of a gamekeeper—La Sabran might lose her influence—and I have need of it now. Just once more—just for my last grand *coup!*" and so determines this intrigue must be stopped and ponders how to do it.

After they have come into Hilda's boudoir he sits so meditative that the Regent calls him "Silent Jean," and laughs; "what are you musing on? Is it that old comtesse who besieges you night and day for shares?"

"*Parbleu!* there are a hundred *old* comtesses and a thousand *young* ones. The women beat the men," says Monseigneur Law, wearily, at which Hilda, though her cheeks are still pale at the remembrance of her escape, bursts into a merry laugh, for she has a reckless, devil-may-care kind of courage.

"Then it is the tobacco tax for which he is always begging me," jeers D'Orleans, joining in Hilda's mirth. "He'll get it for his India Company some time when I am harder up than usual. My financier Jean dreams every night how he will do me out of the tobacco revenue of France. But it is only a little thing—a *small* matter of a hundred millions a year, or so. Eh, Midas! How much will you give for the tobacco tax?"

At this mention Law brightens up   The tobacco tax of France is the last financial *bon bouche* he hungers for. Something he's going to buy *soon*—some favorable day when Philippe has no more money to squander on his mistresses and his *roués*.

With this they drift into more general conversation, D'Orleans telling Hilda that Law has come in very despair to the Palais Royal this evening to get away from his usual levée of the nobility imploring him for stock. "*Parbleu!*" he laughs, "the King's Stockbroker is growing so popular the Regent is dethroned."

"'The King's Stockbroker,'" echoes Hilda, who has not heard the term before.

"Yes, has not De Prie told you?" chats Phillippe. "His little Majesty yesterday at his Court of Versailles was shown a new map of Paris.   Examining it with precocious air, Louis exclaimed : 'I do not see the Rue Quincampoix upon it.'

"'It is there, Sire,' answered Dubois, pointing to the street.

"'That the Quincampoix?' replied his Majesty. 'It is in ordinary ink !   Order my printers to put it in *gold letters !* It is the place from which the money comes from my stockbroker, with which I buy my bonbons—good Monseigneur Law !' *Pardieu !* They say De Conti, who was standing by, grew pale. You know how well he loves the King's stockbroker," chuckles D'Orleans.

In his laugh Hilda joins, but not Monseigneur Law. This hate of De Conti is one of his bugbears. So much the more reason De Sabran must lose none of her influence over the Regent by reckless unfaithfulness. He however forces himself to join in the conversation, though his gray eyes, when they meet Hilda's, have reproach in them—perchance menace.

But she says carelessly : "Old gloomy ! what makes you so savage ?   Has that driveller, Saint-Simon, snubbed you again with his ducal rights ?"   And giggles in his very face, for she knows Uncle Johnny—of all men—dare never tell tales of her. .

Upon her badinage D'Orleans breaks in, saying : "We came to take you with us to the opera. There is time for the last ballet. You should see how well

the theatre looks in the new wax lights furnished by
Monseigneur Law, who gives us all good things."

"Is it a command, Sire?" she asks, looking at
D'Orleans.

"It is never a command to *you*," he says in careless
good nature.

"Then, if you will, please excuse me this evening—I
am tired."

"Very well," answers Philippe, "you will be brighter
for the supper afterwards. You will come to my supper
party at least?"

"Is that a command, Sire?" she laughs.

"No, but an entreaty."

"Which is to me a command," replies Hilda, for she
has a very gracious way with this prince, whom she does
not love, but who is very kind and generous to her.

"Then it will be not *adieu* this evening."

And the two gentlemen take their departure,
D'Orleans bowing over the fair hand she extends to
him, and kissing it with courtly grace.

She listens to their departing footsteps, and sinks
upon a chair in careless attitude, and wonders whether
this night has made an end of Raymond's love.

But catching glimpse of her fair self in a neighboring mirror, of which the room has plenty, hope comes
to her and lights her eyes, and she grows radiant.

Just then one of her women—the one De Moncrief
has applied to to obtain audience for him—the one he
has in his pay (for Hilda now is cursed by the pomp of
state, and many waiting and tiring ladies, and some of
them are bribable)—comes in and asks her if she will
see the Procureur du Roy?

She answers sharply: "No!"

But for reply gets Cousin Charlie's laugh, and the
woman passing silently out, Hilda remarks in freezing
tones: "Has not old age taught you good manners?"

But he comes quickly to De Sabran, who gazes at
him with menacing eyes; then with audacious senile
finger chucks her under her fair chin.

"What—you dare?" she hisses, and rises, with one
white gleaming arm uplifted to reach her bell rope. But
he stops her with these words: "I dare to laugh; of
course! I am giggling at—." He comes close to her and

whispers in her ear: "D'Arnac, the gamekeeper! that's what I'm giggling at! ha! ha!"

And she, looking at him shudders, and tries to mutter: "What pleasantry is this ?"

"Oh, ho! D'Orleans will think it very pleasant. The young gallant, the Comte d'Arnac—the one you love the best upon this earth—comes in the evening, disguised in humble clothes—and you, putting your arms about him—beg him for his love. Oh, this will be a merry tale, at which the Regent will shake his sides. He's growing very jealous now, I'm told, and *you* the favorite of all his beauties. He may find some excuse for breaking Raymond on the wheel, as he did last week to the young Comte de Horn, because they say, his second choice, la Parebere, looked kindly on him."

"I have no fear of Raymond. Raymond would never murder a poor stockbroker like Comte de Horn!" she mutters.

"Egad! he may though—*one*—the King's Stock-broker," jeers De Moncrief.

Then his tones grow strident, and he seems to become taller and tower over her, and says: "I had come to implore—I now come to demand!"

"What?" Her face grows very pale.

"That you leave Mademoiselle Quinault alone—unharmed! I will not have my plans destroyed by you!"

"Y-e-s."

"I now demand MORE!"

"What?" Her face grows even paler now—her lips tremble—anguish is in her eyes—as she meets his—and they droop before them.

"This! *Think I am a boy again ?*"

"Im—imposs—i—ble!"

"Love me! IMAGINE I AM RAYMOND!"

And his eyes grow luminous, and he utters senile chuckles, as she in all her loveliness sinks down before him, her hands uplifted in a silent prayer, that she knows, even as she makes it, will never be granted. His eyes are too longing—his joy too great!

And gazing at the wondrous beauty that will now be his boy Charlie jeers: "What I have waited for so long—

what has been refused me so often—the triumph of Cupid over Venus!" then chuckles: "It is a long joke that has no turning!"

Two hours after, at the Regent's supper party, surrounded by the perfume of flowers gathered from almost the corners of the earth—amid the blaze of lights upon the gleaming shoulders of the fairest beauties of France—amid the flow of sparkling wine—whose laugh the lightest; whose *bonhomie* the best; whose wit the brightest? Cousin Charlie's!

For he is as a boy again, and as his gaze falls on Hilda de Sabran, her eyes as they meet his grow piteous, and her lips tremble, and her glance is that of the slave looking at her lord.

BOOK III.

THE STRUGGLE ON THE QUINCAMPOIX

CHAPTER XIV.

"THAT AWFUL WOMAN SPECULATOR!"

THE EVENTS of the preceding night leave curious complications behind them.

Monseigneur Law, though he has the business of a nation on his hands, finds time to ponder over what he has seen, and decides to make a curious appeal to Raymond in person.

"This inopportune love affair of Hilda's must be stopped at once," he decides.

This being in his mind, he writes a very courteous note to Raymond, begging he will call upon him at his earliest opportunity, which is sent by one of his hundred flunkies; for now he has almost kingly state, private gentlemen aspiring to wear his liveries for the greater convenience in their stock speculations.

This note arriving at the Rue St. Honoré, creates a sensation.

D'Arnac has just finished telling his sister a *portion* of his adventures of the day before, when the genial Mr. Lanigan interrupts.

Making his bows, Lanty remarks easily: "I'm just fresh and breezy from the country this morning. I have come in to get an outfit sufficiently grand to do honor to Comte Dillon and one or two lackeys to serve him. Bedad! this morning I varnished his boots, and it seemed loike the good old toimes."

"You returned the comtesse safe to the convent?" asks Mimi, hurriedly.

"Safe as a trout to her native stream, though she didn't seem to wag her tail so happily as fishes do on reaching water. Sure! the poor little girl put up a frightened face as Dillon led her in to the awful Mother Superior. But the general has an Irishman's tongue, and oh ! the blarney the comte poured out upon the abbess, who had been in a mortal fright all day at the loss of her charge, and had been telling her beads since early morning. She was just about to notify ye—and frighten ye to death—when we popped in upon her. But when she forgave the little comtesse, ye should have seen how Mademoiselle Julie plucked up spirits. Faix! Monsieur Raymond ye'd have cried yer eyes out laughin' if ye'd heard her description of ye as the butcher that abducted her. Begob ! if she recognizes you at the altar, heaven help the bridegroom. We found the letter—the precious epistle that we think Cousin Charlie wrote—just outside the convent gate. If ye'd give this to Monsieur d'Argenson, sure I think it would add to the little girl's safety."

"Which I will," says D'Arnac.

"At once !" cries Mimi.

So taking coach, Raymond and Lanty drive to the office of the Lieutenant-General of Police, where D'Arnac explains the affair to D'Argenson, presenting Comte Dillon's compliments, and giving him notification of his change in locale.

Looking over this note, the policeman remarks grimly : "I think we have the old fox Moncrief on the hip. Fortunately, you did not kill *all* of his bravos. I have my hand on one of them now—Geronimo, the Corsican."

That worthy ruffian being sent for, such a representation of his affair is made to him that he gives D'Argenson all the information that he wants.

And in the course of time, report of this matter being made to D'Orleans, it rouses him to great rage against Charles de Moncrief, for the Regent is very angry at the manner his edict has been carried out. He mutters savagely : "Abducting an heiress from a convent—sacrilege!" And would make short work of the Procureur du Roy were he not at present too valuable to Monseigneur Law.

So Philippe simply dockets this affair and waits until De Moncrief is no longer useful; then he will call him to account.

But unconscious of this, Cousin Charlie goes skipping about the street, as if a second boyhood had come to him, reasoning: " Now is my run of luck ! My fortune already fine shall be colossal ! La Quinault is safe from the revenge of De Sabran. She is an ambitious little puss, and aspires to my cousin Raymond's hand in marriage —an impossibility ! By the ambition of the actress I will destroy this marriage of D'Arnac that would rob me of the estates I long for—under the will. Little Jeanne is my trump card for that ! "

Coming back from his interview with D'Argenson, D'Arnac is received by Mimi, a curious excitement in her bright face. She says : " Two notes for you. One from Jeanne—the other left by a gentleman in waiting, from the Comptroller of Finance."

" From Law ! " mutters Raymond, astounded.

" From Uncle Johnny ! " ejaculates Lanty, who has followed close behind.

Opening the first of these, D'Arnac reads :

I thanked God and you last night for protecting me. I am well—though of course not quite myself. As you attend to all my business affairs, I venture to suggest that you will not forget to-day is the date of issue of the third shares of the India Company. Please get my stock for me. Lanty (if he has returned) will do the struggling with the crowd as he has done before.

This matter being mentioned to the Irishman, he remarks: " Bedad ! it's a fine business La Quinault picks out for me ! It would take ten giants to fight through the crowd at the India Company to-day. A lot were killed in the crush last time, and now there'll be a hundred—the excitement is growing so divilish and intense. But I'll do my best for little Jeanne and myself. I have stock also. Perhaps that other note is something about it."

Raymond, opening Monseigneur Law's communication, returns, knitting his brows: " I cannot understand it ! "

" What is it ? " asks Mimi, anxiously.

" It is simply a most courteous request that I shall

call on him forthwith at his office, and apologizing that he cannot come to see me, as he has the finances of a nation on his shoulders."

" "A private appointment," cries Lanty. "That will do the business of the stock, without me risking me life to get it. Get mine also. I'll get ye the proper vouchers. Please do it! I mayn't come out of the crowd alive, fightin' man though I am!"

"Very well," says D'Arnac, "we'll go together!"

He would step out to the carriage again, but Mimi beckons him back, and whispers: "Be very cautious with this Monseigneur Law. No matter what wrong he may have done your comrade, don't take up O'Brien Dillon's quarrel. That gentleman, I imagine, will soon be strong enough to fight his own battles—to work his own revenge. Be cautious what you say. Remember you are going to meet the brightest intellect in this country—perhaps in the world."

Thus warned, D'Arnac steps into his carriage, Lanty remarking as they drive along: "Be St. Patrick! it'll be the making of yer fortune, Gineral. If he gives ye five minutes' interview ye can borrow a million, and if he gives ye twenty minutes' private talk the usurers on the street will lend ye the earth. A duke waits six hours, and only gets two words with him. Ye've never been on the Quincampoix?"

"Never but once—the day I crossed it to your cabaret to arrange about Dillon's leaving for Vienna."

"Sure then ye've been losing the fun of yer life. It's the world's battlefield. Some men fight for honor and glory, and others fight for money; and when ye see 'em, ye'll think those that fight for money fight the hardest!"

But they can't drive into the Rue Quincampoix—the crowd there would block a cavalry charge. There is not space enough for surging men and women.

"Begob! there's not room enough for fleas, let alone horses and carriages," remarks Lanty, philosophically.

Dismounting, they finally force an entrance through the struggling throng from the Rue aux Ours that has been set apart, by royal edict, for the nobility; those of commoner clay, arriving on the same general battle ground by the Rue Aubry-le-Boucher.

Here they see a sight the like of which Raymond has never seen before, and as he struggles with the jostling crowd hopes he will never see again.

One solid, squeezing, writhing, fighting mass of men and women struggling to force their way up to and into the offices of the India Company; for it is the day of the third issue of the shares, and a thousand *livres* premium is bid for them now, even before they are circulated.

But Monseigneur Law's servant is in front of them, and his liveries give them a little advantage. Finally, in the course of half an hour of squeezes, of crushes, of prodding with elbows men who curse them in even unknown tongues (for so many nationalities have come to Paris to struggle for gold that the place is like the Tower of Babel), by taking advantage of every little swaying of the crowd, they reach the private entrance, which is not so densely thronged, and finally gain the private reception room of that great company.

This they find full of the *noblesse* of France.

Princes are gesticulating like stockbrokers, and bidding, and crying for privileges. And comtesses and duchesses, who have thrown away rank and etiquette, are jabbering to each other in the jargon of the street, bidding for "daughters," "granddaughters" and "mothers," and puts and privileges with as much vivacity and vigor as any other bulls and bears.

In this throng great favor is shown to Raymond. The Comte d'Arnac's name is no sooner announced than a gentleman-in-waiting says, with a profound bow: "Monseigneur Law will see *you* sir, at once."

Dukes who have been waiting by the hour, and princes who have been cooling their elbows from six o'clock in the early morning, begging for a minute's interview, look with envy upon D'Arnac. One man, the Prussian, Versinoble, whispers in his ear: "I'll give a half million *livres* for the information," as the door opens and Raymond gets audience with this man of men—this Colossus who can make other men rich.

Cousin Charlie, who is one of the directors of the India Company, and has the privilege of entry behind its financial doors, whispers to Raymond as he passes along the hallway: "Oh, ho! cousin—a speculator also!"

"Yes," says Raymond, "a little.   Besides, I'm looking out for Mademoiselle Quinault's interest."

"Oh! she is rich, I understand.   She will have a glorious dower when she weds," remarks the Procureur.

But D'Arnac passes on and, the door being opened, steps briskly into the sanctum of Monseigneur Law, who, rising hurriedly, gives him so cordial a greeting that it surprises the young man.

"I hardly thought you would remember me," replies Raymond.   "You have not seen me since Marseilles."

"But once," whispers Lass, "last night!"

And his tone is so significant that D'Arnac understands very well to what he alludes, as the financier goes on hurriedly: "It is in regard to that I have asked you to do me the honor to visit me."

"Indeed?" says Raymond, forcing himself to smile. "I am glad you see me in a better coat."

"I am very glad the Regent did not recognize you in masquerade," returns Uncle Johnny, who has apparently made up his mind to frankness.

"Pooh!" laughs Raymond, lightly.   "I could soon have explained to his Highness that it was an accident which robbed me of my uniform."

"An accident that sometimes happens to gallants," sneers the financier, his eyes growing keen and searching; for he thinks it is to be a battle of artifice between himself and Raymond.

"Yes," iterates D'Arnac, "an accident. And as you have come to the point with me, I will be equally frank with you." And he tells in a very few words to the gentleman who stands gazing at him astonished, his adventures of the day before—except those connected with his visit to De Sabran.

Lass listens to him, his brow clouded, and finally mutters: "These police outrages under my edict will cause the common people to hate me.   But this makes my request to you so much the more timely.   I wish to make an appeal to you to give up something that I presume you hold very dear; not as a gentleman—though I might do it on that account—but as a patriot—for I know you love France!"

"An appeal to me—for what?" asks Raymond, astounded in return.

"An appeal to you to give up the love of a lady with whom you once eloped. Whom you were to have met one evening, had not her husband returned from Vienna to take your place—whom you would have met again at Marseilles, had I not prevented it. Of an affair that I believe that you are now continuing—to the injury of France. Of course it is a gentleman's privilege to deny such things—but before you do—let me call your attention to certain facts."

With this Monseigneur Law continues: "You know the financial state of this country when I came here—bankrupt. You see the wondrous change to-day —that France is the mistress of the world—because she is the mistress of its pocketbook; gold—not armies, makes power upon this earth—for without gold no armies can exist. The longest purse wins the battle between governments."

Then he explains to Raymond the glorious future he has mapped out for France. How by her colonies she shall become strong. That the riches of the New World—of the Indies and the Canadian fur trade—shall flow in upon her.

"Now," he says, "will you be the one to thwart me?"

In this appeal John Law shows perhaps more subtlety of intellect, more power of judging his man, than in many another more complicated and important action of his life; for he has guessed D'Arnac loves his country and his country's honor.

He had brushed O'Brien Dillon out of his way, for he knew no such appeal made to him against his own personal honor as a husband would have been listened to for a moment.

He will put D'Arnac's passion aside by an appeal to his patriotism—to his love for the glory of his native land.

"Now, will you stand in the way of France?" he asks.

"I—" stammers Raymond, "what do you mean?"

"I mean that if Hilda de Sabran loses her influence over Philippe d'Orleans (as she will if he but hears of her assignations with you) that I no longer will have influence over him to obtain the edicts that I wish for the glory of France."

"And your financial aggrandizement," returns Raymond grimly.

"There you are mistaken. I have gained some wealth, of course—but it is a little. Where I have made millions, others have made ten millions—and it is this fearful greed that is this country's greatest danger. Where I have added one million by legitimate capital, to the India Company, its greedy speculators on the street have made it ten. If they bid up these stocks too high—some day there will come a fall—and when ruin comes upon them they will not forgive me. But if they do not anticipate me too much, if they give me a little time to develop and build up the growing colonies —sordid as they are—the wealth of the India Company will equal their greed, and France, in her territories, shall dominate the world. See, I have opened my hands to you. Be equally candid with me."

"I will!" returns D'Arnac. "I have no love for Hilda de Sabran!"

"Impossible!"

"I once thought that I loved her, but now I know her, and her treachery. My passion is of the past. Last night I came, not to sue for her love, but to tell her that if she did not spare Jeanne Quinault I would not spare her."

With this D'Arnac goes on and tells the astonished financier *all* that had passed between him and De Sabran, and concluding, says: "Protect Mademoiselle Quinault from the arts of the mistress of the Regent, and you have nothing to fear from one who does not love her."

While he has been speaking, the gray eyes of the man to whom he has whispered this, gaze searchingly at him. As he finishes, the financier says: "I believe you!" and utters a sigh of relief.

Then he adds suddenly: "I will protect Mademoiselle Quinault! Be assured I shall take such steps that no further danger shall come to your ward."

"On your head be it!" answers D'Arnac.

"With pleasure," returns Law, his face lighting up. Then he goes on, almost laughingly: "Now that business is over, can I not do anything for you financially?

"Yes," answers Raymond; "you can prevent my getting crushed to death."

"What, you have shares in the India Company?"

"No; but Mademoiselle Quinault has, and I act for her! also for another friend of mine.   Here are the vouchers.   Would you not kindly pass with me to your office, and see the stock is issued that they call for?"

"With pleasure," replies Law, and the two pass through the hallway, the financier going into the main office of the bank, where hundreds of clerks are struggling to satisfy the demands of the surging crowd, from the onslaughts of which a great barricade of timber has been erected; otherwise the counter would be scaled and the clerks would be overwhelmed.

After a few minutes the great financier returns with the two packets of stock, hands them to Raymond, and says: "If I can be of service to you by my advice—it is yours!"

"Buy something?" laughs Raymond.

"Not now," whispers the great man.   "Their greed is overreaching them.   There will be a fall.   I am glad of this, though I have nothing to do with it.   That is the work of my friends, the Brothers Paris, who think they are ruining me.   They do not guess I pray to heaven each night that the India stock will not go up."

Even as he speaks there is a roar among the surging crowd outside; news has come to them from the brokers on the street that the stock of the India Company is falling.   And men's faces grow a little anxious —perchance a little pale—but not as pallid as they will before night.

For it is the inauguration of the first great bear raid in the history of the Paris *Bourse*—the one engineered by the Prince de Conti, D'Argenson and the Brothers Paris, the company in opposition to that of Law, called "The Anti-System."   And from their offices in the Rue aux Ours (appropriate name street of the bears) they have sent forth their heelers and their brokers to destroy the credit of the India Company and sell its stocks down till ruin comes upon all who have bought on margins.

So now worse rumors come from the market, and women begin to cry and shriek and tear their hair, and men to curse, at which Monseigneur Law says: "Look

at that woman—look at her tearing her hair. This
is my little revenge for the misery she has caused me.
That woman pursues me by day—by night—in my
office—in my home—in even my chamber—the awful
woman of the Quincompoix!"

Following Monseigneur Law's eyes, Raymond starts
in astonishment; for a woman with business mien and
fearful, ferocious eyes, and wildly gesticulating umbrella, is uttering cries of horror, which D'Arnac
nearly returns, for in that dread female speculator he
sees—his Aunt Clothilde, the Comtesse de Crevecœur.

CHAPTER XV.

THE BATTLE OF THE BROKERS.

BUT Raymond has little time for horror. One of the
wild glances of Clothilde catches him. He is behind
the counter of the bank talking to Monseigneur Law,
and a sudden joy comes into the widow's greedy heart
—the wild hope of a sure tip on the market.

With the strength of a virago she forces her way
through the crowd, and bending over the counter,
reaches out a fat hand and grips D'Arnac by his coat-tail,
then whispers: "Raymond, my nephew! Raymond!
for the love of God ask him—are they a buy or a sell?"

But even before D'Arnac can reply a hoarse roar
goes up from the throng, and there is a cry outside
that the India stock has gone down a thousand *livres* a
share at a jump.

With one despairing shriek—"My margins! Holy
Virgin! my broker may sell me out!" Clothilde fights
her way through the surging crush, punching with her
umbrella right and left ahead of her; and careless of
the imprecations and curses that greet her enforced
passage, disappears on her way to the street, the crowd
heaving like storm-tossed waves about her and engulf-
ing her.

Monseigneur Law chuckles in Raymond's ear: "Go
out and see the fight—this battle of financiers. It will
be worse than the battle of soldiers."

"*Pardi!* then you have the self-control of a great
general," returns D'Arnac, gazing on the face of the

financier, which is cold and pitiless, a smile curling his mobile lips, his grey eyes above them quiet as the sea before the squall.

Taking his advice, Raymond steps out, and on the stairs meets Lanty.

"Have you seen what has become of my aunt ?" he asks, concern in his voice.

"Ah, don't bother yer head about her," replies the Irishman. "Faix ! she's well able to take care of herself ! Askin' your pardon for mentioning it, some call her ' the badger' on the street, she's got such an appetite—for money. She did old Papillon out of ten *livres* a share on fifty ' darters' he sold her the other day."

Not particularly pleased with this description of his relative, D'Arnac turns his eyes about, looking for his aunt, and, to his relief, sees her fighting her way down the street towards the offices of the great brokers. He can see her easily now, for the crowd is not so thick in front of the India Company; perhaps they do not hunger so much for the new issue, now that the parent ones are falling.

"Would ye like to see the notables of the street?" gossips the Irishman, proud of his knowledge. "There's Dures Leriche talking to Farges, they've both made sixty millions. That's André and by my soul, here's our curiosity, Quasimodo Junior, the chap who rents his hump back to write contracts on. Do you spot him ? And there's old Papa Chambrey; I call him papa because he has such a nate article of a darter. Mayhap, she'll have a nate dower also !"

But a hoarser roar comes up from the crowd. Again the India stock has fallen.

"Come with me to me broker," mutters Lanty. "If this diviltry goes on there's no telling where I'll land meself to-night. Perhaps in a jail—perhaps in a madhouse." For the stock, as well as they can judge from the conversation about them, has gone down five hundred *livres* more.

So they hurry along the street, impeded by the crowd, in which Raymond thinks he sees every familiar face in Paris, for in this battle for wealth courtiers jostle tradesmen and princes haggle with courtesans.

Gaston Lenoir brushes past clothed in the liveries of Monseigneur Law, which he has taken to facilitate his entrance to the Bank Royal and offices of the India Company.

Poetical Monsieur Voltaire is there, smiling his sarcastic smile. He says lightly to Raymoud: "Eh, Comte, have you come here to see this comedy *in*humane?"

"Begob!" answers Lanty, "I suppose you mane making an inhuman profit out of stocks. That's what you like best I believe, Mr. Poet."

But Lanty's humor freezes in him now. As they get near the main offices of the brokers, from the cries of the throng that are buying and selling and fighting and screaming, they discover the India stock has broken again.

It has fallen to 6,000 *livres* a share, and the affair now takes a threatening aspect.

The faces about them grow pale, for nearly all have bought for a rise! Stocks have been going for the last six months—up—up—higher and higher, and lately no one has ever dreamed of a decline.

But down goes the market!

Securities are thrown overboard right and left, and now the quotation falls to 5,000 *livres* a share—3,000 decline since the morning.

There are faint cries from despairing women; and men who have been fat grow thin with anguish at their losses.

Raymond, looking carelessly on, hears a deep sigh at his elbow, and turning sees the perspiration rolling from Lanty's face, that had been ruddy but is now pallid with anguish—even terror. This Irishman, who had risked losing his life and limb in many a pitched battle, with devil-may-care recklessness, trembles as he fears he'll lose his money.

"God of Heaven!" he gasps, "my margins! If that little Hollandaise broker, Van Tamn, sacrifices me, I'll lose the 'Turk's Head Inn,' my Cabaret, and me chance of winning Marie." Then he whispers suddenly: "Wait for me!"

"Where are you going?"

"To my broker. I'll kill him, by the God of Heaven! if he sells me out!"

With this wild cry Lanty disappears in the throng, making his way towards a sign that Raymond reads:

VAN TAMN,

Dealer in Securities and

Loaner of Money.

D'Arnac would follow him, but as he presses on a crowd gathered about a fainting woman impedes him, and seeing her face he grows pale himself. It is his Aunt Clothilde.

He whispers: "Is she dead?"

"No. Fainted when the stock fell to 5,000. But there will be deaths to-day," says one man desperately. "That infernal Law has tricked us all."

And others mutter: "Curse the financier who has ruined us!"

Aided by some few Samaritans, for even in this crowd of Mammon there are some who have not left humanity behind, D'Arnac gets the fat and fainting Clóthilde into what had once been a cobbler's shop, but is now rented at enormous rate to one or two speculating brokers. In this place he props his aunt upon a chair.

Then, seeing outside in the street the great doctor of the Regent, Monsieur Cheval, he hurries to him and whispers: "One of your patients, my aunt, the Comtesse de Crevecœur is fainting in that shop."

"Don't keep me from my business!" cries the man of medicine to him severely. "Don't you see they're ruining me here?" And he bids wildly for some of the stock, which is promptly sold to him, to his great disgust. For now the quotation falls below 5,000 livres a share.

"Come to your patient!" whispers D'Arnac hoarsely.

"I can't. It will be my ruin!" whimpers the doctor.

"It will be your death, if you don't! Do you suppose I'll let you juggle here with my aunt's life hanging in the balance? Come!" And his athletic hand closes upon the collar of the disciple of Esculapius, and he drags him *nolens volens* into the cobbler's store; then says sternly: "Do your duty by your patient."

Kneeling by Clothilde's side, this man of medicine (who is thinking now but of Mammon) feels her pulse with trembling hands, and the roar of a declining market coming from the street drives him distracted. He suddenly cries in agitated voice: "Oh, my God! it falls—it FALLS!—it FALLS!"

At this, Clothilde, who has partly recovered, whispers, the fear of death upon her: "My pulse falls! Oh,. doctor, my pulse falls, *Mon Dieu!* I am dying. Help —the priest!"

And he snarls: "Hang your pulse. It's the stock of the India Company. It's 4,500 *livres* a share."

This awful quotation acts better than a tonic on the nerves of the woman speculator. She staggers up, a desperate look in her eyes, and whispers: "Raymond —for God's sake—if you want me to live through the day, go to that villain Law—you have his ear—and beg him, in the name of a woman whose fortune he has ruined, to tell you the truth."

"Did the ' villain ' ask you to buy these securities?" jeers Raymond.

"Yes, he did!"

"How?"

"They all said they would go up, and the scoundrel Law did not deny it," cries Clothilde with feminine unreason. "Find out, if my stocks are held, whether they will recuperate." And she begs in piteous tones: "Raymond, ask him for the love of God!"

"Remain here," answers D'Arnac, sternly, "that *canaille* crowd is no place for the widow of my uncle. Don't leave this office!" And he departs on his errand.

But this is what Clothilde can not do. The quotations ringing in her ears from the street outside are horrible. The parent stock—the mother—is being offered at 4,400 *livres* a share—misery! It is sold down to 4,300—despair! Then, can she believe her ears? 4,200.

Flesh and blood can not stand this—at least Clothilde's can't, and she flies out upon the street again, with haggard eyes and dishevelled hair, imploring: "For the love of God spare the mother! Don't sell the mother so low, gentlemen! Spare the mother!"

At this a hideous snicker comes up from the crowd. But still the stock goes down, and the battle of the street becomes more awful in its despair and agony of greed.

Brokers, who can't force their way into the crowd, hang out of second story windows, and sell their customers' securities from this point of vantage; while some of their clients implore them with tears in their eyes, from the street below, to spare their stocks and .not to ruin them.

As for Raymond, forcing his path along the Quincampoix, after a little he gains the offices of the India Company, but here is informed to his consternation that Monseigneur Law has left them.

" Where ? "

An officer of the company with pale face and trembling limbs (for the crowd surging about the offices are now very threatening) fortunately has seen D'Arnac closeted with the financier this morning. He suggests in whispers that the Comptroller is probably at his own house in the Place Vendome.

Filled with his errand, D'Arnac bolts out of the Quincampoix, and luckily getting a *voiture* on the Rue St. Denis, drives to the great house, or rather palace, of the Director of Finance.

Before its doors is gathered another, perhaps a greater, throng, begging and imploring to see this man who holds their fortunes in his hand. Some are muttering threats; but these are made in undertones, as there is a company of soldiers on guard about the building and every entrance is heavily sentried. Uncle Johnny, knowing the fickle nature of his public, has taken his precautions accordingly.

His rank in the army giving him entry, Raymond after a fierce battle with elbows, hands and feet, reaches the reception room of the great man. It is filled with imploring princesses, demanding dukes, begging comtesses, and struggling barons, together with a few of the great speculators, who have succeeded in getting in to beg for just one word with Monseigneur Law, and cry out in agony when they are refused.

As D'Arnac approaches the entrance to the private apartments of Monseigneur Law, which is guarded by twelve soldiers with fixed bayonets and loaded guns, he thinks he will have but little chance of interview. A gentleman-in-waiting has just announced to the Marquise de Prie: "I am very sorry, your ladyship, but Monseigneur Law says an interview will be impossible for six hours. He has the cares of the nation on his shoulders."

"But my little stocks—my poor *little* stocks!" implores the vivacious Madeline, tears in her bright eyes; "What shall I do? What shall I do?"

"Wait!" answers the officer of the financier. "Wait!"

As the pretty Marquise turns away, D'Arnac, getting the ear of the official, begs to be announced.

A moment after the gentleman-in-waiting astounds the crowd by proclaiming: "Monseigneur Law will see General D'Arnac *for one minute.*"

Raymond rushes hurriedly through the guard, pursued by the envious looks of all within the room, and one lady, the beautiful Locmaria, screaming: "I will see him too. How dare he keep me waiting!" tries to force her way after Raymond; but the crossed bayonets of the soldiers stop her.

D'Arnac, more fortunate is ushered by bowing flunkies into the private office of the great man, and stares astonished; for this gentleman, whom he had supposed would be closeted with the Regent and the great officers of the bank and treasury, is coolly seated at a very exquisite *déjeuner à la fourchette*, and, apparently between courses is studying intently some pharo combination that he will use upon the coming evening, to the despair of his adversaries at cards.

"Will you join me, General?" says Law pleasantly; "though I believe I sent word you could have only a minute. That was for the benefit of the crowd outside. They are rather anxious for me, I imagine, some for my money, others for my blood, eh! D'Arnac? But soldiers have quick appetites. Sit down and tell me what you want, as you eat."

Then he looks curiously at the young man and laughs: "Is it a hint on stocks?"

"Yes, just one word," answers Raymond. "My aunt—that awful woman of the Rue Quincampoix—" (here a sickly gleam comes into the financier's eyes) "begs me for the love of heaven to ask you is she a ruined woman? The shares are now 5,000 on the street."

"No, about 4,000," interjects Monseigneur Law, glancing over a slip of paper that a secretary who has come in hurriedly has just placed before him.

Then he whispers almost to himself: "Now is my time! I have prayed God for this financial flurry, squall, or panic—whatever you choose to call it—for the last few nights. I did not wish to make it myself, but it has come and cleared the financial atmosphere. It has shaken out the gamblers who buy for quick turns. Stronger holders will take their places, and this lesson will make the general greedy crowd less sanguine. They will not inflate my balloon *too* rapidly. That is my great terror! But you can tell your aunt that if her stocks are held for her, she is safe. If she has been sold out on margins, of course I can't help that!" He shrugs his shoulders. Then he says suddenly to D'Arnac: "Buy some yourself."

"Why?"

"Because I want you to—as a favor to me," purrs Uncle Johnny. For into his mind has flashed this sudden idea. "This is the man for my purpose! Here he is—made to my order for the moment! A man of standing—a man who has kept aloof from speculation."

"Where will I get the money?" suggests D'Arnac, jeeringly. "Shall I sell my estate?"

"No, this letter to my broker!" And Law writes hurriedly a few lines, then says: "Take it, and regard it, not as a favor to yourself, but as a favor to me."

Raymond glancing at it, reads the following:

To the broker Papillon:
  Buy what Comte d'Arnac orders. I guarantee his credit. Send his stock to the Bank Royal.   JOHN LAW.

"How much shall I buy?"

"As much as you like. Not less than one thousand shares. Better say two. I do not care if you make it three or four. But buy them QUICK! As soon as the purchase is made—and be very careful of this—swear Papillon to secrecy. That will make the ineffable scoundrel SURE to tell. Quick! Go—or I fear the guard outside may have to use their guns upon the crowd, and that would be terrible."

For the murmur of discontent and riot now rises up so loudly that it forces its way into the very room in which they are sitting. And listening to this, Law sneers: "These very people that curse me now, will bless and worship me before to-night!"

With these words ringing in his ears, Raymond squeezes his way out, leaving part of his coat in the hands of the crowd, such is the fearful crush.

But getting to his *voiture*, that he has told to wait, he drives rapidly to the Rue Quincampoix, and finally, struggling and fighting, aud leaving another part of his garment in the hands of the Philistines, he eventually succeeds in forcing his way into the office of Papillon, the great broker of the time—the great scoundrel of the time—who is slowly and curiously tolling a bell in his office, which seems to produce a direful effect upon the market, most of the brokers selling it down.

The India stock is weak, even at 4,000. For this financial charlatan has organized a clique to do his bidding. When he rings his bell in a certain way, every precious scoundrel in his coterie produces every selling order that he has and sells stocks *down*. When Papillon rings his bell a different way, every one of this exquisite band of scoundrels takes every buying order that he has in his portfolio and buys stocks *up*.

Getting to Papillon, Raymond astounds that gentleman by commanding: "Stop jingling your bell—Read this." And glancing at the mystic signature, this broker dares not juggle with the friend of Monseigneur Law.

"What are your orders, M. le Comte ?" he whispers.

"Buy two thousand shares at once."

"Of what ?" says Papillon.

"Mothers of the India Company," answers D'Arnac.

"What is the price ?"

"About 4,000 livres, but weak."

"Buy!"

Papillon, going into the crowd, executes his order, and the shares stop descending for a moment. A moment after he returns and says: "To buy was easy, To sell would have been more trouble. Your commission is executed."

Then whispers Raymond impressively: " I swear you to secrecy about this order and Monseigneur Law's note! "

"As God is above me, no living man shall know!" mutters Papillon, but even as he says this he seems to have received some cipher order, for suddenly he commences to ring his bell.   Three taps, one after the other rapidly.   With this a number of brokers who have been executing only selling orders, suddenly pocket these; and taking their purchasing ones from their portfolios commence to buy.

The stock rises and the crowd cheer, and the India stock goes up to 5,000 *livres* a share.

Papillon whispers eagerly: " Will you sell now ? "

Raymond replies: " No, I'll sell when Monseigneur Law orders—not before! " and strides away, bearing receipt in his pocket that 2,000 original shares of the India Co. have been purchased for his risk and account.

Then he finds Clothilde a fainting wreck upon the street, and gives her comfort.   She says: " Yes, the stock is rising!   I'm safe if my villain broker has not sold me out.   I cannot find him anywhere! "

" What broker is it you fear has played you false ? " asks D'Arnac sternly, for he knows very little about the ethics of stock transactions, and thinks like many others have done since that the poor broker who sells his clients' stock after their margins are uncovered is a thief —that the customer should ruin the broker—but never the broker save himself by client's loss.   Therefore he mutters savagely: " Show the scoundrel to me! "

She whispers: " He is the Hollander, Van Tamn."

They hunt about the street for Van Tamn, but cannot find him in the crowd, and they inquire, but no one has seen Van Tamn.   Some say he has absconded probably, and laugh and jeer—for wrecks are numerous upon the Quincampoix, and money has been borrowed by the hour at usurer's interest, to protect accounts.

Not finding him in the street, they seek him at his office.   But to their astonishment they see Lanty patrolling in front of it, an admiring crowd cheering him as he passes up and down with a naked sabre in his hand, and pistol ready.

At this Clothilde sets up a shudder and cries out:

"Has the usurer absconded? Has Van Tamn *sold* my stocks?"

"By the Lord! he's sold NOBODY's stocks!" answers Lanty. He would have sold mine, but I kept old Van Tamn shut up in his office. I told him he would issue only to find my sword through his body! Then, by my soul! the sneaking fox tried to sell me stocks out of his second story window. But I blazed at him with my pistol until he retreated. So, thanks to me and my sword, Van Tamn's customers are safe."

At this delicious news Clothilde, falling on her knees before the Irishman, astonishes him by kissing his hand and blessing him as her savior, as do many other of Van Tamn's customers who were short in their margins that day.

Then Lanty, opening the door of the office, says: "You can come out now, old man; the margins are secure." For with a roar the stock has mounted to 6,000 *livres*, Raymond shouting with the rest; because now he is a speculator, too; and greedy, like all speculators are. He, who sneered in the morning, shouts with delight and triumph in the evening with every upward move that makes him richer.

And so the battle goes on; stocks recover to 7,000. Then the Brothers Paris and their clique and following make another onslaught; for a minute the upward rush is stayed.

But little Charlie de Moncrief is now in the foremost of the throng, raising his withered hands to Heaven, as if praying to his God, and chanting: "Seven thousand *livres* for a thousand shares!"

"Sold!" cries the youngest of the Brothers Paris, a bizarre and stalwart creature of wild mien and bushy beard and hair. And with the word he smites poor Cousin Charlie right upon the nose and places him *hors de combat*.

Then with a wild yell the members of the Anti-System follow their chief and sell the stock down.

Slowly it declines to 6,500, Raymond looking on, his face growing slightly pale, for the fears of the speculator have come to him as well as the joys.

There is a cry of triumph from the Brothers Paris as the stock goes down and down and is offered at 6,200.

"Egad!" whispers Lanty, "this is a battle."

"Then if it is a battle," replies Raymond, "I FIGHT!" And he mutters: "Who are these *canaille*—these Brothers Paris—that dare force *my* stocks down and make me poor?"

Striding up to Papillon, the broker, he whispers to him: "Buy the market up to 7,000 *livres* a share. Take all that's offered. Don't ring your damn bell! I want the profits myself!"—for the broker is about to toll the signal.

The two fly out on the street together, and to Raymond's ears comes the cry of triumph of the younger of the Brothers Paris shouting with exultant voice: "I'll sell a thousand mothers at sixty-two hundred!"

"Take them!" cries D'Arnac; "send them in to Papillon; and take this also, for decrying the value of maternity." And he knocks the younger Brother Paris down.

Then Papillon is buying right and left, and all his clique not waiting for his bell, sail in again, and such ferocious effects as now take place were never seen in trade before, as in this first great fight to a finish of bull and bear; for brokers fight and tear each other's hair and smash each other's faces, and some are wounded with clubs, knives and daggers.

But with another buying rush stocks mount again. Orders seem to come from everywhere to buy. The Brothers Paris are routed, and the bulls get their glut of bruin's blood that night, though the bears had woefully worried them in the morning.

"I have four thousand shares for you," whispers Papillon in Raymond's ear. "Here are the reports."

"Does that include the thousand I bought from that Brother Paris—the one with the bloody nose, I don't know his infernal name?" says Raymond sternly, for it seems to him Papillon has purchased more than he returns; and the profit on them now is very large, for the parent security of the India Company, as they speak, is being bid for at the rate of 8,000 *livres* a share.

"Yes, these are all," mutters the broker. "Have you not made enough? Would you like to sell now?"

"No. I sell when Monseigneur Law directs," laughs Raymond, as he stands gazing on the scene, which is now gaining an excitement that is weird. The roar is louder than ever, for the bulls have now no mercy.

And over this wild battle of brokers who still fight on, as darkness comes upon them, the red oil lamps of the Rue Quincampoix gleam, as the stocks of the India Company are bid up and bulled until they reach 8,500 *livres* a share, and the people cry: "God bless the great financier!"

And Cousin Charlie, covered with dust, whispers in D'Arnac's ear: "God bless you, too, Raymond! You saved the market."

"Oh, ho! even you, Monsieur le General, are now a financial fanatic!" laughs Monsieur Voltaire, who is standing beside him, smiling upon the scene.

Now some one coming into the crowd cries: "Bravo! the Academy of France has just elected Monseigneur Law one of its members—one of the *immortals!*"

"As a financier?" asks one.

"As a statesman?" queries another.

"As the boy who'll make us all rich, and bate the divil out of the Brothers Paris!" yells Lanty, now very happy.

"No!" answers Voltaire, sarcasm in his voice, and a sneer on his mobile features: "AS A GOD!"

At this the crowd burst into a wild huzza. And looking on it, the poet sneers again under his breath: "Fall down and worship him, ye sons of Mammon, as the Israelites did the golden calf—the calf that one day will be your ruin, as theirs was to them!"

But the crowd, luckily for the poet, do not hear this, and they shout again: "Long life to the King and Monseigneur Law, his stockbroker!"

CHAPTER XVI.

"THE CHEVALIER LANIGAN.'

This awful excitement is fatiguing; and Lanty suggesting: "Would yer honor deign to favor my cabaret in the Rue de Venise, by accepting a supper from me?"

Raymond immediately acquiesces.

"You will let me pay for my meal, I hope," he remarks.

"Faix! I'll do nothing of the kind—it would cost ye *too much*. My cabaret is an expensive place. . Prices have gone up again," grins Lanty.

"I rather think I've made enough to pay for one supper," laughs D'Arnac merrily. Next he says, with a prolonged whistle: "*Pardieu!* it's 800,000 livres on the first two thousand I have and Heaven knows· how much on the other!" then suddenly adds: "There is some good in Uncle Johnny after all."

"Bedad!" says Lanty, "I think he's a good friend of all of us, though I was feeling like killing him this morning, when stocks went down. Just see what a business L'Epée du Bois will be doing to-night."

On entering the cabaret, these prognostications are true. The place is crowded, and did not the host himself get a table and do the honors D'Arnac would only have the pleasure of looking at others eat, drink and enjoy themselves.

"Ain't the prices going up?" whispers Lanty. "Listen to the darlings *bidding* for the food. It's running a little short."

And Raymond, turning about, sees Lenoir, now in the plain clothes of a gentleman, bidding against the rich Mississippian, Fargis, for a chicken— the last in the house. Mutually exciting each other's appetite, they run the price up to two hundred *livres* for a skinny fowl.

"Pardieu! you've got the purse of me," cries Lenoir, "you miserable upstart of finance, but I've got the sword of you!" And, drawing his rapier, he spits the fowl in the aghast waiter's hand, and devours it before the very eyes of the rich and hungry Fargis, who begs him humbly for a little piece of it, but gets nothing.

Satisfying his appetite, Raymond makes way for others who are still crowding in; for, though the larder is running short, there is plenty to drink, and wine is flowing freely—and money likewise.

None are so reckless in their prodigality as stock operators who have made a lucky turn. Money comes quickly—it goes faster!

At the door D'Arnac says hurriedly : "Lanty, good-bye! I've a gentleman to thank this evening."

"Uncle Johnny? Sure! though I never thought

I'd thank Uncle Johnny for anything, ye can give him me compliments also."

Taking carriage again, for the terrible jostling, struggling and pushing of the crowd has wearied even D'Arnac's strong limbs, he arrives at the great house of Monseigneur Law and finds it surrounded by another crowd—but not the threatening one of the early afternoon.

The Place Vendome is filled with the carriages of the nobility, and equipages are driving up, followed by their footmen with lighted flambeaux, to the great entrance of the house.

A number of the *bourgeoisie* are looking on, and a crowd of most disreputable tramps, mendicants, and beggars, are wildly cheering, as if this great commotion in securities had somehow put money in their pockets.

Then Monsieur le General Comte D'Arnac is announced and enters the great reception salon of the house.

The room is filled with the fashion and beauty of France.

In full evening toilettes, the white arms and snowy shoulders of beauty gleam under a myriad wax lights. Among them, La Marquise de Prie upon his arm, strolls Uncle Johnny, God of both man and woman ; the ladies being even more profuse in their protestations of delight at the happy turn financial affairs have taken than the gentlemen. One duchess with tears in her eyes is thanking Lass for her fortune even as Raymond comes up.

As his eyes light on D'Arnac, Law cries out: "You bought just at the right time. Let me congratulate you!"

Then excusing himself to La Marquise he steps to Raymond and whispers: "Have you sold?"

"No. I told Papillon I would sell when you directed."

"Humph! that is more difficult to judge than when to buy!"

But their conversation can last no longer Too many are anxious to catch the ear of the king of gold.

A princess edging between says: "I made my little boy pray to God for you to-night, because to-day you saved his estates for him, dear Monseigneur Law. '

"*Pardi!* Madame la Princesse, for that you should thank General d'Arnac," replies Lass, shortly.

"General d'Arnac?"

"Certainly! He is the man who bought stocks at the right time, and turned the market. Monsieur d'Arnac is wiser than I, and will explain the affair, Madame la Princesse," and introducing Raymond he leaves him with the lady.

This remark of the financier being noised about D'Arnac finds himself quite a hero among lovely women and gay and reckless men.

But though beauty smiles on him, Raymond, thinking of his coat, turns to leave the function. At the door he is encountered by a gentleman-in-waiting who says: "Monseigneur Law would like a word with you."

Following this official, D'Arnac finds himself once more closeted this day with the financial genius of the hour.

"You have ordered your stock sent in to me at the Bank Royal?" says the financier shortly.

"Certainly!"

"Give me the list of your purchases." Looking over this Lass chuckles: "Oh, ho! you bought *six* thousand shares instead of *two*, and bought them *up!* Humph! You are a speculator, *mon general!* But hardly, I think, a perfect one. Anyway you are a bad broker. Bad brokers bull the market when they buy. In fact, you were just the man for the occasion." Then, looking over the account again, he says: "You'll owe me to-morrow 3,380,000 *livres* plus commissions."

"My God!" shudders Raymond, who has hardly gone into figures on the affair, "How shall I pay you?"

"Oh, do not pay me at all. The security is good. You will have stocks in my keeping to the value of 5,400,000 *livres*—2,000,000 profit now. The last quotation was 9,000 *livres* a share. I shall not tell you when to sell. When you think you have enough, let go. I will, however, hint that the stocks at present can pay interest on 10,000 *livres* a share, and the market must be a rising one, for the Anti-System must buy to fill their short contracts."

Then he laughs, as Raymond turns to leave: "What a bad business man you are! Let me give you a receipt for the purchases you have made." This he does, chatting as he writes: "These purchases show you to be no speculator. There is sentiment in every one of them. You had better keep away from the Quincampoix. You wanted the market to go up—you jumped the prices on yourself. *Apropos* of sentiment, please present my compliments to Mademoiselle Quinault, your ward. Tell her that I am at her service."

And, Raymond taking his departure, this man of cold blood gazes after him, a placid smile crossing his clear cut features as he thinks: "To-day I *bought* this man and he does not know it. One limb cut from the De Conti-D'Argenson faction. He's in love with little Quinault; that is what makes Hilda so vicious."

As for Raymond, he drives home tired and happy, but anxious to see his sister—perhaps to brag about his success in stocks—a thing that most young speculators are given to.

Arriving at Mimi's hotel, he tells his story to an excited listener, who finally gasps: "How much have you made?"

"I don't exactly know," remarks Raymond in careless financial grandeur. "Perhaps about two millions on my purchases to-day."

"Good heavens!" she cries. Then says viciously: "And *you* told me not to speculate."

"And I beg you not to. I would not have you such a woman as our aunt, Clothilde, for all the wealth on the Rue Quincampoix."

"Then soon I shall be a pauper," ejaculates La Marquise. "Provisions, rents, wages—everything—are going up to such enormous figures. It's a fearful thing to be a housekeeper in Paris now."

"Yes; chickens are now worth two hundred *livres!*" jeers D'Arnac, and tells Mimi the story of the auctioned pullet.

This inflation of everything is true, as Mimi speaks. But in the course of the next month becomes even more marked, for stocks go up and up, and everything in Paris—from real estate to dry goods—increases in value with them; De Conti, D'Argenson and all their clique, fighting against this to no purpose.

One day De Conti tries even to ruin the Bank Royal, bringing in securities, and demanding payment for them

not in bills, but in silver and gold—something that
Monseigneur Lass is very loath to furnish him.   He has
already carried away three wagon loads of precious
metal, when the Regent summoning him to his presence
says: " In attacking the credit of Monseigneur Law, you
are attacking the credit of France.   Stop demanding
specie payments—or—even for you, my cousin, the
Bastille."

From this De Conti has retired, howling out his rage,
and declaring in the presence of the Regent that he is
being robbed.   But for all that, desisting in his attempts
to empty the exchequer of the Royal Bank.

As for the Brothers Paris they are groveling in the
dust; they have lost millions trying to force down a
market that will not down.

Tremendous fortunes rise like the castles of Spain—
in a night.   Perchance they may fade away with the
morning's awakening; but at present they seem as strong
as the rock of ages.

So the ball goes merrily along, and Paris becomes the
most luxurious city earth has ever born.   *Fête* follows *fête*
—each more extravagant than the one before.   Money
seems to be worth less than the dust of the pavement.

Poplinière opens a buffet table at his own expense,
for the ladies of the opera; where they may be his guests
each day, so that he can invite members of the nobility
to dine with the fair ones of song and dance; and thus
squeeze his way into society.   For that is now the object
of all the great Mississippians who have made enormous
fortunes.

Fargis gives a six days' *fête* of more than royal magnifi-
cence.   And in all the great houses purchased by the gamblers of the street entertainments of reckless prodigality
are given.   Musicians play the sweet melodies of Lulli;
dancing girls pose after dinner in the barbaric nudeness
of Ancient Rome, as the financiers of France cook
dainty morsels gathered from the four corners of the
earth, in chafing dishes heated by burning bank bills.

Then comes the second stage.

Some of the nobility, lured by the enormous dowers
showered upon the daughters of rich speculators, begin
to ask their hands in marriage, and wealth buys blood
and title.

Hearing of these marriages of nobles with the *bour-geoisie*, the fair actress of the Theatre Français' eyes become bright, and she murmurs to herself: "I have two millions—besides, I think he—." Then she begins to blush and laughs: "If I could get a title !"

For the prevailing craze to become one of the *noblesse* is upon her, as upon all.

Wealth they have. Now they cry: "Give us social rank !"

In proof of this one fine morning late in November D'Arnac and his sister are just finishing breakfast when the "Chevalier Lanigan" is announced.

"Who can it be ?" says Mimi, in surprise.

"Deuce if I know," mutters her brother. "The valet is grinning as he announces him." Then he gasps: "Great heavens! it's Lanty!"

As the genial Irishman comes in eagerly and excit-edly, remarking: "Bedad! didn't yer know me *old* title that I've revived with me *new* fortune ?"

"Your *old* title ?" mutters D'Arnac, struggling with an astonished smile; as, occupied with military duties, he has been little in the trading portion of the town, having taken Lass' advice and left his securities dor-mant for the present.

Meanwhile, Madame la Marquise stares at Lanty. His appearance is too impressive for her to laugh, for his eyes, though eager, have the pride of a Hidalgo. His long, gaunt limbs are clothed in the finest silken hose. His doublet and cloak are covered with Spanish lace and decorated by flaming ribbons. He is dressed in the acme of the latest fashion as to clothes, rapier, hat and wig, and walks with the mincing gait of a court dandy.

"You have news from O'Brien ?" whispers D'Arnac, for the fellow's appearance indicates nervous excite-ment.

"Divil a word from him for the last two days, but I've notice from him he's preparing to move on the inimy. I think the courier will be coming soon from Vienna with his papers," returns Lanty, making his bow to Madame la Marquise. Then he says sud-denly: "I'm on business of me own—the business of

me life.   I want both ye, Giniral, and yer condescend-
ing sister to help me out on me weddin'."

"Your wedding!" ejaculates D'Arnac.

"Your wedding!" echoes Mimi.   Then, with feminine curiosity, she queries: "Who is the bride?"

"I'm comin' to her in a minute," answers Lanty.
"Here's the card of invitation," and he produces two
pieces of pasteboard, upon which the following announcement is printed in the script of the time:

Monsieur Georges Chambery

requests the honor of your presence at the

marriage ceremonies of his daughter

Marie Mathilde

and

Le Chevalier Lanigan

of Devil's West, County Clare, Ireland

Grand Mass, at Notre Dame

Midday, December 10, 1719

Grand Fête Champagne, the same

evening, at Monsieur Chambery's

Chateau de Montfermiel

Mon Dieu! you are going to marry the daughter
of Chambery, the rich Mississippian who has bought
Montfermiel, poor old Comte de Beaufleur's pretty

country place at Ivry Why, he's worth forty millions!" cries D'Arnac, excitedly.

"Divil doubt that! I counted the securities when I signed the marriage contract. Perhaps I might have done better—there are richer than he on the street. That leather dealer is worth sixty millions, and Dame Chamard they say has bagged eighty. But I'm continted with forty millions, as Marie is the purtiest girl in the Faubourg," remarks Lanty, complacently. "Besides, I'm a millionaire also. I sold both my inns when I revived the house of Lanigan."

"Worth a million and going to be married to a pretty girl! What is her *dot?*" asks Madame la Marquise, with feminine curiosity.

"Five millions down, and five millions more when I get the bride into society, which, by the blessing of God, will be on me weddin' night. You see, I promised me father-in-law that I would have all the dukes and duchesses and comtes and comtesses at the *fête*, and if I fulfill me agreement Marie's dowry is to be doubled."

"Sit down and tell us how you won her," laughs Raymond.

"Sure, I *bought* her!"

"Bought her?" ejaculates Mimi. "BOUGHT her? How?"

"*I purchased her on the Rue Quincampoix.*"

"Do they deal in such securities there?" says Raymond, smiling.

"Old Chambery did, though he didn't know it when he sold. Ye see, I'd been in ambush for him, and when one day he offered a 'darter' for sale for ten thousand *livres*, up I snapped him quicker than a fox does a rabbit. And the old gintleman, not having the stock with him, gave me a written promise to deliver a 'darter' for the sum of ten thousand *livres*, writing out the contract on the hump of Quasimodo, then and there, and receipting for the money, which I paid him on the hump also.

"All the time I was sayin' to myself: 'Divil take ye, Lanty, ye're not the man I think ye, if, instead of a dirty piece of paper of Monseigneur Law's, ye don't bully old Chambery to deliver up pretty Marie to ye as the "darter" he sold.'

"With that I bolts off to Chambery's house, and gettin' chance word with the girl, I said: 'Marie, ye're mine! I've got yer father's written contract to deliver ye to me!' And didn't she grin with joy as she saw me writing a little note to the old gintleman, which read about this way:

> CHAMBERY.
>   BROKER.
>   In your absence I've taken possession of the 'darter' you sold me on the Rue Quincampoix to-day.
>   Yours,
>   THE CHEVALIER LANIGAN.

"At this Marie's beautiful eyes opened wide as a cockle's in biling water and she gasped: 'What do you mane? Ye're not going to take me from me father's house *before* you marry me?'

"Ah, don't fear, me little darlint,' I said emphasizing my remarks with a few ante-nuptial kisses. 'It's only part of me little game of brag. Ye just run away and go over to your intimate school friend Mademoiselle Laure Brochard, and don't come out of your hiding place till I give ye word, and in two hours I'll have ye the affianced bride of the Chevalier Lanigan!'

"So the mischievous minx makin' up a bundle of clothes, to raise up in her old pater the *worst* fears, I walked her away. But at the corner of the street we parted, Marie going to intimate friend Mademoiselle Laure, and I returnin' to the Turk's Head, to smoke my pipe and quietly await the explosion of my petard.

"By me soul! in about two hours it came in the form of Chambery shrieking and tearing his hair, and followed by about twenty archers of the guard, to rescue his purloined daughter.

"Well, in they came, frightening the people eating in the café.

"What the divil are ye doing, ye old baste, taking the appetites out of my customers!' said I.

"And old Chambery putting eyes on me shrieks out very wildly: 'My darter!'

"'Oh, the darter ye sold me,' I said. 'Did ye get me note statin' I had taken possession of the goods?'

" 'But she isn't the darter I sold you!' he shrieked.

" ' Be jabers! Marie's the one I want for my money,' laughed I.

"Whereupon ye should have seen him tear his hair and cry out he was undone! It nearly made me sick laughing he was so like Monsieur Punch after the clown has run away with Madame Judy! But he screamed out to the archers to search the house, which they did, and they not finding the girl he got on his knees before all the crowd and begged me for the love of the Virgin to give her back to him.

" Then I said, sternly: ' Send the archers out of the house!'

"Which he did. Crying out that dishonor had come upon him.

" ' Dishonor has come upon me by yer foolishness, old man,' said I. ' Come with me!' and he followed me, expecting to find her—but he didn't.

"He only found an empty room, with paper, pens and ink, and two naked swords upon the table, at which he shuddered. I locked the door and he grew more frightened still and would have cried out, but I whispered ' Silence! or ye're past praying for. Ye've put insult upon the future Lady Lanigan! Be me soul! for this I'll have yer life. Take up your sword! *En garde*!'

" At which he grew white and sickly and begged for his life, protesting he meant nothing against my honor.

" ' Is it nothing that you've been going about crying "the *future* Lady Lanigan is undone?'" whispered I, the look of a duelist upon my face.

" ' Spare my life, and I'll make reparation.'

" 'There's only one reparation in yer power, and that I don't know that I will permit ye to make.'

" 'What is it?' groaned he. ' Please permit me to make it.'

" ' On that table,' said I, 'there are pens, ink and paper. Sign there, within the minute, your consent to the nuptials of your daughter Marie de Chambery and the Chevalier Lanigan, of Divil's Nest, County Clare, Ireland. Then the public shame you have put upon the name of the future wife of me heart will perchance be done away, and I'll let ye live!'

"My sword being at his throat, he sat down and wrote his consent to the weddin' as I dictated, and then gasped: 'My darter! what have ye done with her?' For the poor fool thought I'd been playing the very divil with Marie.

"'Don't trouble yer mind about yer darter,' laughed I. 'Put yer brains upon the big *dot* ye'll give her.'

"At which he turned horrified eyes upon me; as I took him with me to the house of old Brochard, and relieved his feelings.

"But after he had seen Marie was safe, and what a trick we had played upon him, the old gintleman turned sulky again, and it was only by pursuing him wherever I saw him, and threatening to have his life's blood if he didn't live up to his written word, and denouncing him as a poltroon, and chasing him from one end of the Quincampoix to the other till the poor wretch didn't dare to make his appearance on the street to buy or sell, and finally by the help of Marie, who always had tears in her eyes when she saw her father, and said he had destroyed her good name, which could only be restored by marrying me, that I finally gained his consent.

"But the cunning old fox made the doubling of his darter's *dot* depend on my putting him in genteel society, which is now the desire of his life.

"So I want you to help me out on my weddin'. I've promised me beast of a father-in-law to have the court and quality visit the ceremony, and enjoy the champagne *fête* afterwards. Will ye come? For the Lord's sake, come. I want all the comtes and marquises, and dukes and duchesses possible. De Villars himself has promised, and the Marquis de Viviens and every officer I have been able to get word with who remembered me in the Flanders war."

"We'll do it!" cry D'Arnac and his sister in one breath.

And they set about aiding the Chevalier Lanigan to make his wedding one of the great functions of the world of fashion as well as finance.

"God bless ye both," mutters Lanty, with tears of

pride in his eyes.   "I feel as happy as an angel.
Bedad !' we'll make it as gorgeous as the feast of Belshazzar."

CHAPTER XVII.

LANTY'S WEDDING.

THIS they proceeded to do; that is, if the feast of the
Babylonian King was the most expensive, luxurious,
and bizarre that could be invented both as regards its
guests and its entertainment.

Raymond obtains the attendance of the officers of
the *Musquetaires,* almost in a body, under the plea that
the Chevalier Lanigan is a very gallant soldier, and
had refused commission both from the King of France
and the Emperor of Austria.   The officers of this swell
regiment, being all nobles, some of the very highest
lineage, this alone should make the affair fashionable.

Madame la Marquise de Chateaubrien passes about
Lanty's cards *ad libitum* among her friends of both the
court of the Regent and the court at Versailles.

Old Chambery goes in person to Monseigneur Law
and begs his attendance, telling him his daughter is
about to be married to an Irish nobleman of highest
lineage, a descendant of the old Kings of Clare.

"I'll come to the ceremony in the evening," replies
Monseigneur Lass.   Then he adds genially: "Give
me a few extra tickets and I'll bring the Regent and all
the rest of the boys."   For Uncle Johnny thinks it is
sound policy to gain all friends possible; and a man
with forty or fifty millions to his credit may be of
assistance to him on the street; though never for a
moment does it enter his head that the Chevalier
Lanigan is his *bête noir* Lanty, of O'Brien Dillon
memory and dread.

"Bedad!" says the Chevalier, looking over the long
list of invitations, "we'll have everybody in Paris
present, except the wits."

"What do you mean?"

"I—I mean Voltaire, Marivaux and the literary
crowd."

"I'll get them for you also," cries Raymond enthusiastically, who has entered into the affair with his
whole soul.   "Little Quinault will be the one to do it."

So he drives to the Français to see Jeanne at the
performance in the evening.

The Chevalier Lanigan has already invited the fair
actress in person.

As D'Arnac explains the errand to Mademoiselle Quinault, she laughs: "Give me enough tickets and I'll
guarantee the whole *Comedie Française*.   And going
about the greenroom she obtains at once Lecouvreur,
Duclos, Baron and Poisson.   Returning from this she
says, enthusiastically: "This evening I'll guarantee
Voltaire, Marivaux and old Crebillon himself, if the
rheumatism does not claim him.   Give me tickets
enough and I'll bring the whole *corps de ballet* of the
opera!"

"Egad! I don't think the wits would feel compli-
mented if I put them in *ensemble* with the *figurantes*,"
jeers Raymond, as Jeanne goes off merrily upon her
errand; for things seem to have been going very well
with la Quinault, since her adventure and escape.

Raymond has not mentioned that he knew the source
of her danger, for very shame of the entailed confession.
He has, however, told her he has made such police
arrangements that she is perfectly safe henceforth; but
his manner as he has said this, has been so full of
concern for her welfare that she has grown happy under
his very words, and the hope that she is nurturing in
her soul of souls, though she dare hardly confess to
herself, becomes more real.

And these nuptials of the Chevalier Lanigan remind-
ing Raymond of his own marriage, he remembers
the day for this is approaching also; and somehow his glances grow more tender as they fall upon
little Jeanne, for he feels that honor will soon compel
him to depart from her side.

So the day of the great nuptial *fête* of the Chevalier
Lanigan arrives, and the gay world of Paris—even the
Court—is eager for it.   Its sun is very bright and
warm, and though it is December, the evening promises
to be mild and beautiful.

The wedding mass is solemnized in great pomp and

state by an archbishop, attended by several bishops and abbés (for the wedding fees are very large), at the great cathedral of Notre Dame.

This is witnessed by a great throng; a good many even of the *noblesse* attending the nuptials of the Chevalier Lanigan, about whose origin and history there are many wild rumors.

As Raymond and his sister gaze on the ceremony, they hear whispered about them such remarks as this: "He isn't Irish, he's Scotch—the natural son of Monseigneur Law."

"No; you are mistaken. He's the elder brother of the beautiful De Sabran," says another—at which atrocious libel on Hilda's charms Mimi bursts into laughter.

But, notwithstanding this, no more gallant figure than that of the robust and martial Lanigan ever strode up the grand aisles of the cathedral, and no plumper bride ever whispered bashfully her responses to the mass that makes her wife than the blushing Marie.

Young D'Aubigné, who has now become a lieutenant in the *Musquetaires,* acts as the Chevalier's best man; for this boy is ready for anything that promises fun, and has a very pretty bridesmaid on his arm, Mademoiselle Victoirine Chamont, whose mother is the richest woman in Paris, having made, almost by accident, eighty millions in the gigantic speculations now taking place.

But, though the religious ceremony passes off very well, it is to the grand *fête* in the evening at the magnificent Chateau de Montfermiel, near Ivry, the grounds of which run down to the banks of the beautiful Seine, to which the *beau monde* look forward with eagerness and rapture.

It is about eight o'clock in the evening that Raymond d'Arnac drives into the grounds, to find half of gay Paris awaiting him, and the other half following after him; his equipage is but one of a thousand that are coming into the place.

With him are Mademoiselle Quinault, her duenna Madame de Caylor, and the poet Voltaire, who has been very happy to accept a free drive to the *fête.* During the journey Jeanne's face is marvelously bright and happy as she turns it on her guardian. Perchance

his manner is even more than usually deferential and
tender because he fears this night may be the last of a
great friendship; for Mimi had whispered to him at
Notre Dame : "Your turn will be very soon—next
Friday is the 15th of December."

So this evening he will tell Jeanne of his coming nuptials as he drives home, and somehow he knows in his
heart of hearts their friendship will never more be just
the same.   Blessings brighten as they take their flight,
D'Arnac's as other men's.

But they are at Montfermiel.

"*Pardi!* they have changed night into day!" ejaculates Raymond.

"Yes, and a fairy day!" cries Jeanne, and clasps her
hands in almost childish joy at the scene.

The grand château is a blaze of light from roof to
basement.   The noble park is illuminated by a thousand
immense flambeaux of white wax; and there are foun-
tains iridescent with lamps of all the colors of the
rainbow.

From a magnificent dancing pavilion of ornamental
wood, covered with tinted silk, steal forth the strains
of a grand orchestra; another, equally gorgeous as to
decoration, is filled with a hundred lackeys in the
liveries of the house of Lanigan—green and yellow—
handing rare refreshments to a thousand guests.

But they have hardly time to note this.   Alighting at
the main entrance, they are soon in the crush.   In the
grand old hall of a noble family, which has decayed and
passed away, the gallant Lanigan, standing by his blushing bride, the plump Marie, who is a mass of diamonds,
lace and silk, and fine fat arms and blushing cheeks,
receives them, his eyes glowing with manly pride.   A
moment after he introduces his father-in-law.

D'Arnac is received with humble bow and faltering
thanks by old Chambery, for giving him the honor of his
presence.   As for Voltaire and Mademoiselle Quinault,
the old speculator is more haughty with them, to the
poet's intense disgust.

So Monsieur Voltaire goes to sneering: "Look at
the mixture! Egad! There's the Prince de Soubise trading jokes with Dame Chamont—not that either of them

are very witty; and the Duc de Bullion chatting with Crozat, the leather merchant!"

A moment after the bridegroom comes up, radiant. He babbles, pride in his eye and joy on his red face: "Faix! I've got a moment off! The Regent's doing the honors; he's got me bride on his arm now. The whole affair's glorious! The champagne corks are file-firing now in the refreshment room! But at the supper they're to be discharged in volleys of a hundred bottles at a clip. I've drilled the flunkies myself! There'll not a man be sober by morning! We throw light refreshments into them now; but at midnight the supper room will be open—then egad! I've got a surprise for all of ye! I have just seen yer sister, la Marquise, and the Comtesse de Crevecœur. Bedad! if the last king of me race could look on me now, he'd say: 'Well done, Lanty! the family's risen again in ye!'"

But others claim the bridegroom's attention, and the throng grows greater still. Fashionable Paris now fills the halls of the proud Chevalier Lanigan. Actresses, speculators, the beauties of the court and the *noblesse* of France.

"Look on this, Lass," remarks the Regent. "This is a great thing—bringing all ranks in touch. See De Conti there. By all the gods! he's asking old woman Chamont's daughter for the minuet. He must want a loan very badly. *Pardi!* I'll take the 'Lady Lanigan' and make their *vis-a-vis!*" which he does.

Gazing on this, Voltaire chuckles: "This mixture of the froth and the dregs will some day make the dregs better than the froth."

But unheeding of the future, every one is very merry now. Squeezed out of the house by the crush, D'Arnac strolls into the dancing pavilion where the beauties of the court are treading the same measure with the magnates of finance; a few *litterateurs* and actresses giving variety to the melange. Little Jeanne is still hanging on his arm, though numerous gallants try for a *tête-a-tête* with her bright eyes, for she is very beautiful this evening in a toilette that is a dream of taste and grace.

The ladies that they meet are not so cordial.

They stroll into another great pavilion and there find performing acrobats and clowns. Here Raymond encounters his sister, and standing beside her the Comtesse de Crevecœur and Cousin Charlie, who is dancing attendance upon his aunt, hoping to get some hint from her that may help him balk D'Arnac's coming marriage.

Mimi is even more gracious than usual to the actress of the Français; for into her heart has come in these latter days a tender pity for the noble spirit she feels will soon suffer a great disappointment, and a generous heart that will be wounded perhaps to death by the inexorable law of class.

But there is no pity in Clothilde's haughty soul for little Jeanne. To her pride of rank she has added now the arrogance of great wealth, for the Comtesse de Crevecœur has made enormous sums in the rise of the India stock. She has great holdings, but has not yet sold; so every day adds to her riches. She says superciliously: "Ah, Mademoiselle Quinault, you come here to see your relatives perform?"

"My relatives?" ejaculates Jeanne.

"Yes; your father was an acrobat, I believe," sneers the comtesse.

"Oh," replies la Quinault, airily, "my father was a much greater artist than these—he could throw a triple somersault."

Looking at her, Cousin Charlie's keen eyes discover that her lips tremble, and this gives him an idea.

If these two women will only hate each other a little more, if he can only bring the actress to take a great revenge upon the comtesse, perhaps she'll do his trick.

So, in his deft way, a moment after, when Clothilde has walked away on his arm, he suggests laughingly: "You should not be so precipitate, my aunt. Mademoiselle Quinault may one day be your niece-in-law."

"*Mon Dieu!*" mutters the comtesse with savage eyes. "Dotard, are you in senile lust going to degrade the family by marrying *her?*" for the Procureur's gaze is upon Jeanne and she is very beautiful this night.

But De Moncrief's hideous grin stops her. "You have other nephews than myself," he chuckles. "These things are not so impossible now. The daughter of the Duc de la Vrilliere is contracted to wed Pamir, the Lyonaise. If cooks aspire—why not an actress?"

"My God! you don't mean RAYMOND!" gasps Clothilde, half fainting at his hint.

"Look at the actress now!"

She glances and grows pale. Jeanne's eyes are fixed on D'Arnac with a happy beam, for young D'Aubigné, chancing to pass, remarks to Raymond *sotto voce:* "I suppose this wedding makes you eager to become a bridegroom, eh, *mon* Colonel?" and laughingly passes on.

Both Mimi and Jeanne have caught the words, and Raymond's sister, who has now an infinite pity for her *protegée*, has passed her arm about the fair actress' waist, and la Quinault imagines D'Aubigné is twitting Raymond about *her.*

Looking on this Clothilde whispers words that make Cousin Charlie wince: "His mistress, yes—but his wife, NEVER!"

"Why?"

"Because," cries the comtesse, anger making her careless, "next Friday Raymond weds ——" She checks herself here, nearly biting off her impulsive tongue and mutters: "A D'Arnac marry a woman of the stage—impossible!"

But she has given a hint De Moncrief has been angling for. "Egad! their juggling with time gives me a fighting chance. The will said December 15th—next Friday is the *last* day," thinks the Procureur.

Then he says suddenly: "Let me caution you about Mademoiselle Quinault—you do not know her wiles."

"You fear this jade has some hold upon Raymond," cries the Comtesse.

"Quiet! let me cloak you. Come into the garden—your agitation attracts attention," mutters De Moncrief.

So he leads Clothilde out of the pavilion, leaving Jeanne very happy upon the arm of Raymond and very proud of him in that dazzling crowd.

It is almost the happiest moment of Quinault's life—for D'Arnac, looking very dashing in his uniform of Colonel of the *Musquetaires*, has been so considerate in his manner, so deferential to her every want and wish this evening that she mistakes what is farewell—for love. The soft strains of the music of "The

Amaryllis" of Lulli float around them.   The scene is
fairylike.   Her escort—her *lover*—the handsomest
cavalier in all the glittering throng.   And Jeanne is
happy, so happy that her bright glances tell the story
of her heart to others who watch her closely.

Gaston Lenoir, who hates Raymond for his success
with one who had tossed his suit aside as not that of an
aristocrat.

Hilda de Sabran, whose wanton soul Jeanne's happy
face fills with all the pangs of longing desire and jealous fury.

So obtaining opportunity (D'Arnac just at this
moment being called away for a little time by his sister) she strides up to the actress and mutters: "You
know me, Mademoiselle Quinault?"

"Certainly," replies Jeanne.   "You are Madame de
Sabran."

"Then come with me—a word with you in private."

"I am at your command," remarks the *comedienne*,
gazing in wonder at the splendid beauty that is before
her, and perhaps rather curious to know what this lady,
who is all powerful with the Regent, can have to say
to her.

Whereon the two pass out together, and people turn to
look at them, for the loveliness of one enhances the
loveliness of the other, as the diamond makes the ruby's
red ray more brilliant, more beautiful—la Sabran robed
in gorgeous colors that she can carry off with barbaric
majesty, la Quinault in lightest tints of lace and tulle
and gauze.   One is as the great red sun—the other as
the rainbow floating round it.

So it came to pass that Cousin Charlie strolling with
Clothilde about the grounds fills her mind with stories
of the actress' love for her nephew, and after a little,
having turned out from the crowd, they sit down upon
a rustic bench, beside a summerhouse that stands
near the flowing Seine, and would talk further—for the
night is wondrous soft for December.

But suddenly from out the rustic woodwork of the
pagoda come words to them that make them very
silent.

Rubbing his hands together with quiet glee, De
Moncrief takes a quick glance through the trellis

work and shrubbery, and notes it is Hilda de Sabran who stands before Jeanne Quinault, saying with pallid lips, but flaming eyes and blazing cheeks: "I have been told that I must spare you. But do not go too far. Don't let me see you glory in your triumph *too much*. Otherwise you may become the veiled and silent one again!"

At this, Jeanne rising with a little cry, for the appearance of Hilda is hardly like that of a sane woman, answers, opening her blue eyes in astonishment: "I did not know that you were my enemy before!" then adds astounded: "Why do you hate me?"

"Why? Because you have the love that is not mine! Because," whispers De Sabran, "you are the mistress of Raymond D'Arnac!"

"I am not his mistress!"

"No!—when his family educated you for that honor?"

"Oh powers of mercy!"

And Hilda bursts into a mocking laugh as Jeanne pale with horror falters out the last.

But this jeer brings fortitude to the persecuted. She cries: "I am not as you are—my love is not as yours—I hope to be his *wife!*"

"You hope to *wed* a noble?" gasps Hilda.

Here her words are suddenly re-echoed, and with an awful voice Clothilde, striding in, says: "You hope to wed the Comte d'Arnac, one of the noblest names in France—and my nephew! You actress—to whom the church refuses sepulchre in holy ground—dost thou not remember the police edict which begins 'actresses and other courtesans?'" and she quotes in harsh and cruel voice a miserable forgotten law of ancient Paris.

Then the two—this mistress of the Regent, and this comtesse of France—burst into mocking laughter, and shower on Jeanne those cruel insults women give to women.

Under them the girl is crushed—but not for long. For she has a spirit braver than those who torture her, and she turns on her tormenters and becomes grand and dominating and whispers: "I'll make you both know I have not aspired in vain!"

"How?" gasps Clothilde.

"I have been called the *mistress;* I WILL BE THE

WIFE!" And Jeanne's eyes glow with inspired revenge and her mocking laughter follows her opponents as they fly from her.

But the game is on! Jeanne Quinault, with all her impetuous soul, will now marry Raymond d'Arnac, if she can do it by fair means or by foul.

But the very hopelessness of her task appalls the girl. She sinks upon a bench pondering "How?"

The light from a great wax taper blazing overhead covers her with soft radiance, as with clenched hands and knit brow, and eyes that have in them tragedy, little Quinault in graceful pose, makes a pretty picture.

Suddenly her musings are broken in upon by a clear-cut incisive voice saying: "Beautiful actress, is this a tableau for your next tragedy?"

Looking up, Jeanne sees Uncle Johnny.

"Yes," she says, "the tragedy of life." Then bursts out suddenly: "You are all-powerful in finance —you make people rich. Will you make a woman very happy? The Comte d'Arnac, my guardian, says that you hinted you would do me a favor. Now I ask it."

"What?" sighs Uncle Johnny, who is always being asked for favors now.

"Oh, I don't want hints on stocks, I only want a title!" cries little Jeanne, her heart in her mouth— "Ask the Regent to give me a title?"

At this there is a merry laugh outside, and Philippe d'Orleans striding in says: "For that, my little actress of the Français, you should apply to me in person."

To this she falters: "I—I thought that Monseign-eur Law's word might have weight with you—you sell him *everything!*"

"Even the tobacco tax!" responds D'Orleans. And he and Uncle Johnny grow very merry for they have just concluded the barter of that revenue.

A moment after the Regent says cheerily to little Jeanne: "And why do you want it?"

"Why? To avoid insult. These great ladies sneer at me! Give me a title—Sire!" cries Jeanne in impet-uous voice. "That I may flaunt it in the faces of these grand dames who despise an actress! Show them that France honors *art* as well as *blood!*"

"It is not such a bad idea, your Highness," laughs
Uncle Johnny, who has something here that he can perchance give, and cost him nothing. "It will make an
artistic era in France, and you will be its hero. You
have brought the people together. Show them that
literature and art may hope for their reward, as well
as trade."

"Humph! It is rather nice, but royalty is not accustomed to give titles to beauty," mutters D'Orleans
consideringly, "*without payment.*" And his eyes gaze
admiringly on the lovely creature before him.

But Jeanne's eyes blaze in return; she says very
haughty in her despair: "That is an honor too high
for my honor, Sire!" and would depart.

Her look makes Philippe half ashamed—he stammers: "Payment of some kind. Perchance if Monseigneur Law would add a million to the hundred he promises me for the tobacco tax——"

"What! and *rob* my India Company?" cries the
financier.

"Oh, I'll give a million!" whispers Jeanne. "I have
two—you can have one of them!" At which both
gentlemen burst out laughing, and to their credit look
shamefaced.

"Egad! We'll not take the little girl's money anyway!—I am glad to learn you are rich enough to
support a title!" laughs D'Orleans. "Well, on your
next triumph—you shall have one!"

"Then next Friday evening!" cries Jeanne. "I play
a new part for the first time in '*La Surprise de
l'Amour.*' Come to the Français."

"Why."

"Because that night I'LL WIN MY TITLE! Bring the
patent of nobility with you. My God! how I thank
thee! You have given me hope!" And she bursts
out laughing, crying, and hysterical.

"Egad! if you value it so much, I'll not forget my
promise," says D'Orleans. "Will you not come with
us to the *fête*? An embryo baroness would look well
upon the Regent's arm—or shall it be a comtesse?"

"No—leave me here! I am thanking heaven now!"

And these two old sinners, astounded at her words,
go silently, perhaps even shamefacedly away.

CHAPTER XVIII.

THE FEAST OF BELSHAZZAR.

LEFT to herself, la Quinault, after the first few moments of ecstatic joy, rises, and wiping away the tears from her blue eyes that now gleam with supreme hope, turns falteringly towards the *fête*, the music of which comes to her in merry strains.

Almost as she reaches the gay throng she is encountered by a grave veteran, who, laying playful hand upon her shoulder, cries: "Come, little Jeanne, and have a walk with De Villars. Egad! I cannot look my host in the face from very laughter, when I remember how Dillon, in the old Army of the Rhine, used to say the Chevalier Lanigan polished boots better than any servant in the army. You were one of us then. Come with your old Chief now. A walk in the moonlight, little Jeanne."

"With pleasure," falters la Quinault; but something in her voice—something in her attitude—catches the old soldier's eye, and he says: "Crying? Who's been wounding the feelings of my *protegée* ?"

"No one ! I—I cried from—from happiness."

"Humph ! a curious reason. Tell papa all about it !"

And Jeanne who is accustomed to confide many of her *little* troubles to this old warrior, and who, perchance, like many a woman, enjoys telling of triumph, babbles out to him the story of how the Regent will make her, if she is a very good actress on the coming Friday, a comtesse of France.

"*Tonnerre de Dieu!* a comtesse !" ejaculates De Villars, amazed. Then he says, gruffly: "What do you want with a coronet ? A comtesse cannot tread the boards. Would you bring discredit on *our* order ? Wouldn't the bills look well—' *Phèdre*, by the Comtesse Fascination ? ' What is to be your ladyship's new name ?"

"I—I don't know—I don't care—I am to be a comtesse. Then I'll leave the boards. Why not—I am rich."

"Ah, ha! For that you must get your guardian's permission. We'll tell D'Arnac of your coming honors.

I saw him in the crowd, only a minute ago. This will be a surprise for our colonel of *Musquetaires.*"

With military strides, he would draw Jeanne back into the festival; but she says, piteously: "No! no! don't tell *him*—not—not just yet!"

Then suddenly tears come into the lovely eyes again, and with them to this old tactician a suspicion that has ofttimes been in his mind. He says shortly: "You have something more to tell me?'

"No!"

"You *must!*"

"NEVER!"

"Well, I can guess. Papa De Villars is accustomed to divine the strategy of men and women." Then he whispers: "You love our dashing Raymond!"

But Jeanne, without a word, slips from his grasp, and runs away, leaving the veteran looking curiously after her.

This catechism, added to the other emotions of this night, makes Jeanne unfit for festival this evening. Seeking Madame de Caylor, and avoiding of all men Raymond d'Arnac, she begs her duenna to take her home; which the fair poetess of passion does reluctantly and grudgingly; for supper is just being announced. And supper is the *summum bonum* of a party to ladies too ancient to attract the glance of man. So leaving message with a lackey to be conveyed to Raymond of their departure, they are about to go.

But chancing to meet Monsieur de Moncrief, that gentleman most gallantly escorts the ladies to their carriage and puts them in, for Cousin Charlie, though he has always been attentive to the young actress, has been devoted to her for the past few weeks, even to bribing one of her maids.

He is just bidding them adieu, when, as ill luck will have it, Lenoir saunters up, and being treated by Mademoiselle Jeanne quite debonairly; she having loathed the man since he dared hint his love to her; this gentleman begins to laugh and sneer: "This is rather early to leave the *fête*—before supper, *too*, Madame de Caylor —has Mademoiselle been naughty—has she listened too much to the light words of gallants—is she to be whipped and put to bed? It is a fine thing for the Comte d'Arnac to be both guardian and ——"

But he gets no further.   With flashing eyes Jeanne whispers, hoarse with passion: "The Comte d'Arnac is my guardian, not my—my tyrant.   If he but heard you, you would get the whipping!"

"Oh, God of heaven! how I would like him to try!" whispers Lenoir, the eyes of the duellist growing cool and deadly in all his passion.   "Tell your guardian how I ——"

But the carriage drives away, in it now a frightened Jeanne, for Madame de Caylor is whispering to her: "For God's sake don't get D'Arnac in altercation with that man.   Don't you know, child, he is the deadliest swordsman in Paris?. Ah, your words have been most dangerous to your guardian!"

And so they have.

Looking on Lenoir's face, Cousin Charlie thinks, why not another string to my bow—and says, laughing: "You are a better swordsman with men than women."   .

"If it had been the man," mutters Lenoir, lingering longingly over his words.

"You would have come off no better than with the lady."

"*Diable!* I could kill him, as I can any other man in France," says Gaston confidently.

"Permit me to doubt not your word—but your sword! I hardly think you could do it!" suggests Monsieur le Procureur with significant voice.

"I would wager my life on it!"

"I will not wager *my* life!" answers De Moncrief, growing slightly pale though his eyes are very eager. "But I will lay ten thousand crowns against *your* life that you do not kill Raymond d'Arnac in open duel this week—twenty thousand that you do not do it by Friday. Do you take my meaning?"

"Aye, and your money, too!" whispers Lenoir. "I accept your wager—it's part of the old Flanders business, I presume," and walks off laughingly.

And Cousin Charlie, gazing after him, thinks very contentedly, "Here's another string to my bow—I have two now—Quinault's love and Lenoir's hate!"

But two strings to one bow sometimes make bad archery!

Not knowing the pleasant surprises his relative is preparing for him, Raymond gets through the evening quite well, though he receives his ward's message of departure with a very bad grace.

But this leaves him untrammelled to enjoy the wondrous *fête* in its entirety, including a most bizarre effect at supper.

This grand meal being announced by several major domos, the great pavilions set apart for this are opened. A smaller one, being devoted to the Regent and his immediate party, in which are Cousin Charlie, Monseigneur Law, the fair De Sabran and numerous gallants and beauties of the Palais Royal clique.

D'Arnac is uninvited to this distinguished table. Monseigneur Law being afraid of putting tinder near the spark—Hilda is safer away from this young gentleman who kindles her soul.

But seated at the head of one of the adjoining tables, Raymond can look into the Royal pavilion, and gets a little side show that makes him laugh. He sees Law buttonholed by Clothilde.

The fat widow receiving introduction from the Regent proceeds to pump the financier as to the market, saying, "Don't sit down to supper yet; I have so many questions to ask you, dear Monseigneur Law!"

"Madame," remarks the comptroller, "I never think of business when I'm hungry."

"But you must promise me one thing," persists the comtesse, who is a woman who will not take a hint, "You must tell me when to sell."

"I will," replies Uncle Johnny, "if you'll only let me eat now."

"Of course," laughs Clothilde, "now that you are a good financier and have promised."

Then comes the supreme effect!

The guests have but just sat down. One hundred flunkies, marshalled in military order, at Lanty's word of command, fire one hundred champagne corks in one tremendous volley.

This is greeted by a cheer, the Regent himself bravoing with delight at this novel salute.

Then they fall to upon a *menu* fit for a club of gourmands. But in the midst of the hilarity, sud-

denly the guests pause, even with their mouths full,
the glasses at their lips.

For bowing down before a gentleman of distinguished mien, comes Lanty and his father-in-law, arm in
arm.   The Chevalier Lanigan announcing in his proudest
tones: "Room for the Austrian Embassador—room!"

"Egad!" whispers the Regent to Monseigneur Law,
"It's the new fellow his Most Imperial Majesty of
Austria has appointed.   His papers were presented to
me to-day.   I hinted to him of the *fête* by note, when
I received his communication; and here he comes on
my invitation."

Then he turns his glance upon the approaching
envoy, which is perchance fortunate, as Uncle Johnny's
eyes now almost start out of his head; his hands tremble and his face grows pale, for in the Ambassador of
Imperial Austria he sees the features that he dreads—
those of the Irishman who has escaped from his toils,
and has come back, he feels in his heart of hearts, for
revenge as unstinted as had been his torment.

Law sinks with a suppressed sigh into his chair, as
Lanty proudly announces: "The Envoy of his Most
Imperial Highness of Austria, the Comte O'Brien Dil-
lon of the Empire, and member of the Order of the
Golden Fleece."

As these words fall upon their ears, Cousin Charlie
and De Sabran, who have been engaged in happy
repartee, suddenly turn, and seeing the sight they fear
most in all this world, Hilda's eyes grow drooping, her
lips quiver, and anguish comes over her beautiful face,
even as she stares.

And Cousin Charlie loses his new found boyhood in
trembling fear and quivering apprehension.

"Bedad!" says Lanty, stepping back and whispering to Raymond,   "Did ye note their faces?   It's a
rale feast of Belshazzar!   Begorra! they see the
handwriting on the wall!"

But D'Orleans, not noticing this, cries out in his
easy way: "I am delighted to see you, Comte Dillon!
I am glad to meet you informally before your official
presentation, so that when you come to me as the representative of our cousin of Austria you also come to
me as a friend."

"By St. Patrick ! Your Royal Highness," remarks
Dillon, easily, "his Majesty of Austria, when he gave
me the honor, said: ' I give it to you, my well-beloved
general, not only on account of the prayers of Prince
Eugene, but because of your ardent wish to visit
your *friends* in Paris.' "

" You have been here before ? "

"No, your Highness," replies O'Brien, kissing the
Regent's hand, and taking a seat next D'Orleans, which
has been reserved for him.

An answer which makes Law, Hilda de Sabran and
Cousin Charlie stare with astonishment.

"You have never been in Paris before?" gasps
Uncle Johnny, as he is introduced.

"No," answers Dillon, quietly, his eyes flaming into
the grey ones across the table till they droop.   " But
to-day Monsieur D'Argenson, your head of police, as
he examined my passports, remarked that some poor
imposter, some dealer in the black art—presumed to use
my title in your gay capital after the battle of Belgrade, but had been punished for the imposition.   It
is astonishing how great names are sometimes stolen.
There was a scoundrel once masquerading in Flanders
as your illustrious self, Monseigneur Comptroller."

But this kind of talk from the Austrian Envoy does
not seem to raise the spirits of Uncle Johnny, the fair
Hilda, or even Cousin Charlie, who has only seen the man
he betrayed twice in his life, and for a moment has a
wild hope the creature he ruined was really an imposter.

But De Sabran's face tells him this is the real man—
the real enemy.

D'Orleans does not notice the sadness of his supper
table, as Dillon chats easily with him, giving him an
account of his fights with the Turks, and mentioning
that the Chevalier Lanigan had stood by his side in many
a pitched battle. Finally getting warm with his subject (and perchance also the generous vintages of the
banquet), he tells such stories of Lanty's love for plunder that the Regent laughs till tears are in his eyes.

A moment after, D'Orleans rises and commands
silence. Calling to the bride, he enraptures the fair
and plump Marie, by saying: " My dear Lady Lanigan, I have just heard such accounts of the Chevalier's

conduct from his friend and comrade, Comte Dillon,
that I congratulate you on gaining for your husband a
most gallant soldier—only when in his most martial
mood, *lock up your diamonds and plate.* I drink to the
health of the glorious Lanigan and his lovely bride."

At this the pavilion rings with shouts and clinking
glasses, and Lanty, rising to the occasion, says "Your
Royal Highness—I am a modest man. In the wars
I have captured everything from a silver candlestick to
a pretty girl—but never have I captured anything so
rich and beauteous as the Lady Lanigan !"

At which the cheers are redoubled, and the hilarity
grows more intense, though neither Uncle Johnny,
Cousin Charlie nor Hilda seem to join in the mirth.

And the supper party soon after breaking up, in the
chance movements of the crowd, Hilda de Sabran finds
herself face to face with Comte O'Brien Dillon.

For a moment perchance she would not speak. Then
compelled by his eyes that seem to dominate hers, she
whispers: "You are here to—to claim me ?"

And his voice, cutting, clear and very cold, seems to
send an icy chill down her fair back, as he whispers:
"When the time comes—*yes !*"

"As your wife ?" This is sighed rather than spoken.

"As my *faithless* wife !"

This sends her away from him shuddering, for his eyes
have an awful gleam now; they have caught the sparkling
jewels of the Turk—the great crescent and its lesser star.

She dare not claim protection from D'Orleans, for
she dare not tell him the truth. She cannot attack the
representative of Austria as she would some common
citizen by the vile police arts of Cousin Charlie.

From this time on, the thought of this man is as a pall
to her spirits, though she tries to be merry and laugh,
as she rides home with the Regent and several others of
his beauties and his favorites.

Monseigneur Law is not of their party. He is communing with De Moncrief. "We are safe from him for
the present," he says to that gentleman, who has turned
a white and piteous face upon him—"As long as we
dominate France we are safe from *everything !* And for
that purpose keep your wits at work, for in the next few
days will come the crisis."

BOOK IV.

JUGGLING WITH FATE.

CHAPTER XIX.

THE THREE LETTRES DE CACHET.

THIS prognostication of the far-seeing financier is true in regard to more cases than his own. The climax comes rapidly on in *l'affaire Raymond*, which, though Uncle Johnny does not know it, is very closely connected with his own.

D'Arnac, happy in the company of his old friend, rides home contentedly in the early morning from the great *fête* of the Chevalier Lanigan. During the drive O'Brien sits opposite to him, talking most of the time with Madame de Chateaubrien, who appears very much interested in his personal adventures in Vienna, for this is the first time Mimi has seen the comrade of her brother.

In all this conversation Dillon makes no mention of his first visit to Paris. He appears to ignore that awful episode of his life.

The drive seems a very short one to Mimi, and they are soon in front of the great Hôtel de Chateaubrien.

"Where are you stopping, Dillon?" remarks Raymond. "Tell me, so my coachman can put you down, and I can call on you."

"Lanty obtained for me some apartments just across the river on the Rue de Vaugirard, though they are not exactly in keeping with my present rank. To tell you the truth," whispers O'Brien, "even with my salary as Embassador I am too poor to keep up my proper style as representative of my master, the Emperor of Austria. Paris has grown so expensive."

Perhaps guessing at his remark, perhaps thinking it will be pleasant for her brother, perchance thinking it will be pleasant for herself—for Dillon's soft accent and dashing conversation have interested the young widow very greatly, Mimi, who has already alighted, turns back and says in her cordial way: "Why not take up your quarters here? We have a great house—only a third occupied. You will be accepting my brother's hospitality—not mine—for he lives here now. Raymond, ask the comte to become our guest."

"Faith, ye do me too much honor, Madame la Marquise," remarks O'Brien.

"Not as much as you will give us pleasure," returns Mimi. Then she adds, impulsively: "Raymond, ask your· old comrade—join your entreaties to mine." Which Raymond does from his heart.

"Then by St. Patrick," replies the comte, "it is very difficult to refuse a man to whom I am under so much obligation as you."

"Say it is *impossible*," cries D'Arnac, "and *come*."

"Faith, then I'll accommodate ye. I'll move. in to-morrow. Don't call to see me—I will be with ye first, if ye don't mind me hoisting the Austrian flag over yer hotel."

"Come flag and all," laughs Mimi.

And with many expressions of good will, O'Brien drives away, to return next morning, and take up his quarters, and lodge his flunkies, and hoist his flag at the great Hôtel de Chateaubrien.

He arrives in time to join in a late breakfast, and the three make a very pleasant meal of it, Dillon looking perhaps more often than it is good manners, for a man with even a faithless wife, at the bright eyes of the charming woman opposite to him.

But very shortly affairs of state take away the Austrian Embassador. He goes to make his official call upon the Regent of France; and afterwards, curiously enough, finds his way to the office of Monsieur d'Argenson, head of police and Keeper of the Seals of France.

While Dillon is doing this, Raymond has had a

hasty conference with his sister and she has said:
"Delay no longer.   Next Friday is your wedding day.
Honor compels you to do what you suggest."

So going to a notary, D'Arnac, in the presence of
that official, signs and acknowledges two documents.

With these he drives to the house of his old chief,
De Villars, and astounds that veteran.   After a
hearty grip of the hand of the maréchal of France,
Raymond remarks, getting to his subject quickly:
"Circumstances have arisen that make it impera-
tive for me to resign the guardianship of a young
lady, in whom, if I mistake not, you take a great
interest."

"Mademoiselle Quinault?" ejaculates the old warrior, twisting his moustache rather nervously.   "Yes,
I love little Jeanne as a father."

"Then be one to her!" says D'Arnac, and places
before De Villars the documents he has brought
with him.

"What the deuce are these?" returns the maréchal.

"One is my transfer to you of my guardianship over
Mademoiselle Quinault, the other is an order on my
notary to deliver to you the securities I hold for her
and a memorandum of the same."

Here the older man gazes at the younger one
curiously, then a sudden twinkle comes into his keen
eyes and he mutters: "Humph! I suppose you've just
discovered, my dear boy, that she is too *old*—and you
too *young*—for such relationship.   That some day
perchance she will marry?"

"Who?"   In spite of himself there is something in
Raymond's voice that makes De Villars start.

. But the maréchal says almost laughingly; very
happy now, because a problem that had come into his
mind about this young lady upon whom he dotes is, he
thinks, cleared away.   "As an actress that would be
impossible.   The unwritten law of the *noblesse* forbids
it," for De Villars is as stern an upholder of rank and
etiquette as any man in France.   "But you yourself,
my dear D'Arnac, may marry a *comtesse*.   Eh, my
boy!"

"I am going to," replies Raymond.

"Of course!" laughs De Villars.   "Yes, you are

right; under the circumstances it is best you are no longer guardian to my beautiful ward."

"You—you accept the office?" murmurs Raymond, and despite himself his voice is sad.

"Certainly! With pride and pleasure."

Then looking over the schedule of securities, De Villars chuckles: "You have brought me an heiress to dispose of in marriage. *Diable!* what a dower little Jeanne'll have. Egad! I'll look out for Jeanne's interests in the marriage settlements!" A moment after he says: ".These stocks should be sold out. Their price is enormous."

"What makes you think that? They've been going up for a year."

"Even a balloon does not ascend forever."

"And now that this is finished," says the young man, hesitatingly, "you—you have no objection to my visiting your ward?"

"Of course *not*, my dear boy!" cries the veteran, enthusiastically. "If the next time you open your lips to Jeanne Quinault you tell her of your coming marriage!" And he gives Raymond a kindly look; for the old gentleman's doting love for Jeanne has made him jump into an awful error.

"I agree to this," says Raymond, with a slight sigh, as he thinks he is now no longer guardian of the prettiest actress in France; though still he wonders at De Villars' manner.

But the old gentleman goes on chuckling and laughing, and says: "*Au revoir!* I'll look after the young lady's fortune now better than you could have done—with love in your head."

And Raymond going away, there are tears in the veteran's eyes as he looks after the young man, and thinks: "Egad—this title episode is a lucky one for little Jeanne. D'Arnac could never have married an actress. As it is I will secure her fortune and remind the Regent of her promised rank."

Thinking over this matter, De Villars, who has not much faith in the inflated stocks of Monseigneur Law, drives off this day to D'Arnac's notary, and receiving from him the securities of Mademoiselle Quinault he sells them all out at the market rate, which has now reached the tremendous price of nearly four-teen thousand *livres* per share.

And then, for the old maréchal is active as a boy, save when the gout conquers him, he rides to the Palais Royal, and getting audience with D'Orleans says: "Sire, I come to ask a favor."

"About the army estimates!" laughs Philippe. "Come to me when I've received the money for the tobacco tax from Johnny Law."

"It is not the army estimates—it is a young and lovely lady."

" 'A young and *lovely* lady!' *Pardieu !* you had better send her in person. She can do her begging better than you, De Villars!"

"She has! Last night you promised her a title."

"Oh, that little insinuating Quinault!" remarks D'Orleans. "*Pardi !* it kept me awake ten minutes last night thinking what reason I would give in the patent of nobility, and what the deuce the people would say about it. Shall I allege because she makes me laugh I make her a comtesse, or because she makes me cry ? "

"Neither!" replies De Villars, "Announce it is because she, at the greatest personal risk, saved a regiment from annihilation, and gave the fortress of Friburg to France. Make her La Comtesse de Friburg, Sire."

"I will," replies D'Orleans, "and I thank you for the idea. The motive will sound very well on paper."

"Then you promise it to me as well as to Made-moiselle Quinault ?" says De Villars.

"Yes, Thursday night, I believe, at the Français. I promised if she acts well."

"Use your own judgment on that, please," laughs the veteran ; "don't take that of the critics!" And goes away very happy that this matter is settled.

So coming with this news to little Jeanne, at her apartments on the Rue de Condé, the old maréchal, taking her playfully by her little ear, says: "Now, at last rebel, you have a master! I am papa and guardian too! Behold this paper! D'Arnac has turned you over to me, bag and baggage—stocks and securities—but only, I imagine, *for a little time*." Emphasizing this last with a smirk, the veteran goes on: "The young gentleman thought it best under the circumstances some one should act as father to you, and I agree with him. As a matter of form, give me your written consent to the transaction, though it is not legally necessary."

"With pleasure!" cries Jeanne, her eyes growing very happy and her face very blushing, for she thinks this is some preliminary to D'Arnac's asking a great question of her new guardian, that Raymond could not conveniently ask of himself—that is—the hand of his ward. She says, hesitatingly, a wonderful redness flying over her fair face: "He—he has said something?"

"*Parbleu!* I brought him to book at once! Trust De Villars, the strategist!" laughs the warrior. "He said: 'I ask you as her guardian, máy I call upon little Jeanne?' I said: 'When you talk to her of marriage.' He said: '1 will!' *Mon Dieu*, you are crying!"

But they are tears of joy, though Papa De Villars does not give Jeanne much time for emotion now. He chatters on: "I have taken a little liberty with your fortune, Mademoiselle."

"What?"

"Sold out your securities."

"Oh, my! *all* my stocks and bonds?" she cries.

"Yes, changed *paper* into *dirt*. I'm investing it all for you in real estate. Egad! I got a pretty price —two and a quarter millions; that will be a great dower for you, Madame la Comtesse de Friburg!" And he bows to her in his old-time courtly way.

"You are *sure*?" screams Jeanne, springing up, but growing pale and trembling.

"I have the Regent's promise."

"La—Comtesse—de—Friburg!" whispers the girl, her eyes burning like stars; then she says suddenly: "Why, that's the place where I showed Comte Dillon and Raymond the mine!"

"Precisely! that's the reason D'Orleans makes you a comtesse."

"And *not* for being a great actress?" ejaculates Jeanne; then pouts: "Anyone could crawl through gunpowder."

"Anyone *could*—but no one *would* crawl through an exploding mine," mutters the maréchal.

"And every one *would*, but no one *could* play ' *La Surprise de l'Amour* ' as I will ! " cries Jeanne. "D'Orleans may say it is for gunpowder, but it shall really be for art ! Even old Baron, who praises no one but himself, said yesterday I was the *comedienne* of France. I had been questioning him, and he said an actress could easier go to heaven than marry a noble. It is astonishing how common people aspire. O-o-oh ! a comtesse ! " With this her fair head is on De Villars' old shoulder, and she goes to crying excitedly but comfortably.

"And is papa De Villars to have nothing for all this ? " remarks the veteran, trying to smooth the soft golden tresses that float about his grizzled mustachios.

"Yes, papa's kisses ! " And she gives him such sweet ones, that the veteran as he goes away mutters to himself: " Egad ! that Raymond is a lucky fellow ! "

Waving adieu, Jeanne suddenly cries to him as he takes farewell: "Next Thursday night if I am not a comtesse, I am not an actress ! " and seizing her part again, goes to studying like one possessed, knitting her brows, and racking her brain, for new and wondrous effects in brightest comedy, and that peculiar pathos of which Jeanne is the mistress more than anyone on the stage.

As for the lucky D'Arnac, coming away from his interview he rather moodily thinks: " Adieu to the most charming friendship of my life "—and turning the interview over in his mind remembers De Villars' remark about the stock market. Sadness produces pessimism and he decides: " Lass said sell my stock when I had enough. The profit will be almost five millions. That makes me rich, even to-day. I sell my own securities at once."

Soon after, Dillon coming in, Raymond informs him of his wondrous luck in stocks, and how he's going to sell them on the morrow.

At which that gentleman says: "Give me a chance in your speculation also! "

"What do you mean ? " asks D'Arnac.

" Well, I mean this. You have only Uncle Johnny's

side of the affair to judge by. *I know what his enemies are doing!* I will guarantee to you the prices of to-day, if you will let me hold your shares three days more and make a profit on them myself. I'm sure there will be one."

"Why?" asks Raymond.

"Bedad! I presume it's betraying a confidence— but still you have a right to ask me that. I have the plans of the other party. They have grown tired of depressing the securities of Monseigneur Law, and now have formed the extraordinary plan of boosting them up to the very heavens in the financial firmament—so high that when the balloon breaks it shall crush everybody— even your friend Uncle Johnny himself.'

"Very well, take your plunge for three days with the securities," says D'Arnac. "If there's a profit from your advice——"

"I'll give you half of it!" cries Dillon, "only I do so want to have my finger in the financial pie!"

"A quarter of *your* profits will be enough for me," says Raymond, and settles the affair.

O'Brien adding: "I know my information is correct."

And his idea is true.

Seeing they cannot stem the tide; with the astuteness of fiends, De Conti, the Brothers Paris, and D'Argenson, have determined to become bulls, to put up stocks to such tremendous figures that no commercial success on earth can pay dividends upon the outrageous prices that they will force them to, and so when the crash comes make the fall greater and the hatred of Monseigneur Law stronger, because of the enormous shrinkage in values and the fearful loss attendant therefrom.

And word of this being brought to Monseigneur Law (for he is very well informed of the plans of everybody —especially his opponents), this astute financier, who is about to announce that he has purchased the tobacco revenue of France, which will bring additional profits to the India Company, fears that his enemies, acting apparently as his friends, will put up stocks so high that when the fall comes they will ruin him and his great scheme of France's colonization at one fell swoop.

But to foresee with Jean Lass is to act. Therefore he goes straight to Hilda de Sabran—for he is afraid to ask Phillipe for what he wants himself, thinking, even if he explains the dangers that will come, the Regent will laugh them off and say: "Why, the higher they put securities the better for all of us—the more money in our pockets."

So, getting word with D'Orleans' mistress, Law says to her: "If you obtain for me three *lettres de cachet* in blank from the Regent you can have from me whatever favor you want."

"For it, will you give me safety from the man I fear most upon this earth?"

"Who?"

"My husband!"

"I will *try* to do so. The Austrian Embassador is very high—but I will try to do so."

"Then promise me that you will work with all your subtle brain for this one object, and I'll *try* to win for you what you desire from the Regent. Is it a promise?"

"Yes."

Filled with this, the fair Hilda uses every art of fascination on D'Orleans, and is more alluring to his jaded senses than she has ever been before—even when she first burst upon his eyes in all her youthful beauty—for now another charm is added to her others—that of a curious timidity, which seems to Philippe a bashfulness—almost a modesty; but it is only a trembling desire to please, and so win what will give her protection from this man whose eyes follow her about the courtly circle with a glance that makes her shudder even in her sleep, for at night O'Brien Dillon's face makes her dreams all nightmares.

And on the afternoon of this very Thursday that Mademoiselle Quinault had promised Philippe to make her triumph at the Français Hilda de Sabran wins from D'Orleans a promise of three of those fatal papers—the invention of Monsieur d'Argenson—which permitted the person obtaining them to imprison, in one of the State dungeons of France, the luckless individual whose name was placed thereon.

"*Pardi!*" says the Regent, "unless you use these with discretion, I'll let your enemies out very soon.

Are they some bothering dressmakers, or has some one been sneering at your charms, fair Hilda?"

"No. I have my eye on the parties," laughs De Sabran. "If you do not like my use of them, of course your signature that imprisons can set free."

"Very well," replies D'Orleans. "Will you be at the Français this evening? I have promised to go."

"Yes."

"Then after the performance they will be handed to you."

Half an hour later, Hilda whispers into Lass' excited face: "I have conquered—to-night the three *lettres de cachet!*"

"Then to-night," says the financier to himself, "I imprison De Conti, though he is a prince of France; D'Argenson, though he is head of Police, and the chief villain of the Brothers Paris, though he is fifty times a millionaire. They will probably get out in a week or two, but in that time I'll put the tobacco tax before the public, and they'll not have a chance to blow up my balloon." For these two preceding days have made Monseigneur Law very nervous. In spite of him the price of stocks has gone up—such is the wildness of the public and the reckless bidding on the street—from fourteen thousand *livres* a share to sixteen thousand.

CHAPTER XX.

A COMTESSE FOR A MINUTE.

IN CONSEQUENCE of this, Dillon comes to Raymond the same Thursday evening, and says to him: "Bedad! I've taken no chance—I've sold out your securities. There are 1,200,000 *livres* to share between us. I feel a little more comfortable now, and you have five millions to your credit at the Royal Bank of France."

"Which I will put into real estate!" replies D'Arnac. "It is the property that a gentleman should own—the land of his country."

"Bedad! I will have to spend a good deal of my nine hundred thousand," remarks Dillon, "keeping up the rale state of an embassador. But it makes things very easy for me at present. And I'll have an estate, too, for estates are cheaper in the Empire than they are here. I have me eye on a castle by the banks of the Danube. Some day you'll come and visit me there with the Comtesse Julie, and perhaps an odd boy or girl or two." For Dillon has by this time learned that to-morrow is the day of his friend's wedding. "I suppose little Quinault will be one of the invited guests as your ward."

"The ward of Maréchal de Villars now," replies D'Arnac, " but she has been invited. I had a battle with the old Comtesse de Crevecœur on the subject to-day."

This is true, and a battle it had been, as Clothilde had fought most vigorously against any invitation being sent to the actress of the Français, to the ceremony that will take place, not in gay Paris, but at a beautiful villa near Versailles, which after the wedding will belong to the Comte d'Arnac, as the *fête* is to be a very private one, the family having as yet hardly gone out of mourning. Besides Clothilde thinks Versailles is safer, for she has still a lurking fear of Charles de Moncrief.

So on this Thursday, Mimi has whispered to Raymond: "Have you told Jeanne yet?"

"No," he says, "but I am going to see her at the Français this evening. I received a note from her to-day—one that I cannot understand. Can you guess its meaning?" And he hands Mimi an epistle that makes her eyes grow teary as she reads:

THURSDAY MORNING.

MY DEAR GUARDIAN:

No, Guardian is crossed out. But it is hard to forget the title that I have given you for the six years in which you have been so kind to one who will never forget it. Papa de Villars hinted that you would come to me and receive my thanks in person at having been such a kind guardian to

Your ex-ward,

JEANNE.

P. S.—Papa de Villars has the gout and will not be at the Français this evening to witness my triumph and to take me home. I believe he relies on you to escort me. J.

The tone of this letter makes Mimi start. Into her head flies a sudden idea that old Papa de Villars may have made a fool of himself in his communications to the young lady, who has written this.

She says hurriedly: "Raymond, take me to the theatre with you. I will talk to Jeanne, and prepare her for a revelation that she may regard perhaps as sudden."

"Very well," answers D'Arnac. "Dillon, I think, will come with us."

At which Mimi gives a little blush and laughs: "If we are to have company, I must look to my toilet," and so goes away.

Some hours after this Dillon, his comrade, and the Marquise de Chateaubrien, find themselves in a box at the Français, looking at '*La Surprise de l'Amour.*"

"Heavens!" whispers Mimi, gazing on the stage. "Did you ever see such acting before? Jeanne is surpassing herself!"

Then the curtain falling on the first act the audience make a tremendous noise; for la Quinault is the great *comedienne* of the time, and as such the goddess of Paris.

While this is going on Mimi puts detaining arm upon Raymond and says: "Don't go to the greenroom now. You may make her nervous. It is her first time in the part."

As for O'Brien, his face red with his exertions at applauding la Quinault, he sits behind la Marquise's shining shoulders, not caring to move. The place is too pleasant to him.

So the performance goes on.

Jeanne, after one bright look at Raymond's box, devotes herself to her art, and perhaps forgets everything else, for she is as one inspired. Each act is a greater triumph than those that come before it.

There is only one act more.

"Egad!" thinks D'Orleans: "The little girl is working for her title, and gaining it too."

Just at this moment De Sabran being ushered into his box, after greeting him, whispers anxiously: "Sire, where are they?"

"What?—the bon-bons for your poodle?"

"No—the papers you promised."

But D'Orleans' reply astounds Hilda. He gives a little start and mutters: "*Pardi!* I had *too* good a dinner this afternoon. I have forgotten them, and forgotten the other also!"

" What—the three *lettres de cachet*?" whispers Hilda
with pale lips. Her whole soul intent upon obtaining
them now; for she has looked across the theatre and
seen Dillon sitting in the box, and his eyes have met
hers, and she is working not for Monseigneur Law—not
for power—not for wealth—but for safety.

"Wait here!" replies Philippe; then adds ambigu-
ously: "I must not disappoint *her!*"

Summoning a gentleman-in-waiting, he goes hurriedly
out, and the royal equipage being brought up, drives
rapidly back to the Palais Royal, and entering his
private sanctum sees two envelopes addressed, that he
in his careless way has left, and a package of three
papers bearing the royal seal and signature of France
—those which convey men's doom to them. Besides
these there is another, bearing also the royal seal and
signature, the one that is to make la Quinault the
Comtesse of Friburg

Hurriedly placing them in the envelopes, the Regent
seals them up, and coming out says to the gentleman-in-
waiting, whom he has brought with him: "Give these
to the two ladies to whom they are addressed, as they
pass out of my box this evening. Quick! let us hurry
to the Français!" He does not wish to lose one
sentiment or one laugh that comes from little Jeanne
this evening, who is acting as if inspired.

But though they drive fast the curtain is just falling
as he returns. D'Orleans is only in time to join in
the ovation that comes after the play.

He says to an official: "Ask Mademoiselle Quinault
to attend me in my box."

And Jeanne coming in, radiant, breathless, but agitated and curiously happy, receives, as they see her in
the royal *loge*, another cry of bravo from the crowd.

But she has eyes for none of it. Even as she court-
sies to D'Orleans she has eyes only for Raymond.
She hardly notices De Sabran—she has forgotten insult
—she has forgotten triumph—in that greater joy—
HOPE!

Almost unconsciously she falters out her thanks to
the Regent, at his honor.

"*Pardi!* don't thank me yet," he laughs. Then as
she bows herself out of the royal box, he says:

"Adieu, Mademoiselle Quinault. When next we meet, I shall call you by a new name."

As she passes from the royal *loge*, the gentleman-in-waiting hands her a package that she clasps to her heart, knowing she is a comtesse of France.

A moment after D'Orleans whispers to De Sabran: "When you leave the box you will receive what I promised. Be very careful how you use them, for I shall require account of what you do with them."

"What do you mean?" asks Hilda.

"I mean," he laughs, "that I am a fool to keep my promises."

This making her fear that he may revoke the same, she answers: "With your permission, Sire, I will say adieu!"

And she passing out, the gentleman-in-waiting hands to her an envelope which she clasps firmly in her hands, hoping it to be her safety from the man whose glances she has shrunk from all this evening.

Coming out of the theatre, she says to her coachman, who has been kept waiting: "Monseigneur Law's as quickly as possible!" and drives hurriedly away.

At the very door of the greenroom Jeanne is met by Madame de Chateaubrien, who is upon Comte Dillon's arm. Mimi says hurriedly: "Have you seen Raymond?"

"No, except in the box. He'll be following his comrade," laughs Mademoiselle, for O'Brien is just now giving her one of his prettiest Vienna bows. Then she whispers into Mimi's ears: "Come to my dressing room and congratulate?"

"Con—congratulate?" stammers la Marquise.

"Ah, some lady's secret," laughs Dillon, and the two ladies enter Jeanne's tiring room.

This is presided over by Madelon, la Quinault's maid, a pert-looking minx De Moncrief has had in his pay for the last two weeks.

But Jeanne is too excited to notice her, and she cries, ecstatically: "Mimi—behold a comtesse!"

At which Madelon pricks up her ears and Madame la Marquise gasps: "What?"

"Oh, did not Raymond tell you? De Villars hinted it to him two days ago. You saw the honor the Regent

did me, by public invitation to his box.   He has done
more! This package "—and she holds it up—"contains
my patent of nobility.   I introduce La Comtesse de
Friburg!"

"Show me!" cries Mimi, eagerly, for she hasn't time
to think how this may affect her brother; and, flying
to her, together they open the packet, and stare amazed
at its contents.   It is no patent of nobility they gaze
upon, but orders of arrest *in blank*, signed by the Regent
and bearing the seal of France.

"Some mistake!" gasps Jeanne.

"Three *lettres de cachet!*" whispers Mimi, with white
lips.

"Ah, I understand !" cries Quinault; "Meant for
Madame de Sabran! We passed out of the box nearly
together. A gentleman-in-waiting gave her a package
as well as me. I have her *lettres de cachet*, and she has my
title. I'll—I'll tell the Regent his mistake!"

With the word, she flies out of the dressing-room,
runs through the greenroom, and by the private entrance
to the auditorium makes her way to the *loge* of the
Regent.

The theatre is now nearly empty, and she finds
D'Orleans' box deserted. A lackey in the Royal livery
says, bowing: "Madame la Comtesse, His Highness has
just left," for the Regent had mentioned her promotion
to his attendants.

And, oh the joy of it!

Panting with pleasure, Jeanne turns away.

But as she steps out of the *loge*, Gaston Lenoir stands
before her. He has come there to ask some favor from
D'Orleans. She would pass him without a word, for she
now fears this man—not for herself, but for Raymond.

This slight of unrecognition adds to this gentleman's ill-
temper. He says, sneeringly, "Madame la Comtesse
forgets old friends." Then an awful significance coming
into his voice; he purrs, "You are seeking your lover—
I mean your guardian ? I am looking for him, too.
Take me to the Comte d'Arnac, that I may say some
pleasant things about you to his face, so I may get the
whipping. Tell your watch-dog this!"

And, looking in Lenoir's cold, steely eyes, Jeanne is

no more anxious to see the Regent of France. She grasps tightly the three *lettres de cachet* as if they were her very life, but utters no word and turns away.

Almost as she brushes past Lenoir, young D'Aubigné comes hurriedly to her and whispers: "Take my arm a moment;" then says, in a low voice: "You will excuse me if I take the liberty of asking you to do nothing to excite that man to any hatred of your guardian, Comte d'Arnac. Would you also—for you can say it and I cannot—ask my Colonel to be guarded in that assassin's presence?"

"You fear," gasps la Quinault.

"A great deal," replies the boy. "Only yesterday, in our *salle d' armes* at the *Musquetaires*, Lenoir was playing with the foils. You know his marvelous skill with them. And the Colonel, though he seldom takes a hand, was persuaded to cross foils with him. Three times I saw him plant his button straight over D'Arnac's heart. They say he tried the same trick with poor De Grammont, before he killed him. Gaston likes to be very sure of his man. You will pardon me for speaking, for I think that it is perhaps on your account Lenoir bears enmity to D'Arnac."

"I—I thank you for it!" gasps Jeanne; and as the young man bows and turns from her she clutches even more tightly to her breast the three blank *lettres de cachet*, and flies back to her dressing room.

"You found the Regent?" whispers Mimi, rising.

"No! Is Raymond here?"

"Not yet!"

"Ah!"

"But that does not matter at present. You must see the Regent and return those *lettres de cachet!*"

But Jeanne answers hoarsely: "*Never!* I throw away my title. I steal *these!*"

"But is this right?" falters Mimi, who half thinks the girl insane.

"Right?" cries Jeanne. "If you see a villain watching his opportunity under society's barbarous code, to murder the man you love, and heaven has placed in your hands a thunderbolt, is it not innocent —nay *just*—nay HOLY—to let the lightning descend and smite the assassin down?"

With this she is at a table, and, writing very rapidly, has filled up one of the dread warrants of imprisonment.

"Now," she cries, "Lenoir, beware! The moment you show your fangs I smite!—See! I mark this with the cross and make it holy!" and she does so and kisses it and murmurs: "It is my Raymond's life"—while Mimi and Madelon look at her astounded; for in her excitement Jeanne forgets her maid.

"Raymond's life?" cries la Marquise. "What do you mean!"

"I mean that the other evening I—I threatened Gaston Lenoir that Raymond should chastise him."

"My God! that awful duellist," screams Mimi—"My brother——"

"Is now safe; this is my talisman—I keep this to imprison the duellist and murderer."

"But what will you say to Madame de Sabran when she demands the return of these?" asks Mimi, with pale lips and trembling limbs.

Nothing! *She will not ask for them.* She wants to humble me—she will destroy my patent of nobility and wheedle the Regent for three more *lettres de cachet.* She hates me because your brother loves me!"

To this the astonished and horrified Marquise gasps out: "Loves you?"

"Yes, he has spoken to my guardian for me. He has told De Villars he would ask my hand in marriage!" But here Jeanne begins to falter: "My God! will he forget now that I have thrown away my title for his life. De Villars hinted to him that I would be a comtesse before he spoke. Will he forget his rank—will he go against *all* France—to marry the *actress* who loves him?"

And Mimi who has on her tongue even now the words that she has come to speak, cannot say them. She thinks in horrified, half-dazed way: "He who has made this misery must tell his own tale. I cannot break this noble heart who has given up so much for him."

She says falteringly: "Let me seek for Raymond. Even now he may be in altercation with that bloodhound who wants his life. If so, I will notify you."

"And I will use the *lettre de cachet* at once!" cries Jeanne. "Don't fail to give me news quick. Send Raymond to me—not here—the lights are going out—at my house! I will take care of the others—but this is the one I cherish! See, the cross has made it holy! It is thy brother's life. He at least will forgive me for throwing away my title for THIS!" Then suddenly she puts her hand upon Mimi's arm and whispers: "No word to Raymond! Promise! So his gratitude shall not burden his love!"

" He should know!" answers La Marquise.

"No! promise me! Oh, my God! if I have destroyed my hope of him!" And Jeanne sinks into a chair and her eyes have tears in them, though she sheds them not.

But in a moment two soft arms are clasped about her, and Madame la Marquise de Chateaubrien murmurs: "Whatever you are to the world—to me you are a comtesse—*my sister!*" and kissing her she goes away.

Then coming to Comte Dillon, who is waiting, Mimi puts her hand within his arm, and tells him for God's sake to find Raymond, and to keep him away from Lenoir this night, but not to let him see Jeanne Quinault until she has word with him.

So the two leave the Français, as its green room is deserted and its candles are being put out.

And Jeanne has made a mighty guess this night!

Hilda de Sabran arriving at the great house of Monseigneur Law is shown into a private room where Charles de Moncrief rises and remarks: "I have been asked to receive you. Law will be here in a few minutes."

" I had supposed *I* was the most important!" remarks Hilda haughtily.

" Yes, but at the moment other things are important also," returns De Moncrief. "Monseigneur Law is very much engaged just now."

Curiously enough the great financier is closeted with the Comte d'Arnac, for he has sent one of his gentlemen-in-waiting first to Raymond's house, then to the theatre, where he learns the young general is passing the evening. And that messenger, catching Raymond just as he is going into the greenroom, has whispered to him: "Monseigneur Law begs to see you."

" Is it very important?"

" Yes, and immediate!" replies the gentleman. " But it will not take you many minutes. I have a carriage waiting for us."

So D'Arnac, turning away, thinks he will join his sister and Jeanne in the apartments of Mademoiselle Quinault.

Being driven to the house of the financier, he is detained for some little time, waiting for the great man who has some important interviews upon his hands.

But at last Law comes to him and murmurs: " I hope I have not detained you, my dear general." Then leading him into a private room, he speaks very hurriedly and earnestly: " I once told you that I would not tell you when to sell your stocks. Now I beg of you to do so—not only for your own sake, but for that of France! You will get nearly the top price, for if the market goes much higher, those who buy from you will never be able to take up their purchases. I beg you—sell your stocks to-morrow."

" That I have already done to-day."

" Ah, it was your sales that kept the market down," replies Law. " I had supposed it was that long-headed old Chambery." Then he continues: " I also ask you to advise your ward, Mademoiselle Quinault, to sell what she has."

" That was done three days ago."

" And the market stood all this and never flinched," mutters Monseigneur Law. Then he cries out: " My heaven! how greedy these speculators are! They are mad—they are crazy—they inflate my stocks, and think I will pay the dividends on any value that they make for them—no matter how ridiculous—how enormous!" And he laughs grimly, but it is a yellow laugh.

" Is that all I can do for you?" remarks Raymond.

" Yes—everything."

" I thank you for your counsel," says D'Arnac, and turns to go. But at the very door he pauses and adds: " The only member of my family whom your advice could benefit now is my aunt, the Comtesse de Crevecœur."

" Ah! the awful woman of the Quincampoix!" mutters Lass.

"Yes!" replies Raymond, "she has made a large fortune—she has immense holdings."

"She has?" cries Uncle Johnny very eagerly; and D'Arnac passes out, having done an awful bad stroke of business for poor Clothilde de Crevecœur."

At the door of Law's house, Raymond is met by Dillon, who says: "I have driven from la Marquise de Chateaubrien's. She wants to see you. Do not go to Mademoiselle Quinault until you have seen your sister."

While this has been going on Cousin Charlie and Hilda have been in controversy.

Looking at de Sabran, something in her face speaks to Charles de Moncrief, and he purrs: "You have won —you have *them*?"

"Yes," she cries. "The three *lettres de cachet.*"

"Ah, that is what Law has been wanting. Let me look at them!"

"Only into his hands!" she says, rebelliously.

"Oh, ho! We are defiant!" he jeers. Then whispers: "Obey me—you know who is master now—with all your beauty—it is I who can make the bird sing!" Meeting his glance, Hilda becomes drooping, but sullen. She tears open the packet.

Suddenly her eyes flame; she cries: "*Mon Dieu!* a miserable trick!"

"What do you mean?"

"One of the Regent's brutal jokes. He has sent to me a patent of nobility for Jeanne Quinault. My God! he has made her the Comtesse de Friburg. Was it to humble me—to flaunt this actress in my very face? But *adieu*, Comtesse de Friburg!" And before Cousin Charlie can lay his astounded hands upon her, in a burst of feminine unreasoning fury, Hilda de Sabran has burned, over a lighted taper, the patent of nobility that was to have made little Jeanne so happy.

"How did this occur?" asks Cousin Charlie, stifling a grin.

And she telling him what has happened in the Regent's box, he says suddenly: "It is only one of the careless mistakes of D'Orleans. Your three *lettres de cachet* were placed in la Quinault's envelope and are now, I warrant you, in that young lady's hands. Don't

you know she will return them for her patent of nobility
—something that would perhaps give her the chance of
marrying the man she loves ? And now you have
thrown Law's opportunity away. *Pardieu !* Idiot—If
Uncle Johnny had seen you ! Go to your house !
Quinault will send a messenger, or perchance even come
in person to rectify this mistake."

"She will not come in person ?"

"Then she will send. Go ! Invent some lie to get
those *lettres de cachet*—or you'll have to reckon with
Boy Charlie in the matter ! "

Then Hilda de Sabran, sick at her-old-man-of-the-
mountain's tyranny, drives away, and De Moncrief sits
waiting—waiting for both the financier and Hilda—
but neither of them come, for Uncle Johnny is gliding
about among the large throng in his great reception
room, and advising them by deft hints to sell their
stocks, to which they mostly turn a very deaf ear;
the market is now rising as a tropical river under a
cloudburst, and the bulk of speculators rarely sell upon
a rising market.

But after half an hour passes Cousin Charlie grows
anxious, and drives himself to the house of Madame de
Sabran. Coming in to her he says, authoritatively:
"Why did you not return ?"

And she answers: "There has been no word about
the three *lettres de cachet.*"

Then, even as she speaks, a subtle gleam of joy comes
over Charles de Moncrief, and he replies: "I will go
to the actress myself and investigate."

Into his mind has come a curious question:
"Why is la Quinault keeping these documents that
will destroy ? Upon whom does Jeanne wish to use a
lettre de cachet ? "

So he goes away with this idea in his brain, while
Sabran sits waiting. She has repented her rashness
now, and the fear of Dillon has come upon her again,
for she remembers his look to-night.

Soon afterwards to her comes in Uncle Johnny, who
says: "Quick ! the *lettres de cachet*—I must use them ! "

But she turns an affrighted face upon him and
mutters: "I did not get them."

"D'Orleans refused you ?"

"Yes," she replies, and lies, for she dare not tell
this man she has thrown away what he considers now is
vital. So she does further damage, for had Hilda told
the truth, Law's bright brain would have found some
way to get the papers from la Quinault.

"You amaze me," he says, falteringly; then his lips
give one spasmodic quiver—but no more. After a .
minute's consideration, he adds: "There has been
some strong influence brought to bear on D'Orleans. ·
He is not used to break his promises. Perhaps they
guess what was my plan. Now God knows what will
happen ! People will not sell their stocks. They're
all greedy for more—more—as if they did not have
enough now ! If I cannot keep this market from rising,
when the flood goes down it will leave us all high and
dry—stranded in the mud of over-inflation. But mark
my words, Hilda—if through any carelessness of yours
—you have lost those three documents I built my plans
upon—remember that in destroying my chances of
success, you have destroyed your hopes of safety—for
with Uncle Johnny gone," (he chuckles grimly) " who
will protect you from your husband's rights over you?
Not Philippe D'Orleans, I'll be bound, for he'll have
enough to think of in caring for himself ! "

Then suddenly he mutters: "That old woman—
D'Arnac said she had great holdings!" and driving back
to his house he sends, late as it is, a messenger begging
to have word with the Comtesse de Crevecœur.

On hearing this request Clothilde arises from her
couch and comes fluttering and excited to the great
home of Uncle Johnny which is still ablaze with lights.

Greeting her with profound deference he leads
her from the throng that still occupies his salon. Closeted with her he says: "Madame, time in finance
is so vital, I have taken the liberty to call you out of
your bed——"

"To give me the hint in stocks you promised, dear
Monseigneur Law?" cries Clothilde; for the market
has closed feverishly and she has a large quantity of
shares on margins, being one of the greedy kind.

"Yes, as it is now *certain* I can at last speak to you,
not as to some women, to whom I would merely say:
buy or sell," replies Uncle Johnny oilily, "but to

a woman of business, who has accumulated, through her own intuitive perception of the laws of finance, a fortune that does honor to the wisdom and sagacity of her sex. Madame, I address you as I would a brother financier."

"What shall I do?" cries Clothilde eagerly.

"Sell!"

"Sell? Why, they're going up."

"Yes! but near the top. I will show you even our books." And he makes such a display to the widow that she ejaculates: "Good gracious! stocks are only worth 10,000 *livres* a share, according to you."

"They sell for 16,000 on the street, but will pay dividends on only 10,000. They will go down. Do you recollect the last panic?" remarks Lass, remembering this woman's agitation on the day of the raid of the Brothers Paris.

At this Clothilde gives a shudder and gasps: "My heaven! do you predict another one?" growing white as she speaks.

"*Worse* than that one! Of course, you must be your own judge—but from the books and from what I tell you I think you will agree with me."

"Thank you, *dear* Monseigneur Law," remarks Clothilde. "I have made up my mind. I have decided to SELL!"

And going home she lies awake all night, thinking how she will get out of her securities before the terrible break comes, fearing she will not get to the Quincampoix in time.

FOR CLOTHILDE HAS DETERMINED TO BECOME A BEAR!

CHAPTER XXI.

THE ONE MARKED WITH THE CROSS.

IN HER apartments Jeanne sits waiting for Raymond, who comes not. Suddenly her heart beats fast, her eyes grow expectant; she hears the sound of entry upon the stairs, and says to Madelon (for Madame de Caylor has gone to bed): "Show him in!" and for one moment thinks it is Raymond.

So Charles de Moncrief, who enters in his stead, sees what wondrous radiance hope and love can throw upon a woman's face.

But as she looks at him hope and love resign to some anxiety unknown to him who gazes on her. She puts a little hand to her heart to stay its fluttering.

His heart is beating fast also. He gives one quick glance up at the portrait of old Richelieu that hangs over the girl, as if to draw inspiration from it, then goes to business.

In his journey from De Sabran's house, Cousin Charlie, according to his wont, has been putting two and two together very deftly. He is now prepared to act, and Jeanne assists him.

Not even waiting for his greeting, she says, eagerly: "You have come from your cousin Raymond?"

"You—you did not expect a visit from D'Arnac this evening?" laughs De Moncrief.

"Why not?"

"Why—he—he—has doubtless other matters on his hands," stammers the procureur, feeling his ground.

"Good heavens! the duel with Lenoir! Find me a king's officer!" And in an instant Jeanne has snatched from off her panting heart a document, one of the kind De Moncrief knows very well by sight, and, looking at it, murmurs: "This cross makes it the *holy* one. Quick! a king's officer!"

But now De Moncrief hesitates no more. He laughs: 'It is not duels Raymond thinks of now, but brides."

"*Brides!*" And hope is in Jeanne's face.

"Of course, BRIDES! You know to-morrow is his wedding day," says the procureur, struggling to keep triumph from his voice.

But Jeanne's eyes now are blank. "His *wedding* day!" she murmurs after him, as a parrot. The words seem to daze her. Then she whispers, slowly, though with but little understanding: "Whom should he marry but——"

"The Comtesse Julie de Beaumont!"

"Who?"

"The young lady he has been affianced to for years——"

"My God!"

"The one whose estates join his—the one his uncle's will commands him to marry."

"Julie de Beaumont!" This is an awful flash of sentiency, and Jeanne suddenly gasps: "The girl he rescued—the cousin he did not wish to talk about to me;" next mutters, piteously: "And yet I *can't* believe!"

"I can prove it," remarks De Moncrief, more coolly now. "At Versailles the Comtesse de Crevecœur gives a *fête* to-morrow night."

"I know—to which I am invited."

Then De Moncrief bursts out, in a tone of horror (acting his part very well): "Oh, that cruel woman! That *fête* is the *wedding!*"

But a more piteous cry comes up to him—that of a great soul in despair, gasping one word, "RAYMOND!"

Then, for hope will have its say, as well as misery, Jeanne murmurs: "It—it *cannot* be. The invitation did not say a wedding!"

"Of course not!" laughs the procureur. "Madame la Comtesse wishes the blow that shall humble the aspiring actress to be a sudden one."

"She wishes to humble me? Yes—yes—I remember —that night she threatened me—and that other woman—De Sabran! who hates me because he loves *me!*" And for one moment Jeanne still has trust, for she remembers the cause of Hilda's hate and cries: "I will *not* believe!"

But he goes chuckling on: "Oh, ho!—yes! yes! The plot is between them. I saw De Sabran destroy your patent of nobility. She sneered: 'The Comtesse de Friburg will never marry the Comte d'Arnac, for she will never be a comtesse!' Clothilde was with her. She jeered also: 'Mistress is high enough for an actress!'"

But here a white-faced woman rises up before De Moncrief and stays his jargon, for she whispers in a voice that makes him still: "The actress will humble the comtesse!"

"Yes!" he interjects, "Madame thought you would enjoy the sight—Raymond in his young bride's arms!"

But a white hand is on his lips, as Jeanne moans, "Enough—*enough!*" then cries: "Madame de Crevecœur shall beg for mercy from the woman whose humiliation would have been her glory. To-morrow night shall see Madame la Comtesse cringing to the power of the actress Jeanne Quinault! I'll—I'll drag him from the altar!" Next gives a piteous sigh and murmurs brokenly: "But I have not the power!"

Then the tempter at her elbow laughs: "Feel in your bosom! Ah! what makes you start! There you have a power that would tear a prince out of a princess' arms!"

And she gasps: "A *lettre de cachet!* Use it on HIM? Too horrible!" Next whispers: "Are you a demon to put such thoughts into my jealous soul?"

"Has he spared your heart?" murmurs the procureur. "Must De Sabran not have *been* his mistress to hate you? Have you had the attention of which she has been robbed? It was his BRIDE he thought of when he became a prude—not you whom he had taught to love."

But she answers hoarsely: "I have no love—I have only *hate!*"

And he whispers: "Quick—the *lettre de cachet!*"

"Yes, before I can repent!"

And with trembling hands, and tears flowing from her eyes, but still determined upon doing her work, she seizes pen, and would fill up another of the dread papers with the name of Raymond, Count d'Arnac. AND WHAT SHE HAD TAKEN TO SAVE SHE WOULD USE TO DESTROY.

But even as the pen is in her hand the music of Lulli's "Amaryllis" comes up from a band outside, and Madelon entering says: "This coronet from the Duc de Villars to the Comtesse de Friburg, and a serenade on her title and the honor France has done her."

Then Jeanne starting up glares upon the diamond insignia of the rank she has thrown away, and the gems seem to mock her, and the music seems to jeer her. But for one moment they make her remember!

She falters: "These were the strains that came to us the other night as we walked together in the pavilions of the wedding *fête*, and I thought—my God! he loved me!" and sinks upon a sofa, her hands twitching with despair.

"Quick ! give me the *lettre de cachet*, I'll fill it up! " whispers De Moncrief, reaching for the paper.

But she, holding it from him, sobs : " I did love him so truly, so well—*I can not do this thing !*" Then cries: " THERE MAY BE A DOUBT ! "

" There shall be no doubt ! " he answers, " You *shall* believe ! What will you take as proof ? "

She sighs: " Raymond's own lips."

And he says desperately: " To-morrow afternoon, if you will come with me, you shall hear it."

" Then when I do hear from his own lips, you shall have this paper. For by my soul! HE SHALL WED NO ONE BUT ME ! " she answers, her lips white, her eyes big with passion.

And he, looking at her, knows she will do her word, and would speak to her again, but she mutters, hoarsely: " Not till *then !* Whatever I do—you are the greater villain ! You would destroy him from the baser motive ! "

And he leaves her standing, a statue of revenge!

CHAPTER XXII.

" USE THIS, IN THE KING'S NAME ! "

BUT as Madelon attends De Moncrief at the entrance, he whispers inquiringly: " She has three *lettres de cachet ?* She filled one up with Lenoir's name—the other two are blank ? "

" Yes," answers the maid. " The one she wrote upon I saw marked with a cross."

" Yes, I noticed it—the one she kissed and fondled —the one she loves—the one for which she threw away her title—has the cross."

Then after one second's consideration he says: " Girl, in the chances of her toilette (for your mistress will keep these papers with her) obtain an opportunity and mark the other two on the back with a similar cross. *Parbleu!* little Jeanne shall not play her hand with Charles de Moncrief with marked cards."

So he passes into the night to ponder on the problem how he can obtain from Raymond's lips the words he wants in the presence of the woman who will avenge them, and how to keep D'Arnac from seeing her; for if the two come together he guesses Jeanne will forgive.

And in this matter Providence is kind to Cousin Charlie. Dillon brings Raymond from the house of Monseigneur Law, straight to the Hôtel de Chateaubrien. Where Mimi meeting him, tells him part of what has taken place this evening; not of Quinault's love and horrible mistake, but of the danger from Lenoir the duellist.

Hearing this, even Dillon looked serious. He says: " Raymond, are you in practice ? "

" Pretty well, but not as I used to be."

" No, faith, we all get lazy as we grow older; and this divil I suppose keeps his hand in with the foils." Then after a moment's consideration, he adds very earnestly: " If anything comes of this, promise to make me your second."

"I will," replies D'Arnac, "where could I find a better ? "

"Then mark my words!" rejoins O'Brien. "When Lenoir forces a quarrel upon you, as this fellow will do some day, act in the affair so that he must be the challenger. Bedad! we will choose pistols—they're getting into fashion now. If you were as strong in the arms and shoulders as I am, I would nominate sabres. Ye could break down his guard! There's nothing like the exercise of the—" Here he stops suddenly, almost trembling, some mighty recollection coming over him, and for a time is very silent.

This kind of conversation makes Mimi very nervous. She says: "Don't put yourself in his way, Raymond. Remember your wedding to-morrow. Promise me you will not go out again to-night."

"But I should tell Jeanne of my coming wedding. She might think it a slight. If she were one of the *noblesse* perhaps I should not be so careful. As she is an actress, I will take good care of her feelings."

To this Madame de Chateaubrien suggests: "Tell her to-morrow morning. Raymond, you know how much depends upon your being able to wed Julie to-morrow. You've preparations enough to make here.

The notary is now in waiting, and has been for the last three hours."

Finally her entreaties have their effect. Her brother busies himself making some last arrangements about his property that the marriage settlements compel.

Then comes the next morning—the morning of the wedding.

They rise by times, as they have much to do, and have just finished a very early breakfast and Raymond is looking at his watch and thinking: "I wonder if Jeanne will be up by this time?"

When, to their astonishment, the Comtesse de Creve-cœur is ushered in, red, panting, excited. "I'm in an awful hurry, my dear children," she says. "I have to go to the Quincampoix at once."

"To-day?" cries Mimi. "To-day you drive to Villeneuve to get the bride!"

"That is what I came about. It is impossible for me to go in person," babbles Clothilde. "Last night I had a very important interview with Monseigneur Law. He has at last given me certain information about my securities."

"What did he say?' asks Raymond.

"Don't try to pump a financier," returns the female speculator, looking very wise and very deep. Then she whispers: "Sell your stocks!"

"Already done," remarks D'Arnac, laughingly. "A bride is sufficient weight upon my mind to-day, without the Quincampoix."

"You were wise in that," says Clothilde. "I say sell, and Law agrees with me; but I haven't time to talk finance. Mimi, you must furnish the escort to Julie. I have a letter from the dear child now. She fears to leave the convent unprotected. She had an awful adventure once outside of the convent walls with a butcher."

"With a *butcher!*" cries Dillon, breaking into uproarious laughter. "Faith, we'll save her from the butcher till the wedding, eh, D'Arnac, me boy?" and playfully nudges Raymond.

"Oh, you needn't jeer," remarks Clothilde. "She did not fall in love with the butcher. I suppose it was some wild schoolgirl freak, for which I hope they gave her wholesome penance. I would! So Mimi, you must go."

"Impossible!" replies la Marquise. "My dress for the *fête* this evening is not yet tried on."

"Bedad!" says Dillon, anxious to take any trouble off Madame de Chateaubrien's mind, "Raymond, supposing you and I and D'Aubigné and De Soubise, who is to stand up with you this evening, ride down. It will not be etiquette to introduce ourselves to the fair Julie, but we'll just take in Villeneuve on our way to Versailles and jog behind the little comtesse's coach at a respectable distance, to see nothing befalls her on her journey. You, Madame de Crevecœur, I presume, will be át Versailles at three o'clock to receive her."

"Certainly by that time," cries Clothilde. "I'll have sold——" but she checks herself and says: "I will have performed my business on the street."

"But," Raymond mutters to his sister, "how will I tell Jeanne?"

"Oh, leave that to me," replies Mimi. "I'll bring her with me to the wedding." For now she thinks that it is best for her to give the information. Some cruel scene would probably arise if Raymond told Jeanne of his coming marriage.

"Very well," replies D'Arnac, "we have not much time to spare; it's ten miles further for our ride," and sends a messenger to the barracks with a note for De Soubise and D'Aubigné.

So it comes to pass, about an hour after this, that Raymond, with his two young officers, in all the gallant trappings and harness of the *Musquetaires*, and Dillon, in the uniform of an Austrian general, ride through the Rue de Condé, past Jeanne's apartments, in which D'Arnac, casting a glance, finds the blinds are still drawn, and passing down the road by Ivry, where the Chevalier Lanigan now holds state, reach Villeneuve le Roy about eleven o'clock.

Two hours later, Madame de Chateaubrien applies for admission to Jeanne's apartments, but is received by Madame de Caylor, who says: "Mademoiselle Quinault has just driven away."

"Where?" asks Mimi.

"To Versailles. This evening she attends the *fête* of

Madame de Crevecœur. I wanted to go with her, but the invitation did not include me."

This horrifies Mimi, she mutters to herself: "If Jeanne only sees my brother and his bride before the altar—if that tells her the tale!" and drives away, determined to be the first to welcome Jeanne at the *fête*, and break the matter to her somehow, if she cannot get word with her before.

This early departure of la Quinault has been caused by a little note she had received from Charles de Moncrief, which had simply said:

At the hostelry of "The King's Arms" in Versailles, at two o'clock, I will prove the truth as I promised you last night.

The information that has produced this note comes, curiously enough, from Madame de Crevecœur herself.

Clothilde has gone to the Rue Quincampoix. The market has been firm, and she has sold a good many of her securities at over 16,000 *livres* a share. But under her enormous sales, the market has necessarily somewhat weakened. The price is now below 16,000 and she feels elated at what she considers her rare tact and sound judgment.

Meeting Charles de Moncrief in the office of her brokers' (where he has come in hopes of finding her, though this she does not guess) Clothilde has said in the playful assurance of success: "I am a little wiser than you, my nephew. Some days ago you advised me to hold my stock. Now, see the market weaken!"

"*Pardieu!* you are successful in everything, even with Raymond's marriage, for which you were kind enough to send me an invitation this evening," has remarked De Moncrief.

"Oh, you know it is his wedding, then?"

"*It must be.* To-day is the *last* day. But you have conquered—I forgive you! Will it be a grand affair?"

"No, a quiet one. You forget I am still in half mourning," says the widow. "I sent the invitation to you so you could be sure the ceremony took place as appointed. De Soubise will be Raymond's best man, and young D'Aubigné of the *Musquetaires*. These gentlemen have just gone now to escort the bride from the convent."

"Humph! Then they all will be in Versailles this afternoon."

"Certainly. I myself have engaged the best apartments in 'The King's Arms' for them, 'till after the ceremony," replies Clothilde. "We will see you this evening?" And she laughs—feeling certain now—right in Charles de Moncrief's face.

But she does not give him time to answer, for at this moment there is a report that the stock of the India Company is at 15,500 *livres* a share, and Clothilde gets to business again selling everything she has in the way of stocks.

This outpouring of securities weakens the market again; the quotations tumble to 15,000 and her brokers congratulate her upon having been so far-seeing.

"By Moses!" cries Van Tamn, "Madame la Comtesse, you have a greater brain than old Law himself! You are a born speculator."

"Am I not?" laughs Clothilde. "I make money whether the market goes up or goes down. These things are not worth 10,000 *livres* a share. See what I will do!"

And with the greed of the speculator, and the rashness of the woman speculator, she orders them to sell double the securities that she had. For Clothilde has learnt in her experience upon the Quincampoix, what it means to "*sell stocks short.*" She is now doing the great bear act.

And these sales forcing the market still further down, the quotation comes to 14,000. But this is in the afternoon, and peoples' faces grow white and many say there'll be a panic before night; but Van Tamn, who is a conservative old fellow, suggests: "Had I not better buy some of those stocks that you have sold and have not got, Madame la Comtesse?"

"No," she cries, "sell *more!* I fill when they reach 10,000."

"Your written order to that effect, Madame la Comtesse," remarks the broker. Then he says: "I presume I shall keep the proceeds of all your long stocks as margin, if you will not buy the stock of which you're short?"

"Certainly! To-morrow morning they will be lower yet. But I haven't time to stay and talk to you," returns the comtesse, for now she must get on her way to Versailles.

So she drives away very contentedly from the Rue Quincampoix, to make a pleasant evening of it in her pretty villa near the palace of the young King; a number of the beauties of his youthful court having been invited to the wedding festivities of Raymond d'Arnac and Julie de Beaumont.

Looking over the market, which has declined to between 13,000 and 14,000 *livres* a share, Uncle Johnny thinks now is the time to announce that he has gobbled the tobacco revenue for the India Company.

He makes public the edict of the Regent.

This is what De Conti, D'Argenson and the Brothers Paris have been waiting for.

Then with a roar, the greedy speculators of the Quincampoix rush in to buy.

"Did you see how that cunning old fox Law forced stocks down, so he could get more before he gave out the news?" is the whisper on the street.

The stock of the India Company commences to rise ! higher—*higher*—HIGHER !

And Madame la Comtesse, riding in easy mind, on the soft cushions of her coach, along the lovely road leading from Paris to Versailles, through the beautiful woods of Meudon, would writhe and tear her hair and scream, did she know what was coming to her and her fortune. For the securities of the India Company, even as she drives into the Place d'Armes and gazes at the great palace built by Louis le Grand, are now bid up on the Quincampoix to 18,000 *livres* a share—stocks which she has sold short—shares which she will have to buy back by the thousands.

That afternoon in beautiful Versailles, at the pretty little hostelry called "The King's Arms," situated on the main drive from Paris, almost where the cross-road leading from Villeneuve le Roy runs into it, Charles de Moncrief receives Jeanne Quinault.

"You are prompt !" he says. "I have made every arrangement." Then shows the way up a short flight of stairs, to a retired waiting-room, the windows of which overlook a little courtyard used in summer for serving open air refreshments to the guests of the house.

Being winter this is now covered by window frames, whose glazed surfaces admit the light of the sun, and keep out the wind when it is cold and cutting.

"If you will wait here, through that window will come to you the information you seek" he whispers.

To which she answers nothing, only waves him away, and hangs her head as if ashamed. But just as he is leaving, she places a little detaining hand upon his arm and says very quietly, but oh! so piteously: "You will not trick me!" Then suddenly she grows tall, stern and menacing, and whispers in a tone that makes him quake: "For if you do, BEWARE! I have another! The Bastille is as silent—its tomb as cold for *you* as for him!"

And so he leaves her, and taking post in front of the house watches.

After a little, a carriage with postilions in the liveries of the Beaumonts, dashes past him, and he laughs: "Behold Julie—the bride!"

Some hundred yards to the rear of this, four dashing cavaliers come prancing on, and looking about, Dillon says: "Faith, I think this is the inn where quarters were engaged for us. We will have a pleasant afternoon here till the evening and wash the dust of travel from us inside and out."

As the gentlemen dismount and toss their bridles to the stable boys who come running out to them De Moncrief strolls unobserved away—thinking: "These gentlemen will tell my story for me."

So it comes to pass that to Jeanne's listening ears there shortly comes a voice that makes her start and wring her hands; for it is one she knows and loves too well.

One quick glance from the window—she can't help it—she must look at him. Then a shudder—for the gentlemen seated at the table have wine in front of them, and D'Aubigné, with a boy's recklessness, has cried: "A health to the coming bridegroom, Comte d'Arnac!"

"Faith!" suggests Dillon, "it would be purtier manners, me boy, to put the bride *first*. I drink to the little Comtesse Julie! Bedad! did you see how she looked at us from her carriage windows! *Diable!* I don't think she recognized the butcher in his colonel's uniform—she gazed at him too coquettishly."

" No, I'll warrant she didn't," laughs Raymond.
" The butcher leading her to the altar will be a rare
surprise to Julie this evening."

"By St. Patrick! she looked too pretty to be a
butcher's bride," says Dillon.

"But not too pretty to be mine!" says Raymond, and
his voice grows tender, as what man's wouldn't, speaking of youth and beauty and innocence that is to be his
own this very night.

At this there is a whispering sigh—from the panting
lips and the breaking heart above.

But just at this moment into the pleasant party
walks Gaston Lenoir.

Cousin Charlie's wager of 20,000 crowns is an
object to this man. The sword play in the *salle
d'armes* of the *Musquetaires* has shown him he has a
certain victim. The week is growing short. He has
lounged about hoping to meet Raymond the night before; but has failed to see him in any of the cafés or
places of general resort.

This morning chancing to speak with De Soubise, that
gentleman has casually mentioned that he will spend
that afternoon at "The King's Arms," in Versailles.
"Ah, you go in the evening to the *fête* of the Comtesse
de Crevecœur—I go there myself," remarks Lenoir.
"D'Arnac I presume will be there?"

"Certainly. He is most important."

"And he will be with you at 'The King's Arms?'"

"Probably in the afternoon. D'Aubigné, I believe,
comes with him as well as the Austrian Embassador."

And this information has been enough to bring Lenoir
this afternoon to Versailles in search of the twenty
thousand crowns Cousin Charlie had wagered.

As he enters, Raymond, his glass almost at his lips,
sees him, and knows the affair is upon him; for Lenoir's
eyes are fixed on his. But as he thinks this Dillon's
hand is slipped into his, and he hears whispered in his
ear the word "Together!" And this makes him very cool.

"You are drinking the bride's health?" says Lenoir.
" *Your* bride, I believe, D'Arnac?" Then he jeers:
"*Pardieu!* what will your mistress say to this?"

"My mistress!" remarks Raymond sternly—"I have
no mistress—I am not in the fashion!"

"Oh, I believe you use another term. *Ward* is I think, the word you use. The little actress of the Français—the one who caught D'Orleans himself last night, so he gave her a patent of nobility, it is said." And he would go chuckling on in this hideous style, did not Raymond d'Arnac rise up in front of him and say: "Dog! you lie! You slander as noble, as lovely, as virtuous a woman as any who graces this earth!"

At this the others have risen also.

"Virtuous!" jeers Lenoir. "Why at fourteen this daughter of a mountebank was one of the wantons of the arm——!"

But Raymond's hand forces the rest of the hideous words down his throat and they stay there, for remembering Dillon's hint D'Arnac has felled the slanderer to the earth.

So in the courtyard these men form an awful tableau of hate and death, and above them a woman with staring eyes is murmuring: "He gives his life for my name and to him I would have given *this*!"

As Lenoir rises slowly he mutters: "You know what this means? *À la mort!*"

"Of course!"

"When will you meet me?"

"To-morrow!"

"Why not now?"

"Now, if you like!"

"Then D'Aubigné will act for me!" says Gaston hurriedly. But the boy shakes his head.

"Raymond, ask me to be your second!" comes Dillon's voice, dominating the scene, in its soft Irish brogue.

"Certainly, I am in your hands!" mutters D'Arnac.

With this O'Brien remarks: "Not quite so quick! We are the challenged party. Time and place belong to us, the choice of weapons also, I opine. This evening Comte d'Arnac has a prior engagement—Ladies *first*, my dear Monsieur Lenoir."

"Well, have your way," mutters Gaston sullenly. "As none of these gentlemen seem anxious to act for me, I'll have my second with you before the evening—only remember, it is *à la mort!*" And his eyes turned on Raymond mean death.

To this D'Arnac says slowly: "I understand you are my aunt's guest—please let no word of this get to her—this evening we will meet as before!"

"But to-morrow?" murmurs the duellist.

"As God wills!"

Then Lenoir passing out, for a moment there is silence, which D'Aubigné breaks saying: "My God! he is the deadliest swordsman in France!"

"I know he is," cries Raymond, throwing off his calm. "But were he the angel of death I would have done it!"

To this Soubise mutters, "Your wedding—it is sad." And Raymond, jeering himself, laughs, "A wedding and a funeral!"

But Dillon, who has been thinking, breaks in: "Leave it in my hands, and the D'Arnacs shall have a lot of christenings *between* ! Bedad! now that we got rid of unpleasant company we'll toast the bride agin—and then go on to your aunt's where I presume there are bridesmaids, eh! young D'Aubigné."

"Let's try a game at billiards," remarks De Soubise. "You, Dillon, I presume are up in the new massé shot that is now the rage!"

To this the Austrian Embassador doesn't answer. He strolls silently out, a curious quiver on his lips, a kind of halting in his gait.

Some half hour after this, Charles de Moncrief coming into the little reception room, the smile of success upon his mobile features, sees a woman kneeling, her face buried within her hands as if in prayer.

"You can make confession to me?" he whispers. "I was once an abbé in the church," then hurriedly exclaims as she makes no answer: "Quick! I have not much time to act now. Give me the paper! You have had proof enough?"

"Too much—too much!" she moans, raising eyes to him in which there is some passion he cannot divine.

And he goes jeering on: "I have just seen the bride. She looks most beautiful. They will make a happy couple."

But while he laughs she has taken from her bosom a paper, and whispered: "This bears the holy cross! You are the Procureur du Roy. If I give this document to you, and charge you to use it in the name of the King, what does the law require you to do?"

"Oh, you need not fear—I'll use it!"

"What does the law require?"

"The law wisely decrees that I must at once give it to the proper officers to be executed on the person whose name appears within."

"And if not?"

"The crime is treason, and its punishment is death."

"Then," cries Jeanne, her eyes ablaze: "Take this and in the King's name use it!" And thrusts the document into his willing hands.

And he in triumph gloating over it cries: "This bears the name of Raymond d'Arnac!"

And she cries back to him: "No! It bears the name of him who to-morrow would have murdered my love, for my sake! That assassin—your friend—Gaston Lenoir!"

And passes out from him, leaving him stricken with despair and broken with disappointment.

But after a time, opening the document in his hand, in a dazed way, a sudden light comes into his eyes; he gasps: "It is *blank!* By all the gods! It's BLANK!" then grins and chuckles: "What a mistake? Fate has been kind to me at last! To-night De Moncrief triumphs!"

CHAPTER XXIII.

LA QUINAULT'S WEDDING GIFT.

DARKNESS has descended upon Versailles. The lamps are twinkling in the gardens of the King.

Amid lovely woods and pleasant grounds on the Avenue de Scraux the villa of the Comtesse de Crevecœur is a blaze of lights. The bridal party, though small, seems a merry one.

The bride is already making a sensation. The innocence of the convent injected upon the gay world of the court and capital produces laughter.

All has gone well in the afternoon.

Madame de Crevecœur, engaged in the exigencies and emergencies of an overpowering toilette (an opera-

tion that to a woman of her portly build is a tremendous affair), has deputed Mimi to receive Julie.

To that fashionable widow the convent-flower is
announced, and, coming in, gives evidence that she is
innocent of the world, even to its etiquette.

And Madame la Marquise smiles as Julie courtesies
quite humbly to the lackeys who announce her, making
her one—two—three—*down!* in schoolgirl fashion.
But the amusement is not all of the widow's side.
After being kissed, the bride cries: "Oh, what a
dress!" and looks at Mimi amazed; for Madame la
Marquise is arrayed, not as the lilies of the field, but
as Parisian *modistes* love to robe women who do not tax
their bills, and give them *carte blanche*.

"You like my toilet?" murmurs la Marquise,
blushing with pleasure; for Dillon will be here, and she
likes to look well in his presence.

"*Like* it? For that lace ruching I would give my
head! Shall I ever have one as lovely as it?"

"One much more lovely is now ready for you!"
laughs the Marquise.

"As gorgeous and with a longer train?" cries Julie.
Then putting inspecting eyes upon the beautiful woman
who stands before her, in convent innocence she covers
her with blushes, for she giggles: "Why, yours has
so much on the ground and *so little* on the body, I should
think you would be cold."

"Come, Mademoiselle *Ingénue*, and see!" murmurs
la Marquise, and hurries this child with candid tongue
to where the maids await her, to robe her in the white
cloud of gauze and tulle, and place the orange blosoms
of the bride upon her fair tresses.

So the *fête* comes on; the crowd is augmenting
rapidly. A number of the juvenile beauties of the
court of the boy king of France mingle with gallants
of the oldest titles and proudest families in France.

Madame de Crevecœur, receiving in gorgeous toilette, announces that the ceremony will take place at
nine o'clock in the private chapel of her residence.
Clothilde, successful in the city to-day, now feels successful at Versailles; this wedding that has been her
ambition next to her pocket—is about to be consummated.

The gorgeous trousseau of the bride—the wedding presents from the immediate members of the family—gleam in an adjoining *salon.* The strains from the king's own band, most condescendingly lent for the occasion by the boy monarch, and which is concealed amid shrubs and flowers, float through the air.

Clothilde, glancing over a note, remarks to Raymond as he stands beside her in the gorgeous trappings of the *Musquetaires:* "How annoying! The Duc de Villars writes me that the gout still claims him. He will not be here!"

"Did you tell him it was my wedding ceremony?" asks D'Arnac.

"No, I only wrote the invitation as I did to other people. I feared De Moncrief then, but do not fear him now. Good heavens! who are these people?"

"The gentleman and lady whose hospitality you enjoyed the other evening!" laughs D'Arnac. "Don't you remember him—the Chevalier Lanigan?" for Lanty is gorgeously arrayed, and his plump little bride, gleaming with diamonds, hangs upon his long arm as if he were the very staff of life.

"Bedad!" he whispers to her, "hold up your head, Lady Lanigan. You'll soon get accustomed to the quality."

So he makes his bow remarking: "It's foine times on the street we've been having to-day, Madame de Crevecœur."

And his hostess, happy at the thought of her grand speculation, laughs: "Very fine times, my dear Chevalier."

So they agree in words, but Lanty knows what he is talking about, and Clothilde, for her own peace of mind, fortunately does not.

"Comte!" whispers Lanty, taking Raymond by the arm, "has the little comtesse recognized ye yet as the butcher with the bloody coat?"

"No. I have not seen her yet—she has not yet been brought down!" returns D'Arnac, wondering if Julie will remember him under his uniform of the *Musquetaires.*

But now there is a hush, Madame de Crevecœur is

entering with the bride, and Raymond, as he turns and glances, is enraptured with the sight.

If Julie had been graceful in her plain convent garb, her fine feathers now make her a finer bird. In tulle and gauze and airy floating gown, she is a dream of innocence—though not the bashful innocence that brides are wont to have. She knows too little of the world for that.

At the entrance of the room her prattle absolutely brightens the fat dowager, who has her by the hand. "*Dieu merci!*" gasps the untutored one. "I never thought there were so *many* handsome men on earth before ? Do you like handsome men ? "

"A little!" laughs Mimi, who has come to Julie's side.

"Well I do *very much !* They love me, TOO!"

"What, already ? " cries Madame de Crevecœur with an awful face.

"Already four gallants followed me from the convent, and one I struck right in his eyes."

"Struck him!" gasps Mesdames de Crevecœur and de Chateaubrien in one astonished breath.

"Only with *my* eyes. He was an officer and wore a uniform, black as the robe of an abbess—but it was sparkling with golden things. And he had such a long moustache. Mimi, do you like long moustaches ? "

" "Sometimes," giggles the widow.

" "Well, I do *very much*. What kind of moustachios has Raymond ? Are they long and soft ? "

But Madame de Crevecœur's stern, pinching grasp is upon the soft arm of the bride, and with a muttered: " Come in! they're waiting for you! " she almost drags the prattling Julie into the assembly.

Then the young court beauties gather about her to be introduced—one, the fair young Ducesse de Longville, remarking: "It is a shame they kept you in a convent, with your beauty."

"Oh, that was to guard me from the naughty men," prattles Julie. "But I am doing finely now. I have had *four* gallants already. Have you done as well ? Besides, I am to be married now. Are you affianced ? "

But before Mademoiselle de Longville can make reply, the bride has turned to her aunt who stands beside her, grim as the statue of Medusa with the Gorgon head, and said: "There's one of my cavaliers —that one in the black uniform—the one with the long moustache. He is the handsomest of the four."

Suddenly the grim smile of Clothilde changes to one of joy. She whispers two words in fair Julie's ear that make her crimson, then beckons Raymond up and he, bowing before the convent blossom, kisses the girl's white hand as Madame de Crevecœur says: "Behold your bride!"

"Oh, he's seen me before," murmurs Julie. "He followed my carriage to-day;" then puts almost a pleading hand upon his arm and whispers right in D'Arnac's ear: "That was because you *loved* me!"

"Loved you!" murmurs Raymond, and the next instant she knows his moustache is very soft and his kiss· very sweet.

"It's lucky that you were the handsomest of the four," murmurs the bride, archly. "Otherwise I should have made you very jealous!"

"Oh, the dear child!" cries Madame de Crevecœur, overcome. "Here's proof of my wise bringing up in the seclusion of the convent. She loves the man selected for her as soon as she sees him."

"Egad!" laughs Dillon, for they have all gathered about the bride. "It's lucky she saw the right man *first*, or your educational ideas might have been shocked."

Catching his voice, Julie turns and babbles: "Why this is the comte—the gallant comte—who rescued me from that awful butcher, with the green and bloody coat."

"Bedad!" mutters the Chevalier Lanigan in Dillon's ear: "She's in love with the soldier clothes and brass · buttons, as many a girl has been before !"

Here, fortunately, Lanty's voice is drowned by laughter that comes up from the crowd; for Julie, turning admiring eyes upon Raymond once more, has suddenly cried: "Where is the priest? Bring us the *lazy* priest."

"Oh, the dear, enthusiastic child!" ejaculates Madame de Crevecœur. Then she suggests: "Go, look at your trousseau and wedding presents. Play with your diamonds till the bishop is ready for the nuptial mass."

"Diamonds!" cries Julie. "Raymond, *diamonds!* Come with me," and drags him to the neighboring *salon* to look at the beautiful gewgaws. Gazing on these, she laughs: "Why, I am more popular than you. All these lovely things seem sent to me."

"Except the loveliest of them all—and it is mine!" mutters D'Arnac.

And she looks upon him and her eyes grow happy. A moment after she suddenly says: "This present is for you," and hands Raymond a letter, the handwriting of which he knows very well.

Opening it he reads:

Raymond—I send you with my blessing on your wedding eve—safety from to-morrow's fatal meeting.

And he mutters to himself: "From Jeanne! She has learned of to-morrow's duel! What does she mean?"

Then suddenly his manner grows even more tender to the clinging girl who stands beside him as he thinks: "My bride to-night, to-morrow may be a widow!" He has little faith that anyone can stop Lenoir's sword after what has passed this afternoon.

How shall he tell his bride of what may come to him? And the brightness of the scene, the softness of its music, its mirth and gaiety seem to him a mockery; for the guests are now treading the stately minuet, the Chevalier Lanigan astounding them by some marvelous steps he has imported from Ireland.

Into this scene strolls Charles de Moncrief, a cynical smile on his face, arm in arm with Gaston Lenoir, whose eyes have a hungry look in them as they gaze upon D'Arnac.

"You are here, just in time, Monsieur Lenoir, and you, too, dear Nephew Charlie," remarks Madame de Crevecœur, "to see the happiness of my life fulfilled, and the wishes of my poor husband consummated. Congratulate me!"

"*After* the wedding," returns Nephew Charlie, suavely. "After the wedding, my dear aunt."

As for Gaston, he doesn't go near bride or groom,

though even as he chats court gossip with some of the fairest women in France his glance is not for them— only for Raymond. His mind has but one thought. In a kind of hang dog bravado he has come to look upon the nuptials of this man he will kill and this poor girl he will make a widow, if God will but suffer him.

It is approaching the hour of the nuptial mass, when into this bright scene is ushered Jeanne Quinault.

Mimi meeting her even in the toilette chamber, before she has thrown off her wraps, looking upon her face, divines she has already learned the object of the gathering.

Jeanne does not permit la Marquise to speak first. She whispers hurriedly, perchance the slightest quiver on her lips: "Is she worthy of him?"

"In youth and beauty, yes; in rank also."

"Of course—she is a comtesse, as I was last night," mutters Jeanne; then sighs: "In the name of mercy, why did you not speak *then?*"

"You stopped my tongue when you confessed your love," whispers la Marquise. And in a few words she explains the late Comte de Crevecœur's will and its effect on Raymond and his bride.

"Ah, now I see De Moncrief's reason," mutters Jeanne. "To-day is the *last* day!" next says lightly, perhaps even mirthfully: "Take me down, Mimi. Let me enjoy the wedding *fête* as the other guests!"

For to-night Jeanne is an actress and will play the lightness of the *comedienne,* if circumstances will but permit her.

Descending the great staircase together, Mademoiselle Quinault is received by the Comtesse de Crevecœur with the ceremony her position as hostess forces on her.

Hand in hand with Madame la Marquise, the actress moves away; Mimi keeping close by her side this night as if to shield Jeanne from any anguish the situation may bring upon her.

Suddenly la Quinault's eyes begin to blaze; she sees Lenoir! Then they rove over the assembly until they come on Cousin Charlie, as he sits with placid smile upon his face.

With a muttered "excuse me," she has left Mimi,

and is at De Moncrief's side, whispering: "Why is
that villain still outside the Bastille? Why?"

"All in good time," he purrs to her. "Wait and
behold your warrant executed."

But here Raymond, seeing this lady who had been once
his ward, and who is still very dear to him, comes hurriedly to her with the convent blossom clinging to his
arm, and says: "Julie, this is my dearest friend!
Jeanne, this is my bride."

And Mimi remarks: "This is Mademoiselle Quinault,
who has long been Raymond's ward."

At this Julie cries: "La Quinault—the great actress!" then murmurs as if astounded: "Why, I
expected to see you at least six feet high. They said
you were so grand! And then I thought—you
will excuse me—you would be so very *fat!* They said
you filled the stage."

"And so she does, and men's hearts, also, *petite!*"
answers Raymond.

To this Julie prattles: "If yours has escaped her, I
will give her all the rest, my husband!" and goes off,
hanging on his arm.

But even as she turns away, she whispers: "I have
seen her before!" then suddenly ejaculates: "*Why, she
is the lady who was in love with the butcher!*"

As these words reach his ear, D'Arnac's eyes meet
Jeanne's; and something in Quinault's look (for strive
how she will, anguish will sometimes dominate even
the *comedienne's* smile) tells Raymond that the chattering of his bride has told the secret of a woman's heart.

But now the wedding march is sounding!

Whatever had been his thoughts at any time about
this being, who seems perchance more beautiful than
she has ever been before, from this moment honor
shuts off even retrospection.

"It is *our* wedding march, my husband!" cries the
bride.

His wedding march—and not HERS! The agony
of it enters Jeanne's soul. The soft music seems dis-
cordant crash. The bright scene becomes blurred to
her sight, for her heart is crying: "This is the last of
him!"

Then—even as the nuptial procession is forming to

go to the little chapel, and Mimi has put one sympathizing hand in Jeanne's—into her misery comes one bright ray. She is giving him the life he would have thrown away for her good name !

Suddenly, through flunkies that stand aghast, and ladies who scream, and gallants who lay their hands upon their swords, a posse of *Sergeants de Ville* make their way; their officer saying: " Madame la Comtesse, the King's name is my excuse !"

" What is, this ? ' whispers la Marquise, growing pale.

"It is my gratitude and your brother's safety!" answers the actress, her eyes aflame. "See the holy cross upon the warrant! Now heaven's thunderbolt falls on Lenoir, who to-morrow would have killed your brother!"

"God bless you!" falters Mimi.

But suddenly la Quinault gasps: " They are passing him! Do they not know Lenoir ?"

And the scene becomes first cruel agony—then awful horror!

Raymond striding to the officer cries: " This is an intrusion, Sir, at such a moment!"

And the lieutenant answers him: "My duty permits no alternative! Raymond d'Arnac, in the King's name I arrest you!"

At this there is fear and commotion among the guests, and the bride is screaming!

And Raymond is muttering astounded: "Arrest ME!"—then suddenly, as if he understands: "Ah, I perceive—the Regent has heard of my coming duel with Lenoir—a bond to keep the peace. Accept my hospitality 'till the ceremony is over and I will, as a matter of form, report with you."

But the policeman says: " My duty does not permit. This affair is too serious. Your arrest is on a *lettre de cachet*, by which I am ordered to convey you to a state prison."

But Jeanne has broken away from Mimi and now is confronting the man crying: " A mistake! *This is my wedding gift!* That warrant is for Gaston Lenoir, the duellist! I know it—it was the one I sent—open the paper!"

"*Pardieu*! as if I could not read!" mutters the police officer, and opening the warrant the name upon the fatal paper reads: "Raymond, Comte d'Arnac."

Staggering back, Raymond in the laugh of despair, jeers: "You gave me *safety* from to-morrow's fatal meeting—*safety* in the Bastille; THIS IS YOUR WEDDING GIFT!"

And Mimi is before her faltering: "Jeanne, revenge upon the man you last night said you loved?"

And Clothilde reviles her with hoarse but sarcastic voice, crying: "The revenge of the *mistress* on the *bride!*"

And he, her victim, has stabbed her with these awful words: "To-morrow I would have given my life for your honor—to-night you give me for my life a living tomb!"

To which she cries out: "I am innocent! Forgive! As you hope for mercy on the Judgment day, FORGIVE!"

But he scarce hears her; the bride is now sobbing in his arms: "Raymond, my husband, they shall not part us! I will go with you!"

My God! he is bidding them good-bye!

They have taken his sword from him, and are hurrying him away.

The lieutenant of police is whispering: "To the Bastille!"

And these dread words have awed the company to silence, which is only broken by a despairing woman's cry: "FORGIVE!"

And he, looking back at her, answers—NOTHING!

Then to the wedding march, the strains of which still float in softest cadence from the flower screen of the *fête*, they lead him out, and Quinault hears the lookers-on whispering: "The revenge of the actress-mistress! Her charms have lured the warrant from the Regent!'

Just from behind her comes a low snickering laugh she recognizes.

With one gasping cry: "Traitor! It is *you!*" she stands confronting Charles de Moncrief, who, looking on her, smiles no more.

For she is muttering: "He did not say pardon. Then why should I *forgive*. Is truth eternal—is God just? when such things as you exist, to make this goodly

earth the home of devils ?" Then she cries hoarsely:
"But beware ! Another fiend has risen up in me !
VENGEANCE IS MINE !"

From her De Moncrief shrinks trembling, for he
remembers she has *another* of those dread documents of
state ; then quietly steals out, and drives as if for his
life to la Quinault's apartments in Paris.

———

CHAPTER XXIV.

AN ACTRESS' LOVE !

As DE MONCRIEF turns away Dillon's soft brogue
comes to Jeanne in sarcastic whisper : "Bedad ! ye
shouldn't play with swords until ye know the trick of
the weapon!"

He may sneer, but he believes !

She turns to him and answers desperately : "They
say I have power with the Regent ! To-night I'll test
it !" then mutters : "Keep Raymond out of the Bastille for two hours, and I'll defeat that villain yet !"

"Begorra !" interjects Lanty, "this is loike ould
toimes ! You and I, Gineral, can head the gentlemen
here, make a short cut to the Paris road, and butcher
the police as they come along with the prisoner."

But Dillon says : "It is not like old times. I am
the Austrian Embassador, and the Chevalier Lanigan, I
presume, does not wish to be made an outlaw for
attacking the power of the Regent himself !"

"Begob! I forgot—I'm married and settled."

But Jeanne cries : "Here is a greater power than
your sword ! Overtake the police ! Give this"—and
she pulls from her finger a diamond ring—"to their
leader. Spend money with them. Ask them to drink
at every wine shop on the road. Delay them so they
will not get to the Bastille before eleven o'clock to-
night. Surely you can get them to drink that much in
a ten-mile ride, dear Chevalier Lanigan."

"By St. Patrick ! I'll try it !" answers Lanty, and
runs out upon his errand.

"Forgive me, Jeanne, that I doubted you a second,"

whispers Mimi, putting her hand in hers. Then she says very anxiously: "What are you going to do?"

"This! Raymond d'Arnac shall not lose estates or bride! Bring Julie with you to my apartments. Get her there in time; by eleven o'clock at the latest."

But suddenly Clothilde is upon her, crying: "What —abduct the bride also, wretched woman? Perhaps you'd murder that dear innocent. God knows what an actress will do!"

And she would go on in this strain, and perchance delay and destroy all, did not suddenly at this moment Van Tamn, the stockbroker, come agitatedly in, his garments disordered with the dust of travel, his eyes wild with a broker's agony of exhausted margins and ruined credit.

Coming up to the comtesse, this old man, bowing, would whisper to her. But she says haughtily: "Enough, broker! No word of business to-night!"

Then he cries: "No word of business, eh? My God! she would put me off and ruin me! Make good your margins! *They now bid nineteen thousand* LIVRES *for the India Company's shares,* of which you owe me many thousands! MORE MARGINS OR I BUY YOU IN!"

At these awful words, Clothilde utters one despairing, ear-piercing shriek; then gasps "*Nineteen thousand livres!*—that villain Law!" and falls prone and insensible and *hors de combat.*

Looking upon her with a smile of disdain, Jeanne mutters to Dillon: "A carriage, for God's sake! Take me to the Regent, quick!"

As O'Brien offers his arm, D'Aubigné coming up, in the eager way of youth, says: "I trust you, too. What can I do for you this night?"

"You are an officer!" answers Jeanne. "Be ready with a fast horse outside the Palais Royal to take what I shall give you, at the corner of the Rue des Bonnes Enfants."

"You will find me ready, Madame!" cries the boy, and goes hurriedly away.

Then Dillon, cloaking Jeanne as deferentially as he would have done a queen of France, escorts the actress to her carriage, passing through the guests, most of whom are already going away with astounded faces.

Driving rapidly to the capital, they overtake and pass a silent carriage, surrounded by armed police. And Dillon remarks: "Egad! Lanty is doing his work;" for it is traveling very slowly.

As they ride on, Jeanne tells O'Brien of the mischance, how it had come about, and of the trick of Charles de Moncrief.

Some little time after, they enter the streets of Paris, and looking at the two remaining documents that she takes from her bosom, by the flicker of oil lamps, Jeanne sees a cross upon each of them and mutters: "There are more traitors than he! Who did this thing?"

"Bedad! some servant maid or attendant, whose hand Cousin Charlie has touched with gold," says O'Brien; "that's his sneaking way."

Then, after a moment's pause, Comte Dillon, who has seen, as embassador, a good deal of the Palais Royal clique in the last few days, remarks: "D'Orleans will be engaged in some revelry, and will not care to be interrupted in his sport."

"I must have audience with him, quick! How can you do it?"

And he answers: "But one man is sure to get the ear of the Regent whenever he wishes."

"Monseigneur Law!" she cries; then suddenly begs: "Tell the coachman to drive to the Place Vendome."

So some little time after ten o'clock this evening, they come to the great house of the financier, through a happy crowd, who are cheering and crying out with joy; for the stock of the India Company has gone up to such tremendous figures.

And Monseigneur Law, whose face is very anxious now, has word brought to him that a lady and gentleman desire an immediate interview. But he is very busy, and answer is returned by one of his gentlemen-in-waiting that the Comptroller of Finance can see no one this evening.

At this Jeanne falters piteously: "I must! Tell him Mademoiselle Quinault implores a word!"

But Dillon, who is looking on her face, and now has some pity in his heart for her, though he has been very angry at the mischance she has brought upon his friend, fighting with his very soul, whispers to the gentleman-in-waiting: "Tell Monseigneur Law that if he will give an interview within a minute to Comte O'Brien Dillon, he will not regret it."

These words seem magic.

Thirty seconds hardly pass, before Law, in his private office, his eyes bright, through apprehension, and with loaded pistols concealed in the desk at which he sits, sees O'Brien Dillon almost support into his presence the trembling figure of the lovely actress of the Français, who says in imploring voice: "For God's sake, save Raymond d'Arnac from prison to-night! He saved your life that evening at the Français—the night of my début—you remember. But for him you would be dead now."

"I am pleased to do anything for you, in my power!" murmurs the financier. "What do you want?"

And the affair being explained to him, Lass mutters between his clenched teeth: "So De Sabran lied to me when she said the Regent refused those *lettres de cachet.* Her passions have perchance ruined me!"

"Bedad! as her passions have made ye!" mutters Dillon. Then suddenly he breaks forth: "I never expected to ask favor of ye, but D'Arnac saved me from the galleys into which you put me. My grasp has been off yer throat because I represent his Majesty of Austria. But there will come a time when I am a simple gentleman again, and then, my Uncle Johnny!" and he smites his palms together in a longing kind of a way, as Uncle Johnny's hands tremblingly steal towards his pistols.

"What do you want?" he whispers hurriedly.

"An interview with the Regent *at once!*" gasps Jeanne.

"Impossible! I fear his Highness is at supper and will not be interrupted!"

"*You* must interrupt him!" cries Dillon.

"Why?"

"Because, if you do this, though I never thought to say these words to ye—if you get from Philippe d'Orleans, Regent of France, an immediate order for the release of the man I love, *ma boucha!,* so that

to-night does not rob him of his estates or bride —
I'll promise, even though it breaks my heart—not only
to forgive ye, but to aid ye, Uncle Johnny. And
perchance, from your looks to-night, ye may have need
of friends some time, not so far away."

. "I'm always pleased to help those who help me,"
exclaims the financier. "Meet me within twenty
minutes at the Palais Royal and I will have what you
want, if I can get it."

So driving to the portico of the great palace, within
fifteen minutes, Monseigneur Law comes hurriedly down
to them, and puts into Jeanne's hand a paper, saying:
"That is what you wish."

Then he looks at Dillon, some presentiment of the
future coming into his face, and mutters: "When I am
naked to my enemies, remember your words."

But they hardly wait to hear. Jeanne has flown to
the corner of the street where D'Aubigné is ready to
mount, and whispered: "Quick! to the entrance of
the Bastille? If they have not arrived, give this to the
officer when he comes up. Raymond's freedom from
arrest. If the portals have closed on him, demand
from the governor his release, and bring Comte
d'Arnac to my apartments, Rue de Condé, as fast as
horse can fly! Do this for me!"

"I will!" cries the young chevalier, but the last
of his words is lost as his horse darts along the Rue
St. Honoré.

Ten minntes after this, as Dillon assists Jeanne out
of the carriage in front of her apartments, another
coach drives up, and with a cry of joy Jeanne is at
its door - whispering: "Mimi—I've saved him—I
think—in time! Bring the bride in—she shall go out
the Comtesse d'Arnac."

So they all come hurriedly into Jeanne's little parlor,
where they are received by Madelon, who appears
sleepy and yawns: "Madame de—de Caylor has gone
to—to bed."

Curiously the lamps are lighted, and as Madelon
drawls that she is sleepy, her eyes are very bright.

Something metallic in the rustle of the girl's dress, as
she turns away, seems to catch Jeanne's ear. She says

suddenly: "Excuse me for a minute, dear friends; I will go to my chamber and throw off my wraps."

But Madelon, from the door of the apartment, flies quickly to her and proffers: "Let me take them off for you, Mademoiselle!" eagerly assisting her with her cloak and hood.

"Thanks! you are a willing child!" replies la Quinault. "Take this paper," and producing one of the *lettres de cachet* hands it to the girl, explaining: "It is of great importance! Place it in my jewel box."

"Yes, Mademoiselle," answers Madelon, with eagerness intense; and with quick step would leave the apartment; going towards Quinault's chamber.

But even as she is at the door, Jeanne cries: "Stop! Did I give you the *right* document? Is there a cross upon it?"

And Madelon, her hand even in the folds of her dress, the document away from her eyes, cries: "Yes, Mademoiselle, there is!"

"Come here! let me be sure."

And the girl approaching, a little reluctantly, the actress pounces on the paper, and cries: "You are right! There is the cross! But," and her eyes are gleaming now with suspicion: "How did you know that? You did not look at it as I spoke." Then she whispers in savage tones: "*Did you place it there?*"

And there is a cry for mercy, as the soubrette is on her knees.

As she sinks down, within Madelon's petticoats there is the clink of gold, and with one quick cry la Quinault has plucked a purse heavy with golden *louis* from the maid's pocket, and is jingling it in the air and laughing: "See, this little viper is rich!"

To which the maid snarls: "You shall not take it— it is mine!"

"Then who gave it to you?"

"I—I dare not tell!"

"You will not answer? Comte Dillon, please take this girl to the lieutenant of police. I accuse her of having robbed me!"

"Bedad! I'll have her there in a jiffy," answers Dillon, who has now some suspicion of what this affair means.

But even as he speaks, the soubrette cries: "The lieutenant of police ! Mercy, Mademoiselle, Mercy !"

And the actress cries: "Who gave you this money ?"

"It was—oh spare me—Monsieur de Moncrief *!*" And the maid astonishes them all by whispering: "He is in your chamber, looking for the other *lettre de cachet !* He came here, and said if he did not get it you would destroy him." Then she suddenly screams: "Madame la Marquise, plead for me ! "

For Quinault's hands are round her throat and Jeanne's eyes now are those that kill; and she is muttering hoarsely: "You expect mercy from me ? You, who have caused the man I love to hate and despise me !"

But Mimi is imploring her now: "Don't kill her—let her go—for heaven's sake ! Raymond will return!"

"Then, *if* Raymond returns, I may spare her !" cries la Quinault, and looking in the girl's eyes she whispers: "Pray for his safety, as you never prayed before ! My own wrongs I forgive—but not *his*—not HIS ! Now go!—Not *that* way ! To your own room; not to my chamber to warn your accomplice ! "

Then a new idea flying through her brain Jeanne whispers into the maid's ear some words of direction and says: "Now go ! you understand ? FLY!"

And Madelon speeding out, la Quinault mutters:

"Now, when he does return—he will surely forgive," and begins to laugh hysterically. "Ah ! I may have some news for you, Julie, that will make you forgive also !"

Here the *ingénue* astonishes them all; she walks to the actress and murmurs: "When I look on your face I can not believe you could do so great a wrong to one who has not injured you!" then suddenly kisses Jeanne and cries: "Give Raymond back to me!"

"If I can ! If I can !" murmurs Jeanne.

But even now the clock strikes half-past eleven, and Quinault gasps: "Will he never come ?"

At the stroke, comes in the maid servant and announces: "Everything is prepared, Madame !"

"Pray, girl, that he comes before midnight !" cries the actress. "For if not—if *not!*" At which Madelon wrings her hands and runs out affrighted; for into Quinault's eyes, as this night passes, Dillon looking eagerly on, sees something of the wild, desperate look of the hunted animal is coming.

Just then the soft tones of the Procureur du Roy are heard from the next room, calling: "Madelon, I can-not find it!" and entering suddenly Charles de Mon-crief starts back and would retire.

But Jeanne is laughing in his face: "Come in, Mon-sieur de Moncrief. Do not be so fearful! We are no strangers. You were doing Madelon the honor to call upon her. Cannot one of us assist you in your search? I suppose you were seeking what you could not find, for I have it with me!" she makes significant gesture to her bosom and whispers menacingly: "You shall see it some day—perhaps to-night—but in hands more powerful than those of a weak woman."

Here De Moncrief, who has eyes only for her, and has not seen Dillon, screams: "Give me that paper, or I will tear it from you!"

And he would advance upon her with desperate hand —but at that moment hears an Irish laugh, and turn-ing sees Dillon, and gasps: "You here?"

"Ah, faith! the more the merrier, my dear Cousin Charlie," whispers O'Brien. "Some day, when I am not Austrian Embassador, you will say: 'the more— the more horrible!'"

At his words De Moncrief would dart to the door, but Quinault cries: "Don't let him escape!"

So the Irishman, stepping to the entrance, De Mon-crief turns from him—he cannot look in Dillon's eyes.

Just here there is a noise of a carriage driving up quickly, and hasty voices come from the stairway. Above them all Lanty's, crying, "Begob! we've got him!"

And Jeanne has given a scream of joy, and the door has been flung open, and Julie is sobbing in Raymond's arms.

But the antique clock in the corner of the room points to fifteen minutes to midnight as Raymond is saying to Quinault: "Forgive, dear friend, I only doubted for a second!"

To this she murmurs, "Oh God, I thank thee! He asks *me* to forgive!" Then suddenly exclaims: "Ray-mond, I give you to your bride! Midnight is near—your marriage ceremony must be instantly performed. The house of D'Arnac must not lose its glory nor its power!"

But Raymond starts and mutters: "There is no .time !"

And she, smiling in his face, says : "But for me, there would not be—See !"

As she speaks, Madelon draws aside the curtains of the little dining-room which has been made into a temporary chapel ; for Jeanne has a religious heart, and worships each day before the cross of Christ.

The tapers are burning as in a chancel, and there is a cushion for the bride to kneel upon as Jeanne whispers : "The altar is prepared—the bride and groom are here !"

Here with a fearful chuckle De Moncrief jeers : "But not the *priest*—I do not see the *priest !*"

And they all cry out : "The priest !"

And Jeanne moans : "I had forgotten !"

To this De Moncrief, triumphant now, laughs : "There is no churchman within reach. The estates will yet be mine ! By the law I triumph !"

But suddenly the actress is standing over him and echoing his laugh, and crying : "By the law you fail ! Charles de Moncrief, you are the Procureur du Roy, and by that title have power to bind in marriage as strongly as any priest."

And D'Aubigné from the door calls out : "A Procureur du Roy once married a King of France."

Then Jeanne goes sternly on: "If I remember right, in your youth you took orders in the church, but lost your diocese through malfeasance in office. Once an abbé, always an abbé." And her voice becomes dominant as she commands : "Go up, and as an abbé do the only good action of your life. Bind both by the civil and the holy law."

And he, snarling at her, mutters: "I have the power, but will not use it! I respectfully decline!"

"You refuse ?"

"I do!"

"Then D'Aubigné," cries Jeanne, "have you, as I asked, kept some of the police outside?"

"They are here!"

"Then take this," and she gives him a *lettre de cachet*. "Tell them to arrest Lenoir on that warrant, and see he is in the Bastille by to-morrow morning. And if Raymond d'Arnac and Julie de Beaumont are not man and wife when the bells strike midnight, come to me for *the other !*"

"Bedad! Give me the other *lettre de cachet* now. I'll save ye a policeman! I'll drag old Cousin Charlie to the Bastille for you. It is any man's duty with the warrant!" cries Lanty eagerly.

At this they burst out laughing, all but Cousin Charlie, who gasps: "You will use the *lettre de cachet* on me?"

"You shall decide that, Monsieur de Moncrief," Jeanne jeers. "Shall to-night be your last in gay Paris? Or will you do my bidding? De Sabran hardly loves you well enough to ask the Regent to let you out."

At these words, a grinding of the teeth from Dillon frightens Cousin Charlie very much, and he moans: "I am at your command."

"Then go up and bind in holy wedlock Raymond d'Arnac and Julie de Beaumont. Quick!" Jeanne falters at the word, but still is jeering De Moncrief as he with sighs and whimpers takes his place at the altar.

Here Raymond comes to her and whispers: "I did not know before. Forgive me! As you love me, forgive me!"

And she laughs: "Pooh! an actress' love — a fleeting passion of the moment! One of the kind that comes to us emotionals of the stage;" then cries : "*Quick*, join your bride—YOU HAVE NO TIME!" And gleams on him with bright eyes hiding a breaking heart. "Go up and marry in your rank! Go up for the honor of the D'Arnacs!"

And he, turning slowly from her, takes the fair young comtesse's arm, and they sink kneeling before the man, who as an abbé, for the moment seems sanctified, as he performs the ritual of the church.

Dillon and D'Aubigné are kneeling also, and Mimi, in a hurried whisper, sobs: "Forget! and live for art!" then sinks in reverence also.

Then Jeanne, standing there as *Phèdre*, dying the

butterfly death, listens to the words that part him from her forever.

And, to her ears, come stealing the midnight chimes of neighboring church, and the soft organ tones of midnight mass. And she moans to herself: "*Their wedding bells!* For *me* no wedding bells will ever sound—for *me* their joyous peal will never ring out! But when their sound for many a happy bride comes stealing to the ears of the actress *whom the church curses* and the people say should only be made A PLAY-THING FOR THE GREAT—I'll know in all their tones heaven has blessed me for this night's ATONEMENT."

Then the solemn voice of Charles de Moncrief, writhing as he utters the words, groans out: "*I pronounce you man and wife!*"

And she responds with one gasping sigh: "*He is hers*, MY LOVE IS DEAD!"

And the actress falls fainting before the bride, as Julie rises—Comtesse d'Arnac.

BOOK V.

THE FLIGHT FROM FRANCE.

CHAPTER XXV

FICKLE PARIS.

INTO this same room, the next afternoon, comes old De Villars. He has at last conquered the gout.

"Madame la Comtesse de Friburg, discharge that stupid servant girl," he snarls. "She has not learned your title!"

To him, Jeanne, with pale face, and eyes big with suffering, falters: "I have none!"

"What! Has D'Orleans neglected his promise?"

"No, he gave me the patent of nobility, but I threw it away. I have no need for title now, for he is wed—wedded to *another*."

"Who?"

"The Comte d'Arnac!"

"Good God!"

"Last night, in this very room, he married the young Comtesse Julie de Beaumont. Good heavens! Don't swear so!" for from the old maréchal's lips oaths are coming worthy of a pirate of the sea.

"The ineffable poltroon!" he cries, "who came to me and promised the next time he saw you to speak of marriage."

"Yes, but you mistook. Raymond alluded to the Comtesse Julie Beaumont, to whom he has been affianced for years."

"God of heaven! did he play a trick on me?"

But she answers, sadly: "No, you mistake. Listen to me!" And she explains the affair to him in

trembling words, he sitting by and twirling his moustache and looking at her aghast, and muttering execra-
tions on Lenoir, and on Raymond and his snip of
a bride, as he calls little Julie.

A moment after, growing more calm, De Villars says:
"I will go to D'Orleans. This matter shall be rectified.
The title belongs to you. You cannot throw it away."

But she, placing in his hand the tiara of gems he had
sent the Comtesse de Friburg that Thursday night,
mutters: "He is wed! I have no use for rank. Now I
am all actress. No coronet shall ever deck my brow
—only the laurels of my art—dear old papa De Villars!"
And Jeanne once more puts her fair head upon
the old warrior's breast, and tears come to her, but
not of joy; for triumph in art will never fill a woman's
heart.

So after a little, going out from her, the old maréchal strides solemnly and sorrowfully away. He is
angry with them all, even with Jeanne for the moment.

But there is another sad-faced man in Paris this day,
in curious contrast to the happy and excited speculators on the Quincampoix, who cry out: "Stocks are
higher yet! We are richer than before!"

Monseigneur Law's face is ghastly white. He knows
the balloon is inflated to the bursting point. There
soon must come a rent; for every *livre* of real value he
has given the India stock, has been multiplied by the
greedy speculators on the street.

The various stocks his company have issued, amounting to something over sixteen hundred million *livres*,
have now reached the enormous quotation of *nine
thousand millions.*

But the higher shares go, the merrier become the
speculators, especially De Conti, D'Argenson, and the
Brothers Paris, who, though they do not buy much
now, keep talking of the wondrous riches of the New
World, all to be lavished upon the India Company, and
through it France.

"*Mon Dieu!* if they would give me time to develop
these colonies in *reality*, not develop them on *paper*,"
thinks Uncle Johnny seated in his office on this day—
the roar of the street coming to him, mingled with the
people's shouts of "*Vive* Monseigneur Law!"—"per-

chance eventually I might make these inflated values
real ones.   At present they mean ruin—my horse has
run away with me!"

But no thought of disaster is in his various sycophants and hangers on; every one congratulates him,
and none but happy faces are seen by him—save ONE!

Early in the day a desperate woman, being denied
entrance to Uncle Johnny's private office, cries out:
"I'll have his blood!"   It is Clothilde, with eager
bloodshot eyes—those eyes so often seen upon the stock
markets of the world—who waits for John Law,
and getting sight of him in the bank, screams: "Let
me at him!   He has ruined me!   He told me to
sell!"

And Uncle Johnny coming to her, says: "Madame,
you made a great fortune; is not that enough?"

"A FORTUNE? when I sold them SHORT by your
advice!"

Then he whispers to her, very low: "Keep them out!
In time they will fall!"

"Keep them *out?*   God of Despair! they're buying
them in for me as I speak. I'm a ruined woman!.
Don't you hear!   Twenty thousand *livres* a share!
Robber, liar!   Twenty thousand *livres!*"

And Clothilde, fainting and despairing, and calling
down the vengeance of heaven upon the villain who
has ruined her, is carried wild, raving and hysterical to
her home.

But though De Villars is sad, he has vengeance in his
heart.   His wrath falls most immediately and practi-
cally upon Lenoir.   That gentleman, by means of
his friends at court, some two weeks after this, getting released from confinement in the Bastille, De
Villars sends for him, and not mincing words over the
matter, says: "Scoundrel, resign from the army that
you have disgraced."

"*Parbleu!* Because I fought a duel or two, and have
perhaps a little more skill, and a little less bad luck,
than those who have come in front of me," sneers
Gaston at the maréchal of France.

"Your outrages in that line are bad enough, but what
I refer to is your conduct in Flanders, juggling away
the lives of brave young officers who were *rich*. Resign!

or a court martial! I may not be able to prove exactly *all* I shall charge you with—but I will prove enough to make you forever detested and forever execrated by every gentleman who wears the uniform of France!"

"*Sapristi!*" answers Lenoir, striving to carry the matter off. "What does it matter to me—a court martial!" I can make money enough in the Rue Quincampoix;" and goes away. But after a little, reasoning that he has no more chance of promotion with De Villars as his active enemy, and that a court martial will come very near to damning him before *everybody else*, Gaston Lenoir sends in his resignation as officer in the army of France and devotes himself to speculation, which now runs to greater riot than before. Everything is very feverish and stocks have now sudden and violent fluctuations, but scarce the rallying power they had a few days before.

The balloon looks as if it were going to burst.

The enormous prices cannot hold. There is not money enough in circulation to keep pace with them, and they commence slowly to decline.

At this, the wiser of the foreign speculators turn their stocks into bank bills and their bank bills into coin and specie, and ship them out of the country. And the end comes nearer.

Then Law, bringing his great mind to bear, tries to strengthen, in very desperation, the specie reserves in the Bank Royal. The Regent decrees, at his petition, that all payments of over one hundred *livres*, from town to town in France, shall be made in bills of exchange, not in coin.

Next driven nearer to the wall Law obtains an edict, that no subject of France shall hold in his possession higher than one hundred *marcs* in gold and twenty in silver.

And suddenly no one seems to have any coin. Nobles and *bourgeoisie* bury it in their gardens and hide it away in vaults, but will bring no more of it to the bank.

So things go on from worse to worse, till in May, 1720, D'Argenson introduces a bill in Parliament, which purporting to be friendly to the company of Monseigneur Law, actually ruins it, for it decrees that after a certain time the shares shall lose half their value. Scrip of 10,000 *livres* is to be worth but 5,000. And though Law pleads, begs, and fights against it, Parliament passes the edict, and thus brands the stock as not worth the price it is quoted on the street. And there is a fearful rush to sell! A panic so great that the Rue Quincampoix is cleared by troops. There is not room for the people who would dispose of their shares in that crowded lane.

The speculators, driven away from there, fly to the great Place Vendome, and there sell stocks not only for money, but for anything they can get for them in the way of trade—horses and carriages, wagons, and even vegetables and things to eat.

Then late in the summer the sponge is tossed up by the Regent, who, though he knows Law meant to make France great, and in his heart honors him and is his friend, yet is tired of fighting a battle he now thinks lost. Forthwith he issues a decree announcing that the Brothers Paris have been appointed to re-organize and put in liquidation the India Company.

And as Law's name is painted *out* and The Brothers Paris' painted *in*, upon the offices of that great company, the iron enters Uncle Johnny's soul. His dream of colonization and commercial grandeur dies.

Then personal enmity rises up to crush this man already crushed. Those who had fawned upon him and begged him for stock cry: "Down with him!" Those who have made money through him sneer at him! Those who have lost it by him curse him! And one, the Comte d'Evereux, even at the Regent's table, Law sitting by, offers to wager that in a month he will be hanged.

Just about this time there comes a courier riding post haste to Raymond, summering on his beautiful estates upon the river Oise, his pretty comtesse laughing through life, beside him; for D'Arnac has resigned his command of the garrison of Paris.

This messenger brings a packet marked "On official business."

As he opens this the fair Julie whispers: "What does it mean?" for she has learnt to read her husband's face, and it is very serious.

He says: "I must leave you to-night! I am ordered on special service."

"For what? Not for the plague—that awful plague that is in Marseilles now, ravaging and killing all? My God! they are not going to send you there—Raymond—my husband!" she screams.

And he answers: "Nonsense! Doctors are needed at Marseilles—not soldiers. De Villars simply wants to see me."

Finally soothing her fears, he bids her good-bye, though she sobs upon his shoulder; then with soldier's promptitude takes horse, and riding for his life, for that is what De Villars commands, the next day is in Paris.

Not even stopping to greet Madame de Chateaubrien, he rides direct to the house of his old chief, De Villars.

That gentleman receives him very grimly. He says: "I have sent for you, because you are a man who can hold his tongue;" then growls savagely, "TOO WELL! I cannot explain the service required of you, though I can guess. But if you will go to D'Orleans——"

"What is it he wants me for?"

"Well, I'll whisper in your ear, but after I have whispered, don't think you heard me!" And the maréchal, putting his snowy moustache against D'Arnac's ear, mutters: "It is to get Law out of France alive!" Then he goes on in low conversational tones: "You always had a kind of sneaking friendship for that bubble-blower, D'Arnac. He made you very rich, I believe, and you are not one who forgets a favor. D'Orleans thinks you will remember it now, even to the risk of your life. As you ride along the streets to the Palais Royal, you will see how well the gentleman who I imagine will be your care shortly, is loved now that his bubble has lost its rainbow hues and become soap suds again."

As D'Arnac goes out on the street and rides to the Palais Royal, he observes how Monsieur Law is regarded by the fickle crowd of Paris, who eight months before had worshipped him. On the walls he sees caricatures of poor Uncle Johnny, driven in a triumphant car, being married to the goddess of shares by the goddess of folly, who officiates as priest.

And another more horrible one, at which a crowd are gathered, jeering—a picture of Law boiling in a cauldron over flames of popular madness; also this extraordinary placard, which it would be difficult for him to miss, for it is posted by the thousands on the walls of Paris:

Beelzebub begat Law!
Law begat Mississippi!
Mississippi begat the System!
Paper begat the bank!
The bank begat bank notes!
Bank notes begat shares!
Shares begat stockbrokers!

Hello! here we are at Beelzebub himself again!

In front of the Palais Royal Raymond sees a strong detail of the *Musquetaires*, for the Regent has determined to save at least the life of this man he knows would have made France glorious in her colonies, if he himself perchance, had not been quite so lavish in his expenditures, and the public had not been quite so greedy.

Passing through the troops, D'Arnac quite shortly finds himself in the presence of D'Orleans and Uncle Johnny, and stares astonished, for the Regent has the atrocious stockbroker placard in his hands, and is laughing at it fit to kill himself, and poking Uncle Johnny in the ribs.

"Egad!" says D'Orleans, stifling his mirth, "I'm glad to see you, D'Arnac, and I think Monseigneur Law, whom you know, is perhaps more happy."

"I have called, your Highness, at the request of the Duc de Villars, to say I am entirely at your command, whether as a matter of military duty, or of personal service," answers D'Arnac, saluting.

"This service," remarks D'Orleans, "is a personal one. I do not ask it as the Regent of France, but simply as Philippe d'Orleans, whom you are privileged to refuse, for it may perchance involve the greatest personal risk."

"I am still at your orders," answers D'Arnac.

"Well, then," here D'Orleans comes close to him and whispers: "This I say to you must be most secret.

I will forgive you if you refuse, but if you divulge, I will never forgive you. It is to get my friend, Monseigneur Law, safely out of France."

"I am under great personal obligation to him, your Highness. I will get him out of France alive, or not live to come back to you."

"Bravo!" cries Philippe, who is happy to have the matter off his mind. Then he adds lightly: "Did I not tell you, my dear Law, that here would be a gentleman who would remember?"

"When do you wish to start?" asks Raymond, with military abruptness.

"Well, this is about my plan," replies the Regent. "I wish you to take some half dozen gentlemen with you, those you can trust—perhaps some of your younger officers. They must not wear the uniform of France, but must be armed to protect if necessary the gentleman they escort. You will go secretly!" Then he remarks, turning to Law, "What time will suit you best?"

"To-morrow evening, with your Highness' permission."

"Yes, that will give me to-morrow to make arrangements," says D'Arnac.

So the affair is very shortly settled. Raymond is to leave Paris the next evening at ten o'clock, and travel rapidly, escorting Monseigneur Law and such belongings as he can take with him, to the Low Countries.

After a few minutes' more conversation, D'Arnac takes his leave, the Regent saying kindly: "I presume this affair will give you many things to arrange. But if you can, General, come to my supper table at eleven."

Passing out from the Palais Royal, Raymond now turns his face towards his sister's house upon the Rue St. Honoré. Here he is received with surprise by Mimi, also the Comtesse de Crevecœur, who is now living with her niece, upon her widow's jointure from the estates of her late husband, her private fortune having been swept away that woeful day that she accepted Uncle Johnny's hint. Clothilde still remembers the financier unkindly. She asks Raymond in vindictive voice, if he has hurried to Paris to see that villain, Law, that robber of widows and orphans, hung.

To this lady's inquiries, D'Arnac simply says that
he has come on military business to the capital—still
being Colonel of the *Musquetaires* it is necessary sometimes to look after his regiment.

A moment after he asks Dillon's address, for that
gentleman, when Raymond had left his sister's house,
had hauled down the flag of Austria, the *convenances* of
society demanding his departure too.

"Comte Dillon," remarks Mimi, perchance the
slightest flush on her fair cheek, "has at present, I
believe, very handsome apartments only a square from
here, on the St. Honoré."

"You *believe* ?" says Clothilde jocularly. "How
many notes have you addressed to him, Mimi ?"

"More than I can recollect," laughs the widow lightly.
Then she adds suddenly : "But Comte Dillon is no longer
the Austrian Embassador."

"No ?"

"He resigned to-day the embassy to his *charge
d'affaires*, and is now a private gentleman. His suc-
cessor is already here, the Prince Esterhazy. I believe
Comte Dillon departs for Vienna to-morrow. He came
to say *adieu* to-day." This last is uttered a little tremu-
lously by Madame la Marquise.

"Then as I shall not see him here," replies Raymond,
"I will call on him myself."

Soon after this he is at the apartments of Dillon.
Obtaining audience, he notes curiously a strange look
in his old comrade's eyes, one unusual to him in the
last few months he has been in Paris ; for with the
honors of the Emperor of Austria upon him, Dillon's
smile has generally been light and his eyes happy.

Now there is a fixed look on his face, and his answers,
even to D'Arnac, are short. He says: "Yes, I leave
to-morrow for Vienna. It was only expected I should
remain as the representative of his Majesty some short
time in Paris."

"You will return soon, I hope ?" queries Raymond.

"That I do not think possible. There are now two
good reasons for my leaving Paris. Faith ! one is, I
like it too much—and the other is, I have business
away from it. To tell you the truth, I may not be back
for years—perchance never !"

"You leave to-morrow night ?" says D'Arnac.

" Yes," replies the other.

"Can you tell me where the Chevalier Lanigan is ?"

" Faith, yes !" laughs Dillon. " The Chevalier Lanigan can be found at his hotel, ' The Turk's Head Inn.'
The Lady Lanigan now takes the cash in his café."

"Good heavens !" cries D'Arnac, "what has become of his fortune ?"

" He has saved some of it, but not all. In fact a
good many of them have lost more. There has been a
pretty general cleaning out in the greedy speculators of
the street. Old Chambery blew out his brains after the
second great fall in stocks. A number of our other
friends have come to grief—only more so !" goes on
Dillon sarcastically. " That scoundrel Lenoir is now
a bankrupt and a beggar, and as for your Cousin Charlie, egad ! they say he won't get off with his life ;
that indictments are being found against him and
two other directors of the royal bank for embezzle-
ment, perjury, and cooked accounts. Law could not
save him if he would. Faith, me Uncle Johnny's
got enough to do to take care of himself. He'll be
lucky if he escapes alive from Paris, though they say
D'Orleans is still his friend and will get him out, if possible, of the country."

"You seem to think you know the movements of the
Palais Royal pretty well," says Raymond lightly.

" Bedad ! and I do, better than some of them think !"
laughs Dillon, but it is a nasty, sneering laugh.

· "Then I'll see you to-morrow," says D'Arnac.

And a moment after, getting upon the street, O'Brien's
last remark comes back to him, bringing with it this
question : " Why has Dillon so unexpectedly resigned
the embassy of Austria ? Is it because he guesses Law's
intended flight, and judges the time is ripe for his revenge ?"

This forces Raymond to a change of plans. He had
hoped to have Lanty's assistance in this affair ; but
now he dare not engage the Chevalier Lanigan, fearing
somehow it may get to Dillon's ears.

So going to the *Musquetaires*, he selects this evening from the younger officers, some four gentlemen,
whom he knows have too much of the soldier in them

to have ever dabbled in the speculation of the street. He simply bids them come with him, to say no word about it to any man ; but to be ready, dressed as private gentlemen, when he gives them word, and appoints D'Aubigné to act as lieutenant.

So these preparations being complete, he turns his attention to selecting the proper route of travel, and decides upon the old way out of Paris—the one he had rode that night with Hilda de Sabran—the road to Mieux. From there he will turn to the north. He chooses this because he knows the route so well in the darkness.

Having made his arrangements D'Arnac calls at the Palais Royal to make his report; and at the Regent's brilliant supper table sees Hilda de Sabran—though her eyes are restless and her smile troubled, beauty is still upon her cheek—she is as lovely as before—she gives him one glance—but it is of entreaty, not love; in fact the glances of her fair eyes to every one within the room are those of fear and pleading this night.

Why? Raymond cares not to guess, and doesn't stay to divine. He has too much to do on the morrow and must have sleep now—for he expects none the coming night.

Early the next day his preparations being completed he calls on Dillon to say farewell, and finds that gentleman hurriedly engaged in packing, and with him, to his astonishment, Lanty.

"Be Saint Patrick! hadn't we better get him to come with us?" cries the Irishman.

But Dillon says sternly to his follower: "No!"

And Raymond now guesses that he has perhaps a harder matter to get Uncle Johnny safe out of France than he has before thought. He cannot bear to think of combat with his old friend. He will try strategy, and to this he devotes his mind.

So that evening he directs D'Aubigné to rendezvous at ten o'clock with the four gentlemen equipped for long and steady riding and armed *cap-a-pie* outside of the barracks on the Charenton road.

At half-past nine o'clock he carelessly strolls to the Palais Royal, on foot; his horse is to be ready for him by D'Aubigné's side.

Admitted by the private entrance, Raymond, coming into the chamber of the Regent, finds Uncle Johnny ready for the journey.

A private carriage filled with baggage is waiting in the great courtyard.

" This will not do," remarks D'Arnac.

"Why not?" says D'Orleans, who has come down with his friend.

" It might be followed. I don't want to fight if I can help it."

" Certainly not! " replies Monseigneur Law.

"What do you propose?"

"This. Get two other carriages. Send one out now—let it drive to the south ; send another out half an hour afterwards—let it drive to the north. If these are followed, they will leave the way clear for Monseigneur Law and myself."

"Bravo!" says the Regent. And shortly after, at his orders, two other carriages are in waiting, and one is driven out very rapidly through the great entrance, turning to the south, and going out of Paris that way. Half an hour afterwards, another leaves, and journeys to the north, under orders to proceed towards Compiegne.

Then the one for Monseigneur Law is drawn up, and the Regent, shaking hands with his financier, the two look at each other for the last time upon earth. Their parting is short, D'Orleans simply saying : " It was my fault—not yours." And Law remarking : " It was the will of Providence, and a woman's unreasoning passion. If I had had those *lettres de cachet!* "

" *Pardi!* " remarks D'Orleans, " let us not cry over spilt milk. Hilda's sorry now—infernally sorry. I've just suggested to her that her husband is waiting for her." At this the two laugh sadly, and bid each other good-bye; Raymond wondering what D'Orleans means.

Then Law steps in, and D'Arnac seated opposite him with two loaded pistols on his lap, directs the driver of the coach to proceed slowly at first, as if in no hurry, and getting to the Port St. Antoine, pass out by that gate and along the road by the barracks of the *Musquetaires.*

CHAPTER XXVI.

THE LAST STAND.

So THEY drive through the streets of the city still lighted brilliantly with the oil lamps, still thronged with the crowds that Law had brought to it, still filled with the trappings of that wealth this man has made to congregate in Paris and *stay there.*

For no matter its fluctuations, whether it has been held by invading armies, whether it has lost enormous sums by outside speculative enterprises, Paris from that day to this has always been RICH!

A great crowd in one of the thoroughfares they pass through is gathered about a new placard that has just been put up, entitled, "The wedding of Monseigneur Law and the Queen of the Mississippis!" At this the Parisian mob are hooting wildly.

Looking on them, Uncle Johnny says: "*Pardi!* If they guessed that I am here!"

Then he gives a sigh and relapses into silence until they pass out of the town near the Charenton road. Here Raymond giving the signal, D'Aubigné and his followers join them, one of them leading a horse for D'Arnac's use.

"Who are these?" asks Law anxiously.

"Your escort," remarks Raymond, preparing to alight and mount.

But his charge says to him: "For God's sake stay with me! Talk to me! Don't let me think."

"Very well. Until we come to the wood of Blondy," remarks Raymond. "There we may meet footpads, perchance banditti." For many of the gamblers who have lost their all in the Rue Quincampoix, and many who never had anything to lose, have taken to the highways to make a living. One half of Paris is robbing, pilfering and murdering the other half. It is the days of Cartouche!

So they drive along, D'Aubigné and his companions following close after them.

Perchance feeling himself at least safe out of Paris, Law commences to chat easily. After a little, turning his conversation upon events that have lately taken place, he gives D'Arnac some curious information.

"I suppose," he says, "to-night there are some more unhappy than I. I at least have the friendship of the Regent. Those who betrayed me have not."

"Betrayed you! Who?"

"Why, your cousin!" breaks out Law. "Charles de Moncrief! He did not tell me the Regent had given Hilda the three *lettres de cachet* that would have shut my enemies up in the Bastille until too late for them to bring about my ruin. And then De Sabran, who let her jealousy and her hate of the emotional Quinault rob me of them! Had I known it that night I would have got them from the actress, she would have had her title—I would have destroyed my enemies —and you, my dear D'Arnac, would not have come as close to the gates of the Bastille as you did!" This last is said with a kind of sighing laugh.

Then he breaks out: "Retribution has come upon them. Charles de Moncrief to-night was charged by the Parliament with treason in embezzling the funds of the Bank Royal, and Hilda de Sabran this evening (so I have it from D'Orleans, who has suddenly become virtuous), is about to be transferred to the authority of her husband, your friend Comte Dillon—who has resigned his post of Embassador of Austria, to take her to Vienna, where I imagine he thinks a perpetual convent will be the safest place for his erring spouse."

"D'Orleans give up the beauty of Hilda de Sabran?" murmurs Raymond, almost incredulously.

"*Pardi!* Did not *you?*" chuckles the financier.

"I had my reasons!" answers Raymond, shortly.

"Philippe has his also!" remarks Law. "Besides, six years is a long time for D'Orleans to worship *anything*, and there are newer faces, though doubtless not as pretty, about the Palais Royal now."

"So that is the reason Dillon is leaving for Vienna."

"That, and possibly because he wants a free hand against his enemies, who are now naked to him. As the representative of the Emperor of Austria, Comte Dillon's hand would be tied!" remarks the financier so easily that Raymond is astonished.

But conversation is here stopped by D'Aubigné riding up and saying they are entering the forest of Blondy.

Thereupon Raymond mounting his horse, with

D'Aubigné by his side, precedes the carriage as it moves along.

Getting through this wood safely, between twelve and one that night, they reach the village of Claye, stopping at the post-house that D'Arnac remembers very well.

Its appearance is the same as when, nearly six years before, he had approached it on his elopement from *Des Capucines* with Hilda de Sabran.

Perchance it is some memory of this that makes him sigh as he dismounts, for the landlady who comes to the door of the little *auberge* is the one who had welcomed him that other evening.

But important matters are on D'Arnac's mind; though every arrangement has been made in advance by couriers preceding the party, both as regards secrecy and speed; a private room being ready to which Monseigneur Law can instantly retire to prevent any chance of recognition by loungers about the posthouse.

That gentleman is immediately conducted to a chamber up stairs, while D'Arnac superintends getting fresh horses into the coach. In this he is slightly delayed; another carriage is standing in front of the *auberge* also waiting for its relay.

As he hurries the sleepy postboys, Raymond suddenly starts, for as well as he can discover by the dim light of a lantern held by one of the grooms, he thinks he sees, for one moment, a familiar figure striding into the stables. It looks like Gaston Lenoir. What can this man want here?

He steps hurriedly to the door of the stables, but sees no evidence of the individual he is seeking, and thinking he must be mistaken soon enters the inn with D'Aubigné to take a little refreshment before proceeding on their way to Mieux.

This finished, D'Arnac rises from the table, to summon Monseigneur Law. In the hallway meeting the landlady he says: "Which room?" pointing up stairs.

And she, remembering him, laughs: "The one at the rear! It is the most retired."

So Raymond springs up the stairs, and opening the door, being in too much hurry for ceremony, whispers: "Everything is prepared!"

He is answered by a scream, part of terror, part of recognition, from a lady, and a shriek for mercy from a man; and stands astonished. By the flickering candle light he sees Hilda de Sabran, her eyes big with astonishment, and Charles de Moncrief, who has fallen on his knees before him, begging him for the sake of his kinship and his blood, not to arrest him and drag him back to Paris to be hung!

"You need not fear me; though I have wrongs enough to wish your death. I am no *sergeant de ville*," he says grimly; then adds sarcastically: "What are you doing here with this lady—the wife of my friend, Comte Dillon?"

"You—you are some emissary of my husband!" cries De Sabran; and leaving Cousin Charlie groveling upon the floor, she strides towards Raymond and whispers: "You can kill me, but you can't take me back to put me in his charge! No Viennese convent of black nuns for me! No dark cell and penitential prayers. No black bread and haircloth dress and disciplinary scourge for life! I die or live *free!*"

Then as he answers not, perchance she thinks that the beauty he once loved may still be potent, and whispers: "You remember this very inn where you first loved me? Where I first looked upon your handsome face, my Raymond, that was never to be mine! You remember?"

And seeing in his glance perchance some tenderness of recollection, she bursts out imploringly: "In that memory I ask you but one favor—don't put my husband upon my flying footsteps. Let me pass out unscathed into another land!"

"He is not in pursuit of you!" answers D'Arnac.

"If not now, he will be. We played a ruse upon him in the city. He thought D'Orleans would place me in his hands to-night. But I know he will pursue me. Do you want my blood upon your hands? If not, keep a silent tongue! Don't tell *him!*" .And her eyes that are very close to his seem to say: "You loved me *once*, why not AGAIN?" as her soft tresses brush caressingly his cheek.

But here Charles de Moncrief, plucking up courage, cries jealously: "Siren, would you make him love you before my very face when you have beguiled me to the risk of my life into taking you with me?" next mutters: "Where is that poltroon, Lenoir, whom I hired to guard me? Did I not give him ten thousand *livres* to protect me from pursuit? Why is he not here?"

So Raymond leaves them, and for the last time looks upon the beauty of this woman whom once he would have made his goddess, had not his friendship for her husband and her own crimes prevented.

A moment after he has found the chamber of Monseigneur Law, who has made a very comfortable meal while the horses have been changed.

Then coming down to the carriage that has been drawn up in waiting, to his astonishment, Raymond sees Hilda de Sabran just stepping secretly in the darkness out of the coach of Monseigneur Law and into the other one of Cousin Charlie which is now driven hurriedly away.

Why Hilda has stepped into the coach of Law for a single moment he has no time to inquire, for the one bearing Cousin Charlie and Hilda, attended by a single horseman whom he now recognizes as the duellist, is already on the post road and has turned, going towards the south and Italy.

A moment after D'Arnac has Monseigneur Law in his carriage, and they, keeping the road to the east, drive towards Mieux.

In the early morning light, just as they are about to enter the town, D'Aubigné, who is riding behind, suddenly puts spurs to his horse, and coming beside Raymond, whispers: "We are pursued!"

"By how many?"

"Two men, I think. They are riding very hard. I cannot distinguish anything more in the uncertain light."

"Then you and I pause here, D'Aubigné, and we'll see what these people want."

So the two reining up their horses, the cavalcade attending Monseigneur Law passes on.

A minute after D'Arnac finds himself confronting his old comrade, O'Brien Dillon, who, with Lanty just in his rear, comes spurring along the road.

"Halt!" says Raymond, sharply.

"In whose name!" cries Dillon.

"In the name of friendship!" answers D'Arnac.

"By St. Patrick! is it you?"

"Yes," replies Raymond, "I'm charged by one whose name I shall not mention with the safety of the gentleman in that carriage."

"Uncle Johnny, bedad!" says Lanty.

"Yes, Monseigneur Law!"

"He is safe from me," replies O'Brien. "I promised him, for your sake, Raymond, that I'd spare him, though it broke me heart to do it. It's what saved ye from the Bastille and gave your bride to ye."

"Thank God!" whispers D'Arnac, a great load lifted from his mind: the fear that he might have to meet in deadly combat his comrade of the sword.

"But," continues Dillon, "I did not swear mercy to the woman who has disgraced my name, and I will pluck her out of me Uncle Johnny's coach!"

"That you can do with pleasure," remarks D'Aubigné.

"She is not with us!" adds Raymond. "Hilda de Sabran neither left Paris with us, nor is with us now, nor will be with us to the end of the journey."

"You give me your word of honor as a gentleman to this effect?" whispers Dillon, his face white with disappointment.

"Certainly!" replies D'Arnac.

"Then which way did she go? I traced her as far as Claye, and thought certainly she was with you."

"Bedad!" says Lanty, "I got word in the stables there of another coach going to the south. There was a very old gintleman in it that scattered his money like water, and a gintleman that rode on horseback beside him."

"But the lady stepped into your carriage!" cries Dillon.

"She did!" answers Raymond hurriedly, "but out of it again and into the other."

Then he stops suddenly, biting his tongue, as Dillon cries: "That's one of Cousin Charlie's little games! I know him! They're in the other carriage, Lanty—six or eight hours the start of us! But I'll overtake them yet! *Both* enemies together! That's enough for me—the two I want! Come!" And with hardly a word of farewell, such is his haste, O'Brien Dillon turns his horse about and gallops off, as if speed were his only object in the world, Lanty following him.

A few minutes after Raymond overtakes Monseigneur Law's carriage. He has been looking back with some anxiety, but on seeing Raymond his face becomes serene again.

Half an hour after, arriving at Mieux, they change their direction, turn to the north, and take a more direct road to Flanders, where, four days afterwards, Raymond acquits himself of his promise to the Regent, and delivers Monseigneur Law safe in the Low Countries.

On that same day in the southern part of France, along the dusty road, in the first light of morning, a post-chaise bearing Charles de Moncrief and Hilda de Sabran passes out of Avignon, Gaston Lenoir riding doggedly behind.

By means of money lavishly scattered along the post route, the greatest possible speed has been attained, and they at last think themselves safe from pursuit.

They are at the commencement of the great Rhone Delta, where the river scatters itself in several branches running towards the sea. Almost directly south, a little to the east of this Delta, lies Marseilles upon the Mediterraean.

There would be safety for them *there* from any man— from any hate; for no vengeance would lead man into the awful pestilence that ravages Marseilles.

The plague has come upon it from the Levant.

The great blessing of being made a free port the year before, by the agency of Law, has brought to it the commerce of the Mediterranean. But in one of the barks sailing from the pestilential East has come a plague as awful as even the black-death of three centuries before.

Fostered by the inadequate sewerage of the city flowing through open gutters into the very basin of the port, and nurtured by the hot sun of this burning summer, this pestilence has grown until it waves the sword of death above all who remain by force of circumstance or force of duty, in the dread city. The rest have fled from it.

As De Moncrief and his party have approached, even before they come to Avignon, evidences of surrounding panic, fear and flight have reached the Procureur's watchful eyes. From Lyons even, there has hardly been a postchaise journeying to the south. All have been coming north. This has made their relays of horses easy and quick.

At Avignon, the host of the inn has whispered to De Moncrief : "*Mordieu!* you are not going *further* south!"

"Yes."

"You are crazy!"

"I am going to Toulon, and so to Italy. There's no pestilence there."

"Ah, that is better—though it is the south!" whispers the innkeeper.

"Oh, that is safe enough!" says Cousin Charlie. "I have no idea of risking myself in the awful plague!" and grows pale at the word. "I keep the east bank of the Durance—forty miles from contagion."

"*Pardieu!* you could not get the postboys to drive you, if you turn towards Marseilles. Every one is coming from there. They die a thousand in a day. So God be with you!" replies the host of the auberge. "You will have a quiet journey. No other carriage these two days has gone towards the south."

So, with the Durance flowing on their right hand, they are journeying rather slowly along the dusty road; for the sun is just rising and the August heat this day promises to be something awful.

Avignon is eight miles behind them. Foaming in its rocky bed, the swift Durance on their right, appears, by its cool current fresh from Alpine snows, to cut them off from the pestilence in the hot plain to the south;— its living waters seem a boundary to the plague.

De Moncrief, feeling safe now from pursuit, they are so far from Paris, looks at the beauty sitting beside him and rejoices that it is all his; for Hilda, as the fear of O'Brien Dillon has grown more distant, has regained all her old loveliness and charm.

Heat has caused a summer toilet.

In its light robes and laces, she looks as airy and cool as does the foam of the sparkling Durance. Her white arms move in graceful gestures, her blue eyes blaze with the opal fire, her beauty is scarcely of this earth as she thinks: "How soon, when safe in Italy, I will cast off this hideous old gentleman, who nauseates me with senile love." Her laugh is now as merry as Cousin Charlie's.

About this time, Lenoir, who has done his work of protecting them and looking after them very well (for he hopes to get a little more than the ten thousand *livres* De Moncrief has paid him for this service, which, in his beggarly condition, has almost kept him from starvation), comes riding up to them, and says: "I see a cloud of dust that seems to be following us."

"How far is it away?" asks Hilda.

"Four miles, I should judge. Even from this hill-top I can only see the cloud of dust rising by the road-side."

"This is curious," mutters De Moncrief. "Few carriages are traveling towards the south."

And De Sabran mutters : "Tell the postilions to whip up!" in a nervous way.

These orders being given, they quicken their speed, encouraging the postboys by a promised largesse.

But after a little, Lenoir coming to them again, says: "The cloud of dust is nearer."

"Drive faster!" cries De Moncrief to his riders. "One hundred *livres* each if you leave those who are behind us!"

And with whizzing whips and biting spurs the post-boys do their work. They pass Caumont quickly, the Durance flowing cool beside them, as if in mockery of the heat and dust of the scorching road.

But they do not seem to gain—perchance they lose a little. The cloud of dust is nearer to them still.

"We are surely pursued by some one!" cries Lenoir.

Their pace is amended again, for De Moncrief offers more money to the postboys. But their horses are jaded with the heat. The postchaise is heavy; besides their baggage, De Moncrief has in it not only a large amount of paper bills, but specie, which weighs heavily —what he has suddenly gleaned up of his great fortune before leaving Paris.

The pursuing vehicle, apparently traveling lighter, still continues to gain. In its dust they can now dis-tinguish (for they look back often and anxiously) four horses dragging the lightest kind of post-chaise used in travel.

De Moncrief shouts: "One thousand *livres!*" to the boys. " Get me to Cavaillon ahead of them who follow after!"

Pushing wildly on, they gain Cavaillon first.   Here fresh horses are put to their carriage.   But just as they are dashing from the post-house, another coach comes flying up, and as they drive away, horror and consternation are upon them, for they hear Irish voices crying out behind them, and one of these is that of O'Brien Dillon.

"We cannot escape him!" mutters Hilda, growing very pale.

Then with desperate eyes and lips that tremble as he speaks, De Moncrief says words to her that make her cower down, shivering: "Holy Virgin! not *that!*"

And the procureur's hands are trembling and his voice is husky as he cries out: "There is *no other* chance! *It* may spare us! That Irish fiend never will!" and he whispers words to the postilions that make the postboys turn pale also.

But he cries to them a sum of money that will make them rich.   And they, turning their horses' heads, and crossing the Durance, make straight south, through the hills leading to the low Rhone Delta.   For De Moncrief now fears the vengeance of O'Brien Dillon even more than the plague.

"*Pardieu!* he'll ·.ot follow us!   He has life and happiness before him!" jeers the procureur, but his laugh is ghastly as death itself.

Half an hour afterwards, Lenoir rides up alongside, his face somewhat pale, notwithstanding the heat of travel. He cries: "God of heaven! you have made a mistake! A white lipped peasant tells me we're going towards the plague!"

"God of heaven!" cries De Moncrief back to him: "That is *where* we *are* going!   The plague is my sanctuary! Marseilles is the one place where that bloodhound dare not follow!"

BUT HE DOES!

Even as they confer, Lenoir begging them to ride back again, and he will fight for them, a dust cloud is seen following after them.

The coach they fly from has crossed the Durance also!

With that De Moncrief bursts out wildly, offering to increase the wages of the postilions, and proffering Lenoir a fortune to still go with him and protect him: "Get into the carriage—rest, that you may fight! Ten thousand ducats!"

With a muttered "Yes," Lenoir springs in.

So they dash on again—*nearer the plague!*

At Salon they get fresh horses once again. But the postboys here refuse to travel any nearer to the pest. The country round them is now apparently deserted by human beings. All have fled to the North, away from this dread disease that sweeps humanity before it.

But one or two adventurous riders, lured by the bribes of De Moncrief, at last agree to take them to Rognac, where a line of guards has been placed to prevent any one escaping from the stricken city to carry the contagion with them. That far the postboys will go—no further!

So they dash on again!

And after a little Cousin Charlie, looking back, sighs: "He has given up pursuit. I cannot see the dust;" then suddenly cries out: "Good God! He's coming too!"

For Dillon has been delayed, like themselves, by fleeing postboys. But now he drives himself, Lanty sitting beside him, they alone occupying the vehicle. And they are gaining—their carriage is so much lighter.

But at last De Moncrief, pouring out money upon the trembling postboys, for he is nearly crazy with terror now, they reach Rognac.

Here they are barred by members of the guard that patrol the road running from Rognac to Aix and the East, isolating Marseilles and its contagion from the rest of France.

"I am a priest!" cries Charles de Moncrief. "And she is one who has come to nurse her father, stricken by the plague."

"We have no wish to stop your going in," reply the men. "Doctors and priests have come and passed into the contagion. But we can permit none to *return.*"

At this Hilda begins to shudder and the postboys throw down their whips.

They will drive no further. The fear of death conquers the love of gold. Even Lenoir whispers to De Moncrief hurriedly: "Give me that bag of ducats under the front seat, and I will stay here and bar his going in after you. I travel no further toward the plague!"

"Take it!" cries De Moncrief. "But earn it!"

At this Hilda suddenly cries: "I'll stay here, too. My beauty will make my husband forgive. Anyway, it is better than the plague."

But De Moncrief says, with a muttered curse: "Do you think I'll lose your loveliness. You go with me!" And holds her in his frenzied arms and binds her to her seat.

But her cries attract the guards. They would come to her did not the procureur call: "Back! She has the delirium of the plague!"

On this, those who would aid her, fly from her. The pest has made all men cowards.

Then, for Dillon and Lanty are nearly up, De Moncrief (no postboys now) driving himself, speeds desperately away into the plague, beside him a frenzied woman, moaning in terror and praying to God to spare *her* and strike *him*.

And the guards say to each other: "Neither will come back again! Youth and age go down together!"

Just then O'Brien, who has seen his prey, comes flying up and cries: " Let me pass!"

"You can go *in*, but not *out*!" they say.

"It is *in* I want to go!"

"Into the plague?"—You are mad!"

"Into the plague I go!" And there is something in Dillon's eyes that make the men stand back—all save one!

Gaston Lenoir, savage at being dogged so long, and hating the man who sits there calling for fresh horses and perchance willing to earn his bag of ducats, steps to the front and cries to Dillon: "Turn back! You go not in! I have sworn it!"

"Faix! to De Moncrief, whose dirty money ye have!" says Lanty, and would spring off to settle this

affair himself.   But Dillon's grasp is on his arm.   He
mutters: "Not you! This is mine!"

"Wirra! He'll make mincemeat of ye!" cries
Lanty—"He's as cunning with the weapon as the divil
with his tail!"

"Don't I know that?" whispers Dillon. This shall be
the duel of the galley slave and the *maître d'armes*—
strength against skill.

Drawing the great sabre he carries by his side,
O'Brien springs from the carriage, and Lenoir and he,
are at last at each other, face to face.   Gaston
is armed with sabre also, and in knowledge of the
weapon no man in France is his equal.

Ever as their blades meet, Dillon knows: "If I fight
him as a fencer, he will win?"

Then Lenoir finds out what wondrous power
the awful travail of the galleys gives to the arm of a
strong man.   O'Brien does not lunge—he cuts with
the giant strength of his mighty shoulders; and every
stroke Lenoir wards, though his wrist is iron, is like a
lightning shock to his arm.   He has no chance to
attack—blows come like hammer on anvil—each one
weakening his wrist—each one nearly paralyzing his
hand from the shock of contact.

Still, if he can but get an opening—just one lunge!
And the perspiration pouring from his brow, Gaston
stands waiting, trying to keep his weapon in his hand,
for his one chance—and thinks it comes.

The great sabre of O'Brien flashes through the
air! He will turn it deftly away.   He throws up
his point.   As he does so, instead of the blow catching his at half sabre's length, it comes close to his
wrist, and the strength of the galley slave triumphs
over the skill of the master of fence.   The contact is
so potent, the blow so strong, Lenoir's sabre is dashed
from his hand. He stands defenceless before his enemy.

Perchance he would go unscathed (for Dillon is
no man to strike an unarmed foe), but with a muttered
oath, Gaston's hand seeks his pistol belt, and that
move is fatal.

For flashing in the sun, O'Brien's sabre falls, and
with a shrieking oath, Lenoir, shorn of his right arm,
near the shoulder, sinks writhing upon the earth.

CHAPTER XXVII.

THE DYING BOATSWAIN OF LA SYLPHIDE.

GASTON would die from very loss of blood but for a young doctor, who, thinking more of the charity of his profession than the dangers of the plague, is journeying toward Marseilles. He, like the rest, has stood gaping in amazement at the sight of a man *fighting* his way into the contagion—and not a doctor, nor a priest.

Under this Samaritan of medicine's hand Lenoir's wound is bound up and the arteries secured and cauterized in time to save his life.

But for this O'Brien does not wait.

"Bedad!" cries Lanty, "they're well ahead of us now!"

"Well ahead of *me!*" mutters Dillon.

"Of *us!*"

"No! for you go no further! You have a wife and family."

"Don't talk of wife and family to me," screams Lanty. "Don't take the pluck out of me when I'm going to follow you to hell!"

"But not there!" And Dillon points towards the pest. "Remember your wife! Think of the child that's coming! Stay for them! Meet me at Toulon! If I come out unscathed—alive—from this plague spot, there I shall need you! Good bye!"

Wringing his hand, O'Brien, alone now, drives into the pestilence that has settled like the gloom of death upon Marseilles.

As he passes through the open country round the town, he sees no living man—there are only bones and vultures.

Into the place he drives. People fly from him, as they fly from one another, for each fear that the other may have the pestilence. The shops are closed. The streets are like those of a city of the dead.

And over all the pitiless sun beats down, drawing from out of the basin of the harbor, which has now become a cess pool, the awful odors of the plague.

The sick lie dying in the streets. The dead lie unburied in the houses or on the ground.

One poor scared wretch to whom O'Brien speaks, points to his own plague spots and flies from him, crying, "Keep from me or you may partake of my despair."

But a priest to whom Dillon calls, turns, and making the sign of the cross, comes to him and asks: "Are you sick of the pest? Can I aid you to a hospital?"

"Faith!" remarks O'Brien grimly, "are there nurses for the sick when there are none to bury the dead?"

To this the man of God replies: "We can care now only for the living—they have hope in this world. The dead have gone. The galley slaves were compelled to bury them, but the galley slaves have all died. You are a stranger here! Why have you come?"

"I seek a man and a woman!" mutters O'Brien between his clenched teeth. For this mention of the galley slave has brought up his awful sufferings and spurred on his vengeance, and he gives a description of Hilda de Sabran and Charles de Moncrief.

"I think I saw a man and woman such as you describe drive towards the basin of the harbor. There's a galley there to which orders were given to sail. It is the only one in port—the only one that has not yet gone away. They may have gone on board that ship, hoping to escape from the pestilence."

A galley in the basin of the harbor! O'Brien Dillon darts for it striding along streets a year before he had crouched through, fleeing from the galleys. This awful degradation—this terrible travail of his life—is in his soul, as he comes to the harbor, and there seeing a galley, strides on board. '

But before him a man and a woman seeking escape from the town, have stepped upon its deck. And the woman, who is very beautiful, has looked about and suddenly uttered a cry: "My God! *La Sylphide!*"

For Hilda de Sabran remembers the glorious pageant that had met her in Marseilles but a year before.

It is the same fairy galley that had borne her in triumph to the *fête* at the Isle Pomègue.

But now the beautiful vessel that was once covered with silken awnings and made picturesque by gilded poop and decorated forecastle, is a wreck. Not the wreck of the storm, but the wreck of the pestilence.

This has broken out upon her, among the confined

wretches of its waist, worse than in the town itself. Under it these galley slaves, huddled together in their chains, have died like sheep. The living have now grown too sick or weary to throw over the dead, who lie, still chained upon their benches.

The officers, standing to their duty, have striven to raise the sails and put out of port. But the sailors who have lived, have deserted this hole of pestilence, for the sewerage of the city flows around them with its awful stench. So there has not been strength enough upon the craft to get up its anchor or its sails; one of these now floats languidly, half hoisted, under the sun.

Of all the officers of the boat none are now alive save the dread *comité*, who lies upon the poop deck, stricken with the plague, the spots of the contagion upon his face and neck and hairy breast, the incipient delirium coming on him.

And he stares at the beauty of the woman and the age of the man who stand before him; then cries: "It is a year ago! This is the mistress of the Regent —the beautiful woman who made me lash the slaves to death, to drive them faster in the race. A year ago— when we were happy here! All save the galley slaves! And I was cruel to them with lash and rod—for which God pity me! I now go to the torment of the damned!"

So he jeers in their faces, as they beg him to take them out to sea, and pour gold before him, and offer him great wealth to get the vessel out upon the breezy ocean, and laughs: "Impossible! All are dead or dying!"

Then suddenly to the *comité* comes what he thinks is delirium.

There is a hoarse cry from the woman and a gasp of terror from the man; another figure is coming on board!

Staring at it, the boatswain with eyes of terror cries: "The ghost of *forçat* number 1392! He who went mad and drowned himself right here a year ago! Mad from the cruelty of the lash!"

Suddenly he says no more—but simply looks!

For the ghost of the *forçat* has cried out with awful mocking laugh: "At last—faithless wife! At last— De Moncrief! who made me a galley slave!"

And suddenly the beautiful woman flies to him, and on her knees screams: "Mercy!"

And he says: "From my hands—yes! For God has stricken ye! The plague spots are on your neck and face!"

And she, staggering from him dazed, turns eyes that roll with horror upon a mirror on the cabin wall, a remnant of the great *fête* she glorified the year before; and seeing the taint of the contagion upon her soft, white skin, she flies to the side of the vessel, and with a shriek of mortal terror springs into the air, her white garments floating about her, gleaming in the sun, an image of despairing beauty which has lost earth, but has not gained heaven, as with one flash she disappears into the inky waters of the basin of death.

Perchance the trembling old man would follow after her. But there is a grip of iron on his shoulder, and a hoarse voice is whispering: "This is a fitting place for us to meet! My God, *La Sylphide!* the very galley where they tortured me!" The sight of his place of torment drives O'Brien Dillon into madness. He drags De Moncrief, his teeth chattering in his head, his eyes rolling with terror, up to the second bench of the waist, on which two corpses lie chained, and three slaves stricken with the pestilence are dying, and there are empty irons for one; one *forçat* had been thrown overboard a corpse.

And he says, hideous laughs coming from him, that are punctuated by the shrieks of the victim he holds in his hands: "On this bench *I* suffered! Behold the impress of my limbs into the hard oak, where I toiled by day and moaned by night, ironed to the deck. This place is for YOU!"

"Good God of mercy!"

"These irons are for YOU!"

But now there are only screams from the old man, as the escaped galley slave chains him in the very irons he wore, amid the dead and dying, and laughs: "Turn about, by heaven! Turn about is fair play!" And so leaves him amid the groans of the wretches dying of the pestilence. Dead men about him—the rest all stricken.

But now Charles de Moncrief begins to pray to the.

boatswain to be released, for his tormentor has left the ship.

But the delirium of the fever is on the *comité* and he cries: "A *new* galley slave! Always for him the welcome of the *bastonnade!* We will row now! We've a strong man here!"

And in his madness of the plague, the *comité*, flying from the poop, falls upon the last galley slave that shall come under his hands—*the new one*—and shouts: "Row!" and tears off his clothes, shrieking: "*Row naked, as in battle!*" And raising again his awful whip, the maniac boatswain cries: "Row!" giving the cadence of the stroke.

From very force of habit, the other three wretches at the bench, spring up shrieking, the lash whizzing over their shoulders, and they force De Moncrief's hands upon the oar.

Then suddenly above the cadence and the time given by the boatswain, and the shrieking slaves trying to move this spar that is now too heavy for their dying strength, comes up one wild howl from Charles de Moncrief, once Procureur du Roy, now galley slave number 1392.

The lash is falling upon him and cutting his old back into pieces, and he is shrieking desparingly as the maniac boatswain laughs: "The *bastonnade!* THE WELCOME OF THE NEW GALLEY SLAVE!"

But it is only a maniac that is shrieking now! and the boatswain falling to the deck, dies of the fever, and the three galley slaves expire.

And the sun is still flaming in the heavens and the pestilence is still coming up from the town, and the priests are still saying their masses, and the good bishop Belzunce is still working at his labor of love and life among the mephitic hospitals; but upon the galley *La Svlphide*, there is no living thing to tell the tale, save a chained maniac who is dying of the plague.

*   *   *   *   *   *   *   *

Twenty-four hours after, Dillon lands at Toulon in an open boat coming from the open sea. Lanty, meeting him, asks no questions. His old master's face tells its tale.

"By my soul! you're faithful, Lanty!" cries the comte, wringing his hand. "You must love me!"

"By my soul!" chuckles the Chevalier, "there's more than me as loves ye in Paris. Madame la Marquise would never have forgiven me, if ye hadn't come back!"

At this, the eyes of O'Brien Dillon, that have become deep set in his head through his night of labor on the sea, and all the horrors of his passage through the plague, glow with a new fire—a new hope.

He has still something to live for!

FINIS.

www.ingramcontent.com/pod-product-compliance
Lightning Source LLC
Chambersburg PA
CBHW021050030726

47496CB00006B/1769